MASTERING Brazilian Jiu Jitsu

RIGAN MACHADO & JOSE M. FRAGUAS

EMPIRE Books
P.O. Box 491788, Los Angeles, CA 90049

Disclaimer
Please note that the author and publisher of this book are NOT RESPONSIBLE in any manner whatsoever for any injury that may result from practicing the techniques and/or following the instructions given within. Since the physical activities described herein may be too strenuous in nature for some readers to engage in safely, it is essential that a physician be consulted prior to training.

Copyright © 2007 by Rogan Machado & Jose M. Fraguas.

All rights reserved. No part of this publication may be reproduced or utilized in any form or by any means, electronic or mechanical, including photocopying, recording, or by any information storage and retrieval system, without prior written permission from Empire Books.

Empire Books
P.O. Box 491788
Los Angeles, CA 90049

First edition
06 05 04 03 02 01 00 99 98 97 1 3 5 7 9 10 8 6 4 2
Printed in the United States of America.

Machado, Rigan.
Encyclopedia of Brazilian jiu-jitsu / Rigan Machado and Jose M. Fraguas.
-- Rev. ed.
p. cm
Includes index.
ISBN 1-933901-33-0 (pbk.:alk.paper)
ISBN 1-933901-34-9 (pbk.:alk.paper)
ISBN 1-933901-35-7 (pbk.:alk.paper)
1. Jiu-jitsu--Brazil--Encyclopedias. I. Fraguas, Jose M. II. Title.
GV1114.M339 2006
796.815'2--dc22

2006026783

Editor: Doug Jeffrey
Design: Willy Blumhoff
Cover Design: George Chen

Dedication

To the memory of Grandmaster Carlos Gracie, the first member of the Gracie family who trained in the art of Jiu-Jitsu.

To the memory of Grandmaster Helio Gracie, a true pioneer who broke barriers and put himself to test in behalf of his beloved art. His study and sacrifice paved the road for all future generations.

Acknowledgements

Special thanks to the members of the Machado and Gracie family, whose permission to quote and peruse from personal notes has given this text its core.

To all the students who provided excellent cooperation and skills while demonstrating the techniques that you see on these pages.

Finally, we want to thank all the students and practitioners around the world whose support and dedication to the art has tremendously helped to promote and popularize the art of Brazilian Jiu-Jitsu.

About the Authors

RIGAN MACHADO

Rigan Machado, whose lineage is linked directly to the art's founder, Carlos Gracie, is one of the top Brazilian Jiu-Jitsu instructors in the world. His long experience in teaching — to everyone from beginners to world champions — and his contributions to the art's teaching methods have brought him worldwide acclaim. Originally from Rio de Janeiro, Brazil, Machado's personal credits include many of the top Brazilian national and international championships. Furthermore, Rigan Machado was one of the first Brazilian black belts who moved from Brazil to the United States of America, where he became one of the leading forces in expanding the art. "Brazil was just the beginning of the grappling movement," says Machado. "From there, the seeds have been spread all around the world. If a student is not from Brazil and he becomes a world champion, then that makes me a good teacher and makes me happy."

Despite his fame, he continues to train with a dedication born out of the love of his art. Machado has also appeared in several movies and television shows, becoming one of the most recognizable figures in the world of the martial arts. Highly regarded as one of the most talented technicians and teachers who ever came out of the Gracie family, Rigan has been instrumental in the development of Machado Jiu-Jitsu as it is known today.

"Finding a harmony between mind and body is the ultimate goal of any martial artist, but the physical techniques must come first," he says. "A calm and concentrated awareness is the key toward the realization of personal potential, of which the technical mastery is the first step."

Drawing from his considerable knowledge, Rigan Machado has written extensively on his art and authored several series of DVD's on Brazilian Jiu-Jitsu through EM3 Video and authored "Encyclopedia of Leglocks" for Empire Books.

JOSE M. FRAGUAS

Jose M. Fraguas had his first contact with the martial arts (the grappling art of Judo) at the age of nine. Practicing as a child under Sensei Lee in Madrid, Spain, Fraguas progressed rapidly until he decided to pursue a different but related martial art style. The seeds of contact sports, however, had been planted.

Recognized as an international authority on the martial arts and author of many books on the subject, he began his career as a writer at age 16 by serving as a regular contributor to martial arts magazines in Great Britain, France, Spain, Italy, Germany, Portugal, Holland and Australia. Having hands-on experience and training allowed him to better reflect the physical side of the martial arts in his writing. He started his training in Brazilian Jiu-Jitsu in the late 1980s with several members of the Gracie family.

"I would love to mention the members of the Gracie family and the Machado brothers who spent so many hours in private and group classes sharing their knowledge with me, but I am afraid that crediting them with being responsible for my Jiu-Jitsu skills would make them feel more pain than pride," Fraguas says laughing.

His desire to promote both ancient philosophy and modern thinking provided the motivation for writing this book. "I want to write books so I can learn as well as share." Fraguas continues, "The martial arts are like life itself. Both are filled with experiences that seem quite ordinary at the time and assume a fabled stature only with the passage of the years. I hope this work will be appreciated by future practitioners of the art of Brazilian Jiu-Jitsu."

He currently lives in Los Angeles, California.

Table of Contents

- About the Authors v
- History viii
- Introduction xvi
- Attacks from the Guard 1

  Closed Guard 2

  Open Guard 137

  Half-Guard 161

  Seated Position 177

- Passing the Guard 203

- **Side Control** 288
- **Takedowns and Throws** 367
- **Attacks from the Back** 415
- **Escapes from the Back** 439
- **Attacks from the Mount** 459
- **Escapes from the Mount** 483
- **North and South** 501
- **Breaking the Grip** 519
- **Epilogue** 529

History

MITSUYO MAEDA AND THE ORIGIN OF BRAZILIAN JIU-JITSU

Born in the Prefecture of Aomori in 1878, Mitsuyo Maeda was meant to change the history of martial arts forever. As a boy, he studied tenshin shinyo-ryu, one of the many traditional Jiu-Jitsu styles found in Japan. When he was 18 years old, his family sent him to the Senmon School in Tokyo and he began training in Judo at the Kodokan in 1897, according to official records. The dedicated Maeda took each and every one of his practice sessions very seriously and soon became one of the more talented prospects trained by Jigoro Kano. A great future for him as a judoka was predicted by the Kodokan masters.

In 1904, Sensei Kano sent one of his top students, Tsunejiro Tomita, to the United States to give a Judo demonstration to President Theodore Roosevelt. Mitsuyo Maeda was sent to assist Tomita. Both men demonstrated at the West Point Military Academy but nobody truly understood what they were doing, because Tomita and Maeda performed Judo kata, a traditional fighting practice against imaginary opponents.

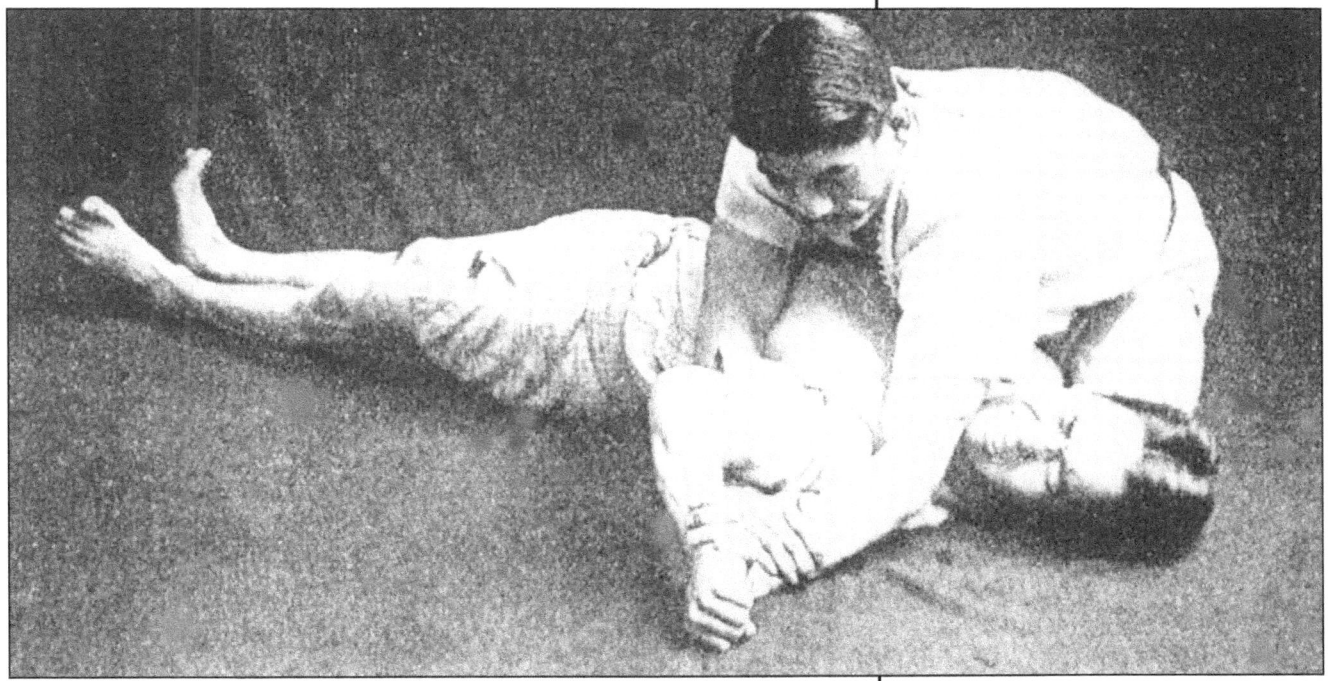

After the demonstration, Maeda was required to fight a powerful, young wrestler. Due to Maeda's lack of understanding of the Western method of Wrestling, the young American pinned Maeda for a while. Finally, however, the Japanese reversed the situation and forced the wrestler to submit.

The Americans were impressed by Maeda's performance, but Tomita was the teacher, so they asked him to fight. Tomita couldn't lose face in front of all the spectators so he accepted the challenge. Tomita failed with a throw and was pinned under the bigger opponent. Tomita had no choice but to give up.

"The dedicated Maeda took each and every one of his practice sessions very seriously and soon became one of the more talented prospects trained by Jigoro Kano."

"Maeda taught Judo at Princeton University and had no problem accepting challenges from anybody who wanted to test his fighting skills."

Ashamed with Tomita's poor showing, Maeda parted ways and stayed in New York when Tomita left for the West Coast. Maeda taught Judo at Princeton University and had no problem accepting challenges from anybody who wanted to test his fighting skills. He persuaded some Japanese businessmen to stake him $1,000 in prize money to challenge all comers. This attitude was directly opposed to the ethics and precepts of Kodokan Judo. Jigoro Kano's rules prohibited students of engaging in challenge matches of this kind. Since Maeda didn't have any success as a teacher, he decided to go ahead and become a professional fighter. A match against a wrestler with the nickname of "Butcherboy" was the first of many in Maeda's career.

Maeda traveled with Japanese associates to other countries like Cuba, Honduras, Costa Rica, Panama, Peru, Colombia, Brazil and Mexico — it was there where he received the name of "Conde Koma" or Count Koma, which became his ring name. Maeda always thought his life was problematic and that trouble was constantly coming his way. In Japanese, this state of constant trouble is called "komaru," so he originally called himself "Maeda Komaru" when fighting. During his stay in Mexico, however, based on his elegance and good looks, an acquaintance suggested he use the name "Conde" (Count). After that, Maeda always referred to himself as "Conde Koma," which can loosely be translated as "Count Trouble." His first fight in Brazil was in Porto Alegre Dec. 20, 1915, and was arranged by Octavio Pires Jr. in the Politama Theater. After Porto Alegre, they went to Rio de Janeiro, Sao Paulo, Salvador, Recife, Belem and finally Manaus. Then the group left to continue the trip in other South American countries.

It wasn't until 1917 that Maeda went back to Belem, Brazil with his English wife May Iris. He loved Belem and decided that was the place to live. Following the same path that he pursued in the United States, Maeda accepted all challenges, and the fights made him famous in the region. His popularity grew as a teacher of a Japanese fighting art, and he was invited to teach Army College cadets, policemen and private students. Among all his students, it was the son of Gastão Gracie, Carlos, who eventually became his most notable protégé.

The techniques used by Maeda in his many challenge fights weren't the same he had learned in the Kodokan. His constant fights against opponents from other styles forced him to alter and modify many of the techniques from Judo and discard many of the sport-oriented movements that lacked useful-

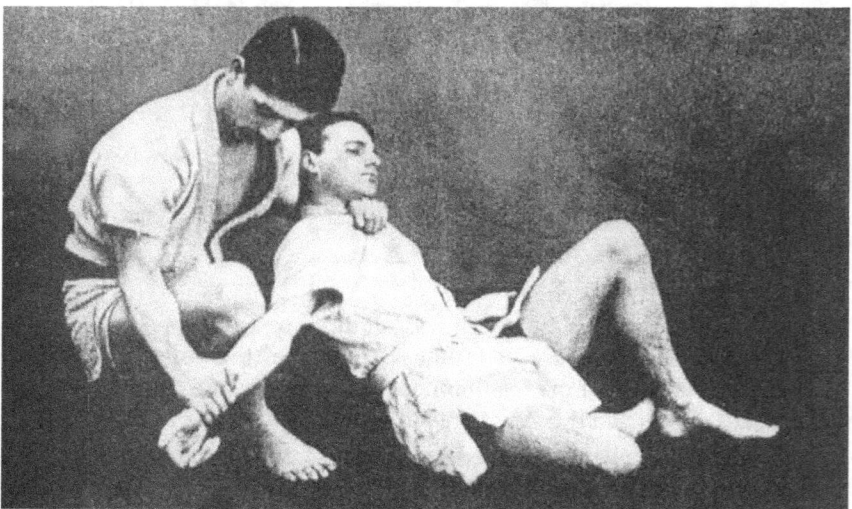

"Koma soon discovered that his opponents were very vulnerable to the lethal samurai Jiu-Jitsu ground techniques discarded by the Kodokan."

ness in real fights. The matches in the Kodokan didn't include fighting techniques against experienced boxers and wrestlers because Judo's technical structure was meant to match opponents who used the same techniques. The attacking method of the opponent was supposed to be matched by the corresponding defense maneuver. Since this was obviously not the case in a real fight, Maeda analyzed the old system of pre-war Judo — known as taryu shiai Judo — and used many of its strategies and techniques to face his opponents.

The old school of Judo was closer to the traditional samurai combat Jiu-Jitsu of Bu-Jutsu. Conde Koma soon discovered that his opponents were very vulnerable to the lethal samurai Jiu-Jitsu ground techniques discarded by the Kodokan when Sensei Kano converted the original, violent art into a "gentle" sport meant to be practiced in a period of political peace. In fact, when Masahiko Kimura encountered Helio Gracie, he remarked that the techniques used by his opponent reminded him of earlier pre-war Jiu-Jitsu.

In 1925, Maeda decided to help other Japanese to immigrate to Brazil because he thought that Brazil was a better place to live, due to all the anti-Japanese feelings in the United States at that time. Maeda worked closely with Japanese officials, scouting Brazil and looking for potential homestead sites. Although all his efforts were useless due to malaria, which made many Japanese return to Japan or move to other countries, Maeda became a prominent individual in the community.

In 1940, in recognition of the work he had done around the world in spreading Japanese culture, the Japanese government offered to pay Maeda's trip back to Japan. He was tempted, but decided to stay in Brazil until he finished the house he had started to build for his family. Tragically, he died of a kidney disease one year later in the month of July.

Authors Jose M. Fraguas (top) and Rigan Machado (bottom) with Grandmaster Helio Gracie.

THE GRACIE CONNECTION

The art of Brazilian Jiu-Jitsu started when Mitsuyo Maeda (Count Koma) decided to rebel Japanese tradition and teach Gastão Gracie's oldest son, Carlos, in return for the diplomatic support Gastão gave him in establishing a Japanese immigration colony in the north of Brazil. Carlos was so fascinated with the techniques he learned from Maeda that when the family moved to Rio de Janeiro in 1925 he opened the first Gracie Jiu-Jitsu Academy. During these early years, Carlos made a great effort to teach different law enforcement groups and police departments the effective techniques Count Koma had shared with him. Carlos, a very intelligent man, dedicated most of his time during the first years in Rio de Janeiro to promoting and publicizing the art and teaching in the academy.

Helio, his younger brother, was physically very frail and doctors prohibited him from participating in any kind of physical exercise that could make his health worse. In fact, Helio was ordered to avoid any kind of physical exercise at all. During the classes that Carlos taught at the academy, all Helio could do was sit on the side and watch the students practice. For several years, that was all Helio was allowed to do inside the walls of the Gracie Academy. For Carlos, the health of his brother was far more important than teaching him the ancient fighting techniques of samurai Jiu-Jitsu.

But the history of the art was changed forever when Carlos couldn't make it to the academy one day for one of his private classes. The student showed up for class and Carlos wasn't there. Helio, only 16 years old, offered to teach the student himself, so the client wouldn't lose a day's practice. Helio told the

"Instead of relying on strength and explosiveness, Helio began to use leverage and body mechanics to achieve the same results."

Rigan Machado with Grandmaster Carlos Gracie.

"Kimura, very confident in his abilities and his superior strength and size, said that if Helio lasted more than three minutes without being defeated, he should consider himself the winner."

student that he knew the moves because he had watched his brother teach them every day for the last two years. The student accepted the offer and Helio Gracie taught the first class of his life.

Later, Carlos arrived at the academy and tried to apologize to the student for his tardiness. But the student replied, "Don't worry; your brother Helio taught me. If you don't mind, I would like to take classes with him from now on." Carlos was shocked but also extremely proud of his younger brother. With the blessing of Carlos, Helio became more active in the teaching duties of the academy. Soon, he found himself teaching the vast majority of the students. Carlos, an excellent nutritionist, focused more and more on the development of what is now known as the "Gracie Diet." A phrase by Hippocrates, to "make your food your medicine," was the trigger for Carlos to dedicate his life to the nutritional aspects so important to the Gracie family training methods. He also allocated time to managing the fighting careers of his younger brothers. With Carlos busy researching nutrition and managing the family's business aspects, young Helio's role in the academy increased. In the art of Jiu-Jitsu, he found the love of his life. But all was not perfect.

While the techniques taught by Maeda to Carlos were extremely effective and useful, they didn't fit Helio exactly. With a small frame and weight of less than 140 pounds, Helio soon found out that many of Maeda's techniques weren't suitable for his slight physical structure. He began a process of analyzing the techniques taught to his brother and modifying them to allow him to use them against bigger and heavier opponents. Instead of relying on strength and explosiveness, Helio began to use leverage and body mechanics to achieve the same results. Subtle changes in the techniques allowed him to devise an arsenal of moves that could be used with much less strength. Out of necessity, Helio Gracie devised a unique fighting system based on proper positioning instead of physical force. Under the guidance of his brother Carlos, Helio started to fight. Although Carlos was worried about his brother's health, Helio surprised everyone but himself when he beat all the opponents he fought. In only 30 seconds, via armlock, 17-year-old Helio beat professional boxer Antonio Portugal and laid the cornerstone in the construction of the Gracie Family dynasty. Fighters such as world wrestling champion Wladek Zybskus and Japanese Jiu-Jitsu champion Nakimi were soon on the receiving end of Helio's revolutionary fighting methods and masterful technical skill.

Not only did Helio Gracie create a name for himself and his family, but also for generations of Gracie fighters to come. His fame reached as far as the "Land of the Rising Sun," and so Japan sent the lightweight Judo champion, Kato, to face the Brazilian hero. It was time for a Japanese master to stop that "rebel," they said. Little did they know that Helio was going to defeat Kato via a chokehold at the Ibirapuera Arena in Sao Paulo, after the first fight between them was declared a draw. A commotion in Japan occurred and the open weight champion, Masahiko Kimura, was sent to regain the honor taken from the Kodokan. On October 13, 1951, the greatest soccer stadium in the world, Maracana, was packed to watch the fight between the Brazilian national hero, Helio Gracie, and the Japanese champion Kimura, who is now widely regarded as the greatest Judo fighter of all time. Helio was 42 at that time and weighed 140 pounds. Kimura, in his prime, was 34 and weighed 195 pounds.

Kimura, very confident in his abilities and his superior strength and size, said that if Helio lasted more than three minutes without being defeated, he should consider himself the winner. Helio fought Kimura for a little more than 15 minutes, and brother Carlos threw in the towel only when Kimura got Helio in a painful armlock. Helio didn't seem to be willing to tap at all, so Carlos decided to stop the fight before any major damage could be done.

Impressed with Helio's performance, the Japanese masters invited him to Japan to teach the modified version of Jiu-Jitsu that he had developed. Helio, understanding the difficulties of leaving his family and his academy to go to a foreign country, graciously acknowledged the compliment but declined the offer.

The many legendary fights of Helio Gracie include the longest fight in history when he faced Waldemar Santana on May 24, 1955, for 3 hours and 45 minutes in a non-stop fight. Searching for fame, Santana, who was Helio's student, had made disrespectful comments about the Gracie family. Helio answered by coming out of retirement and challenging him to fight. Although Helio lost the fight, his courageous performance won him the hearts of the Brazilian people. During his fighting career, Helio also issued challenges to some of the greatest boxers in history such as Primo Carnera and Ezzard Charles, but the most notable was when the great Joe Louis declined to fight against the Brazilian master.

During his entire life, Helio Gracie has proven to be a courageous and determined individual. With the support of his older brother, Carlos, he created one of the most efficient styles of self-defense known to man, and he left his own blood in the ring to perfect it. Carlos became very spiritual in his later years and tried to reach higher of level of consciousness by dedicating more time to meditation and perfection of the Gracie Diet. Both brothers made a tremendous contribution to future generations of martial artists all around the world. Carlos died at age 94, filled with the peace he sought, while quietly taking a bath. Helio Gracie is recognized as the father of the Jiu-Jitsu style he developed, which is now known around the world as "Gracie Jiu-Jitsu" in his honor.

"Impressed with Helio's performance, the Japanese masters invited him to Japan to teach the modified version of Jiu-Jitsu that he had developed."

THE ULTIMATE FIGHTING CHAMPIONSHIP

In November 1993, the history of Brazilian Jiu-Jitsu reached a major turning point when Rorion Gracie, the eldest son of Helio Gracie, created the Ultimate Fighting Championship. The event was televised on pay-per-view and attracted the attention not only of all the martial artists in the world but also of politicians who tried to stop the event due to the lack of safety rules for the fighters. The problem was that the UFC was never meant to be safe for the fighters. Fighters were fighters and they were there to fight. Only two rules governed the event: no eye gouging and no biting. Everything else was allowed. It was as raw as it could get.

With a cage called the "Octagon" designed by famous film director and Jiu-Jitsu student John Milius, the UFC was meant to duplicate the vale tudo (anything goes) no-hold-barred fights that the Gracie family had done in Brazil for more than a half-century. It was meant to prove which techniques and fighting styles were truly efficient for one-on-one fighting. The limited rules allowed representatives of every style to use any technique they thought suitable. There were no weight classes, no time limits. It was as real as a sport could get and marked a dramatic turning point in the explosion of Brazilian Jiu-Jitsu around the world.

Royce Gracie, one of the younger sons of Helio Gracie, represented Brazilian Jiu-Jitsu in the UFC. The "Gracie Kid," as he was referred to by many at that time, ran over all his opponents in the first four UFCs. He displayed a calm strategy and submitted all his opponents using the techniques his father Helio had developed over the years. Martial artists and fighters from all over the world were shocked to see how the smaller and weaker

Rickson Gracie, a legendary Brazilian Jiu Jitsu master and champion.

"The problem was that the UFC was never meant to be safe for the fighters. Only two rules governed the event: no eye gouging and no biting. Everything else was allowed. It was as raw as it could get."

Royce could not only control bigger and heavier opponents, but also choke them at will without getting hurt. He methodically closed the distance, got into a clinch, took his opponents to the ground and finished them with a clean choke or armbar.

The aftermath of the UFC took the popularity of Brazilian Jiu-Jitsu (or BJJ as it came to be known) to every corner of the world. Soon, countries such as Japan were offering great opportunities for other Jiu-Jitsu fighters to prove the efficiency of the art against skilled fighters. Rickson Gracie and Jean-Jacques Machado were two of the main proponents of the art who regularly visited Japan to fight. With the success of BJJ fighters, the demand for instructors became overwhelming and many Brazilian black belts decided to move to the U.S. to share their knowledge. Nothing would be the same in the world of martial arts as Brazilian Jiu-Jitsu suddenly reached every corner of the globe.

MACHADO JIU-JITSU

One of the first groups of instructors to teach Brazilian Jiu-Jitsu internationally were the Machado brothers. Carlos, Rigan, Roger, John and Jean-Jacques, the sons of Luiza (the sister-in-law of Carlos Gracie), have been instrumental in developing and expanding the art within the U.S. They began to practice at an early age and soon found themselves training alongside other members of the Gracie family, spending many hours perfecting their techniques at Helio's famous family ranch in Teresopolis. With their main headquarters now in California, their passion and dedication for sharing Jiu-Jitsu caused a great number of students to embrace the art. Known for not holding back any knowledge of the art, Machado students soon became a leading force in BJJ and MMA competitions around the world.

The Machado brothers understood that to have good students, time and effort had to be expended on their part. They unselfishly dedicated a great amount of their time to bring out the best in their students, instead of focusing on their own competition careers. They felt driven to give others the gift of Jiu-Jitsu that they had received. While Rigan, John, Roger and Jean-Jacques relocated to different areas in the state of California to better expand the art, Carlos Machado moved to Dallas, Texas, where he opened an academy and taught legendary karate champion and television and film star Chuck Norris, the star of *Walker: Texas Ranger*. Norris soon became a true believer

"The Machados researched, grew, and expanded the art of Brazilian Jiu-Jitsu in every technical area."

of Brazilian Jiu-Jitsu and threw himself into learning it. He also helped to promote the art through his show by giving the Machado brothers several guest appearances in many of the series episodes. The Machado brothers' reputation soon spread and other martial art movie stars offered them guest appearances in their action films.

The friendly and easy-going attitude of the Machado brothers that caused other open-minded martial arts experts to study and learn under their tutelage. These various masters already had excellent reputations in their own styles, and the Machados took the opportunity to observe and absorb technical and tactical elements from other non-grappling fighting arts and incorporate them into the structure of Machado Jiu-Jitsu.

Although Machado Jiu-Jitsu is not a new method or different style of Brazilian Jiu-Jitsu, the five brothers have made important additions to the art by incorporating elements from arts such as Wrestling and Sambo into their arsenal. They incorporated useful material and blended it into the strong technical structure they already possessed. This approach soon proved itself in trials by fire when Rigan and Jean-Jacques entered the Abu Dhabi Combat Club tournament in the United Arab Emirates with excellent results, beating some of the top grappling stylists from around the world, including world judo, wrestling and sambo experts. In 1999, Jean-Jacques gave the greatest grappling performance ever witnessed when he won all his matches by submission and was awarded the title, "Most Technical Grappler in the World."

But the true benefit of their methods have been proven by their students who have become national champions and won many important sport Jiu-Jitsu championships around the world. With open minds that allowed them to research, grow, and expand the art of Brazilian Jiu-Jitsu in every technical area, the Machado brothers have become the most sought-after Brazilian Jiu-Jitsu instructors anywhere. They are a leading force in its growth, not only in the United States, but also around the world.

"The five brothers have made important additions to the art by incorporating elements from arts such as Wrestling and sambo into their arsenal."

Introduction

MASTERING THE BASICS

The art of Brazilian Jiu-Jitsu comes directly from the efforts of Grandmasters Carlos Gracie and Helio Gracie although, after more than 70 years, substantial differences in the way instructors teach the art, as well as new training methods and techniques, have developed.

Before beginning, it is vital to analyze and understand the nature of Jiu-Jitsu training in comparison with other martial arts methods. In other styles, students must develop skills in three different areas: basic techniques (fundamentals), forms and live sparring against an adversary. Only one of these three aspects requires interaction with another live opponent: sparring.

Mastery of any physical endeavor that involves two people is twice as difficult. Therefore, one must not only develop one's own skills, one must learn to respond, predict, flow with and counter another. It is very easy to drive a car at 90 mph when there is no traffic, but it is much more demanding when the street is packed with cars driven by unpredictable humans and frequently uncooperative drivers.

This is the most important fundamental understanding of training in Jiu-Jitsu. Unlike the majority of other martial arts, Jiu-Jitsu techniques must be applied and perfected against live opponents. There are no forms or shadow-boxing. This simple fact makes everything more complicated. However, Jiu-Jitsu also owes much of its legendary effectiveness to this approach. Because training requires an adversary, after many years of practice, the Jiu-Jitsu exponent has a much higher level of practical application as compared to students of any other arts.

THE NATURE OF THE ART

All Jiu-Jitsu practitioners should accept the fact that mastering the basics is the only way to reach the higher levels. Indeed, it is the key that opens the door to the advanced movements. The efficiency of Jiu-Jitsu, like any other fighting art, lies in the mastery of the basic movements. In the long run, you will find out that — if you lack the fundamentals — it is a waste of time to learn 100 different new techniques because you won't be able to apply these movements against a skilled opponent. Instead of accumulating an arsenal of new techniques, it is far more important to constantly work your basics.

Knowing 100 different choking techniques won't help you if you lack the basic and fundamental principles. You need to understand how the fundamental principles work from all angles and countless variables and master these well. The number of variations that you know will give you more opportunities to defeat your opponent, but they will be meaningless if you don't have what it takes to make them work.

The secret is "body feel" and "body mechanics" on the ground. These two attributes can only be developed through long sessions of drilling the basics, and not necessarily fighting. Stated simply, drilling in the basics is the trick to mastering the art. Professional basketball and football players drill every day but rarely do they play a full game at practice.

In the beginning stages of training, it is imperative to learn how to apply the basics. During this phase, you learn the essentials like changing the angle and positioning to suit your game plan. At the same time, you learn how to prevent your opponent from controlling you. This is a progression of the

"All Jiu-Jitsu practitioners should accept the fact that mastering the basics is the only way to reach the higher levels."

"You can't learn a language without learning the vocabulary, and you can't learn Jiu-Jitsu, or any martial art, without refining the basics."

more advanced control of body mechanics and body feel that you developed in your first years of "boring" and "tedious" repetition of the basic positions and techniques. Only when you have developed these attributes to a high level can the advanced techniques be applied at will. New movements won't bring out these important attributes of fighting, but they will help you to create a game plan that becomes unpredictable to your opponents.

Obviously, a Jiu-Jitsu competitor with a superior number of technical movements will be more difficult to defeat than someone who only counts 10 techniques in his arsenal. It is similar to a chess game. Technical options and possibilities are two important principles in elite competition.

One mistake most beginners make is searching for "shortcuts" — only to learn that there are no shortcuts. You can't learn a language without learning the vocabulary, and you can't learn Jiu-Jitsu, or any martial art, without refining the basics. When the level of the game increases and your opponents are more knowledgeable technically and, therefore capable of stopping your techniques, you will need a better strategy, a better understanding of the basic techniques and how they can be used under different scenarios and situations.

This involves the ability to modify the basic techniques to fit the movements and physical ability of the opponent you are facing at that moment. The key word here is "adaptability." It is not a "new trick" that the competitor needs but a deeper understanding of what he has and how to adapt it to make it more effective or adapt it to ever-changing situations. Many people try to look for or invent new movements instead of going deeper into the understanding of the fundamental techniques. They look for the answer outside where they should be looking inside of what they already have.

All the new techniques found in competition are extensions of the fundamental principles and movements of Jiu-Jitsu. In this work, you'll find a great number of basic, intermediate and advanced movements that will give you an "edge" in training and competition. These movements have been developed by the best Jiu-Jitsu practitioners in the world and currently are used by the

"Most beginners mistakenly search for 'shortcuts'— only to learn that there are no shortcuts."

world champions. To be able to perform these techniques, the competitor needs to master the essential principles and techniques of the art and combine these with the important physical attributes (body feel, strength, balance, et cetera). Attributes developed through many hours of drilling the physical techniques is the so-called "secret" to making the techniques work against an uncooperative opponent.

Think of each technique you learn as a unit composed of several segments or sections. For the sake of explanation, let's say that each Jiu-Jitsu technique is divided into 10 little sections or segments that make the movement possible. Try to work each section separately until you really master it. Then move to the next one. Polish and perfect each segment to the maximum of your possibilities and never try to jump from segment 3 to segment 8 with a simple push of strength or brute force. Once you have mastered all the sections which compose that single technique you are learning, begin to add a more solid use of your body weight and strength, not as a substitute for the lack of polished technique, but as a back-up element to your game.

Never try to compensate for lack of technique with pure strength. This approach will work against a lighter and less-experienced opponent, but it won't be of any use against a heavier foe, let alone against a more skilled practitioner. Using strength to accomplish the technique will eventually limit your future skill as a Jiu-Jitsu practitioner. Work on developing skill in technique and strive to understand the essence and principles involved in the movement instead of forcing your way through it. Finally, it is extremely important to understand the essence of how the art works and how this affects the structure of the techniques used in a confrontation. Jiu-Jitsu was developed as a self-defense art — not as an attacking method. The main emphasis of the art's structure is to protect and preserve the student's physical integrity. Jiu-Jitsu is a defensive art in nature. Obviously, this doesn't mean that a Jiu-Jitsu practitioner can't attack his aggressor in a fighting situation, but it is important to understand that the very essence of Jiu-Jitsu as a martial art is defensive.

This means that the Brazilian Jiu-Jitsu practitioner will perform the movements based on what his opponent gives him. It will be the opponent who will set the final technique used by the BJJ stylist. There is no other task at hand for the BJJ practitioner than to complete the other half of the equation. Your technique will be the result of your opponent's movement. Don't get obsessed with trying to get the armlock or the rear choke; let the technique "occur" naturally. If it is not there, it simply doesn't belong there.

Be relaxed at all time and feel your opponent's intentions and movements. He, without realizing it, will "give you" the right technique to apply on him. In the higher levels of the art, there is nothing else to do but fill your opponent's gaps. Some people — with a sport-oriented mentality — wrongly describe this fighting approach as passive, when in fact it is the very nature of an excellent self-defense system.

IMPROVING YOUR GAME

Finding the proper way to improve your game is one of the most difficult things to do. After years of training, every Jiu-Jitsu practitioner reaches a point described as "hitting the wall." It is here when more training won't necessarily bring the desired results. More is not better anymore. The choice of your training partner is paramount here since your improvement will be based not on your partner's general skill but in his ability to bring the best out of you.

At this point, your partner becomes your "training coach." Try to put yourself in a worst-case scenario and work from there. For instance, if your guard

"You need to understand how the fundamental principles work from all angles and countless variables and master these well."

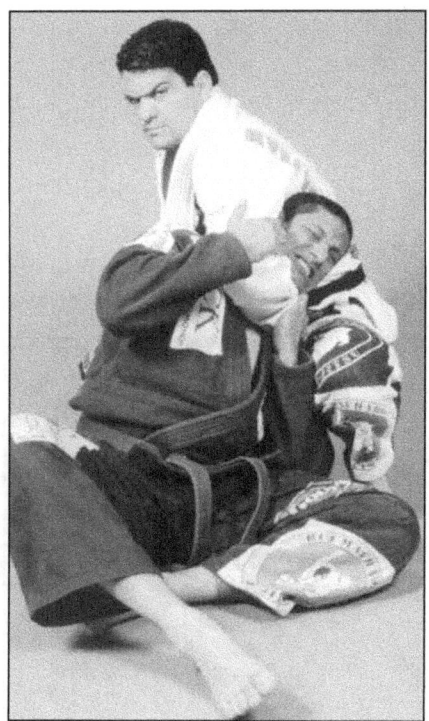

"There are four phases to achieve mastery of any physical technique: to learn, practice, master and finally functionalize it."

is your weak point, dedicate the beginning of your personal training to work other aspects of the game. When you are tired, ask your partner to try to pass your guard. This is a difficult situation for you due to two factors: 1) you are already exhausted and, 2) you are going to work on the weakest part of your game.

You must always try to stay calm. This specific training should be highly technical. Ask your partner to attack your guard using a flowing approach. Don't let the egos come into play here. "Play" is the key. Have your partner feed you with several approaches. Ask him to not use brute force but technique and deception. If your partner doesn't follow what you are asking him to do, replace him. This is your way of improving and if he doesn't cooperate, choose someone who does.

MAKE IT FUNCTIONAL

The road to excellence is long in any sport, and Brazilian Jiu-Jitsu is no exception. From the very first moment when a practitioner learns a technique until he applies it successfully in a world championship, there are many hours of hard training and progressive technical development.

There are four phases to achieve mastery of any physical technique: to learn, practice, master and finally functionalize it. We'll analyze each one separately and explain how the different concepts apply to each one of these training phases.

1) *Learn*: This is the very first step. The instructor teaches the student the movement (technique) and gives him all the necessary technical details to perform the technique correctly. He walks with the student through all the basic elements and principles that build the foundation of that particular movement. The student now has all the information about how to perform the technique correctly, but he still lacks the training. This is the reason he doesn't perform it well and has difficulty executing it. It is important to be neither aggressive nor to use a combative mind in this phase. It is paramount to empty and relax the mind, trying to absorb as much as information as possible about the fine details of the movement.

2) *Practice*: Now that the student has the basic information, the next step is to practice what he already has (in his mind). This phase is extremely important since all the fundamental body mechanics for that specific technique will be built during this phase, which means that he must pay very close attention to how he inputs the information into his system. Taking time while absorbing and working on the little technical details of the movement is very important. The mind should navigate the body. Don't rush and try to use force because all the data that you'll be putting into your body will be incorrect. Relax and work slowly, little by little, paying full attention to each small detail that the teacher corrects.

Progressively, and only when the student has a fair amount of control on the "little details," should he start to increase the speed used to perform the movement. If he feels like he is having problems in achieving any "segment" or "section" or if the movement is less than correct, then he should slow down the pace and work on that particular aspect of the technique until it is fully corrected. Paying complete attention to each small detail is extremely important in this phase of training.

3) *Master*: This is a tricky word that brings confusion to the practitioner. He already has a very good level of skill in performing the technique as a "mold," but now he needs to add a new element into the equation... different opponents who give him different scenarios. Here, the practitioner doesn't need to think about the small details of the physical movement anymore — because these should be already in the database — but he needs to be able of fit the technical movement into the structure of different, uncooperative opponents. Uncooperative is the key word, because no two opponents in the world have the same way of moving, giving the same exact energy back or trying to counter the technique.

This first aspect of mastering the technique has to do with the operativeness of the technique in itself and your ability to understand how the technique should be used against different kinds of opponents. You should research and go deep into the essential principles of the technique and its possibilities under different kinds of circumstances (opponents). When facing a problem, don't try to find the solution outside the fundamental principles of the technique but analyze this new situation and try to find a way using the essence of the principles that compose the basic movement.

Don't randomly change the technique for the sake of change, but make the technique fit into the new scenario as you maintain the basic principles of it. In this phase of the technical development, the training partner again is a very important element of the equation. To a certain extent, your training partner should be at least as skillful as you are and, in a perfect world, a much better Jiu-Jitsu practitioner. Why? Simply because he is the individual who needs to set the environment for you and needs to think ahead of your technique. He is the person who will set the circumstances for you to improve your game.

Ideally, your training partner should be your instructor/teacher, and that's why private classes are very important at this stage. Only someone with more understanding, skill and knowledge than you can truly take you to the higher levels of this phase. No beginner will improve your technique at this level. Only someone with a deep and mature understanding of the art, its principles and the complete spectrum of the training phases in the art will be capable of getting the best out of you.

"Many people try to look for or invent new movements instead of going deeper into the understanding of the fundamental techniques."

4) *Functionalize*: At this level the practitioner already has a) a sound technical foundation; b) a deep understanding of the fundamental principles that rule that specific technique and; c) the ability and precise body feel to use it against different kinds of opponents. Now he needs to kick it up another

notch and develop a plan of how to use the given technique against different opponents (size, weight, and physical characteristics). Then he should begin to incorporate combination attacks that involve the study and analysis of how to interrelate and combine that specific movement with other techniques, creating a network of technical solutions.

Each one of the techniques composing that network should have been taken to the master level. Otherwise the technical network will have important flaws that will bring problems to the practitioner. For instance, let's take the triangle as the main technique. You have to learn to adapt this movement against someone who is skinny and against someone who is heavy with a strong neck and shoulder muscles that will impede the movement. Then you must study how to interrelate that movement with, for instance, the straight armlock and omoplata.

Now that you have three different options from one single given point in combat, you'll have to be able to attack with one and, as soon as your opponent counters this one, move into the other successively, creating a constant menace for him. He will be only humanly capable of covering a limited amount of attacks. When one door closes, another opens. It is this stage, where you develop a complete game plan, that brings together the fine skill in techniques with the proper tactics and strategies of when and how to use the technique against any kind of opponent and under any kind of situation. To reach this very advanced level, the student needs to be able to modify the techniques against different opponents and combine it with others to create a tactical network. It is only here when you can really say that your Jiu-Jitsu techniques are truly functional.

Unfortunately, and due mostly to today's "fast-food" mentality, the urgency of passing belt tests or winning sport competitions, these phases are overlooked and easily forgotten in many Brazilian Jiu-Jitsu schools. It is true that without using the four-phase approach you can become a world champion anyway. But if this happens, it isn't because you found a "shortcut" to excellence. Instead you cut yourself short in your true Jiu-Jitsu potential, allowing a great deal of understanding and talent to be lost somewhere along the way. The road you'll take will depend on the degree of personal imperfection for which you're willing to settle.

CHOOSING AN INSTRUCTOR

Being able to perform all Jiu-Jitsu techniques won't make you an instructor in the art. Doing and teaching are two completely different things and as such should be understood separately. As a student, you should be able to perform the physical techniques with a skill level accorded your rank. As an instructor, the physical ability won't make your students good Jiu-Jitsu practitioners. It is the ability to communicate, break down and pass the technical knowledge that is important here. Many great champions, in all kinds of sports, lacked the ability to break down everything they were capable of doing and teach it to their students. They were talented athletes but with no ability to create other talented athletes or good students.

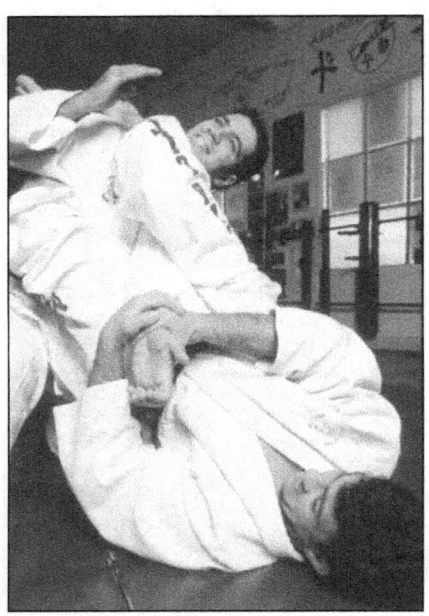

"Teaching Brazilian Jiu-Jitsu requires an extensive knowledge of how all the pieces of the puzzle (techniques) fit and the fundamental principles that every single technique exemplifies."

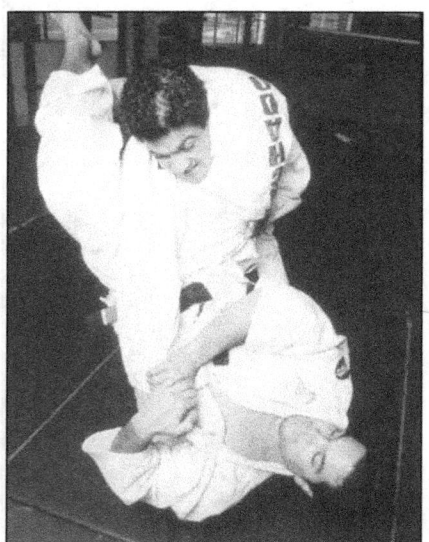

Teaching Brazilian Jiu-Jitsu requires an extensive knowledge of how all the pieces of the puzzle (techniques) fit and the fundamental principles that every single technique exemplifies. A good teacher will have a progressive program that will allow the student not only to physically improve, but also understand how the different techniques are interrelated and how those can be combined in a practical format.

Although it is very common to see an instructor giving techniques in a random manner, this approach is definitely not the most appropriate for students to understand what they are doing. An instructor should start showing the student the basics of the art. The basic techniques develop the most fundamental principles found in the art. Most importantly, this is teaching the student the necessary body mechanics for future technical growth. Like any other martial art system, Brazilian Jiu-Jitsu has a set of fundamental techniques that a good instructor should emphasize in the early stages of learning. These basic techniques should be backed up with several drills — not fighting drills — that improve the student's ability to move his body on the ground. The drills eventually will make it possible to perform the technique properly.

Beware of instructors who show too many techniques in a random way without giving a strong foundation to the student. Be cautious of those teachers who allow beginners to spar almost immediately — focusing on a competition approach and how the techniques are supposed to be used in a tournament — and force them to struggle in a grappling situation without previous intensive training and understanding of the basics. These types of instructors will push the student to perform the technique via pure strength and muscle, but this will eventually cut the student's progress in the art since all the basic information added to the database has been wrong. It is easier for these kinds of instructors to have students spar than to dedicate time to correct and teach the art properly. There is a time for everything and sparring in Brazilian Jiu-Jitsu should be incorporated into the student's program at the right time.

A good instructor will get any student — regardless of level of understanding and physical ability — to learn and apply a basic movement. It is up to the instructor to be able of dissect the technique and communicate the intrinsic principles of the movement to different levels of understanding. An experienced instructor will teach an armlock differently to a white belt, a purple belt and a black belt, depending on their expertise and knowledge of the art. It is the ability of the instructor to break down the information according to the student's level (technical and understanding) that sets a master apart from an average instructor. There are no bad students; only teachers incapable of making the student good at Jiu-Jitsu.

Find a teacher who dedicates time and attention to explaining the art and the techniques properly; someone who has a teaching structure and the correct methodology. No art or subject of any kind can be properly taught without a correct structure and format.

"Never try to compensate for lack of technique with pure strength. This approach will work against a lighter and less-experienced opponent, but it won't be of any use against a heavier foe, let alone a more skilled practitioner."

Finally, when looking for a Jiu-Jitsu instructor, simply remember that the students are a reflection of what the teacher is. Pay attention to the students, analyze how they train, how they move, and how they behave with lower ranks, such as explaining the techniques. See if they "compete" with the lower ranks or help them to improve. If you are planning to join a school and find that all the students do is "roll" indiscriminately, fight with no sense of technique or finesse and focus excessively on competing, maybe you need to keep looking.

TOURNAMENTS AND COMPETITION

Tournaments are an important part of most martial arts styles, but when practicing a martial art you must take into consideration what the real goal of the art is because ultimately a martial art is something different than a sport. Rules in competition, in any kind of competition, set the direction in which the physical techniques of the art/sport will evolve.

The ultimate goal of Jiu-Jitsu is to control and submit your opponent. Only these aspects represent the true superiority of one fighter over another. The problem arises when two excellent competitors meet and the "ideal" submission technique is blocked and countered by the other fighter. This situation provokes both participants to try to stall and play with the rules — using excessive force to get out of a position in which the opponent gets more points even if the fighter is not truly in any danger.

Jiu-Jitsu competition rules vary and change according to the specific tournament and those running it, but the essence of our Jiu-Jitsu training — when practiced at the school — shouldn't be governed by the set rules of the sport. Training in the art of Jiu-Jitsu and being good at it should be our main concern, not simply winning tournaments. Jiu-Jitsu is first and foremost a martial art and a sport second. When you step onto the mat and you are rolling with your partners, you try to do your best, regardless of how many points are awarded in competition for any specific movement.

Develop your game plan based on the concept and principles of a martial art, and later on, if you feel interested in competition, learn the rules and try to use them appropriately without forgetting that trying to control and submit your opponent is the main objective of Brazilian Jiu-Jitsu. In a perfect world, referees should only award points for either controlling the opponent clearly and with a full controlled technique for a certain amount of time (several seconds) or for putting the opponent into a submission and making him tap. This way, the competitors should have to train to fully control and totally submit their opponents.

Once you get into a tournament, make sure you know the rules and how to play with the regulations to get the best out of them. There is nothing wrong with using the rules of competition to your advantage. However, always keep in mind that sport competition has limits and regulations that don't measure your self-defense abilities, your personal involvement or the totality of your skill in the art.

In competition, the participants are grouped into similar levels of rank and skill. Therefore, as much as possible, it is a match against theoretical equals. As a result, the key element in sport Jiu-Jitsu lies in other surrounding aspects of the technical training. Physical conditioning, strength training, power training, cardiovascular training, psychological make-up, are these key attributes that will make a difference at the end.

The best illustration is the iceberg analogy. The tip of the iceberg, the fraction that shows, represents the physical techniques of the art — the basic movements. All the rest, the physical attributes necessary to make that "tip"

"Training in the art of Jiu-Jitsu and being good at it should be our main concern, not simply winning tournaments."

work in a fight, comprise the 90 percent that is below the ice. They are underwater, where you can't see them...but that certainly doesn't mean they don't exist.

Every martial arts system requires certain physical attributes from the practitioner to be able to fully apply the individual techniques of the art. Standing fighting arts require specific attributes such as timing, mobility, reflexes, eye-hand/foot coordination, etc. Grappling arts like Brazilian Jiu-Jitsu rely mostly on physical sensitivity, body positioning, isometric muscular strength, limberness, etc.

Since the "perfect" execution of a single technique depends on the practitioner's level of attribute development, it is important for the students to allocate time to develop these necessary attributes for their chosen arts. Analyze the attributes that specifically apply to Brazilian Jiu-Jitsu and work on them hard. By doing this, you'll improve the effectiveness of your technique. Do the attribute training once you have already developed a high technical level. Attributes without refined technique is useless. It is important to bring the building blocks in the proper order to establish a strong foundation. Technique first... everything else follows.

Today's competitors are more knowledgeable about all the technical possibilities available at arm's reach. Hopefully, the knowledge of an additional technique may surprise your opponent and allow you to score a decisive point or completely submit your opponent, but with all the technical advancements, an exclusively technique approach simply is not sufficient. The competitor needs to be an athlete if he wants to become a Brazilian Jiu-Jitsu champion. The physical techniques now have to be supported by other "supplementary aspects" of fighting because the game has improved tremendously in the last decade.

The hours you spent on the mat are called "flight time." Leave the ego at the door and don't try to fight your partners. The school is not a competition or tournament, and it is not a fight; it is the place where you learn the art. If your partner doesn't cooperate, then ask him to slow down and make him understand that both of you are helping each other. Anybody with enough muscle power can fight and force his way through a technique. Doing it with refined technique and skill is reserved to the few who excel.

One good way of training intelligently is to roll with your opponent when no submissions are allowed. Neither you nor your opponent can go for a submission, armlock, choke or leglock. This takes the pressure out of trying to submit the training partner and allows the practitioner to smoothly roll with the opponent, which will eventually develop many of the important attributes in sparring or competition. In this specific training drill, there is no destination or submission so we can enjoy the journey more consciously and improve one of the most difficult aspects of the art of Brazilian Jiu-Jitsu — flow with your opponent.

Finally, set a progressive training plan that allows you to get better and improve your game. Start working hard on the basics; work on the small details that make the technique work. Leave the brute force at home and think of finesse instead of strength. Try to discover how all the positions you are learning interrelate to each other, how you can move from a defensive movement into an attack, how to reverse an armlock and end up submitting your opponent with a choke, or how to escape from a headlock and finish your opponent with a leglock. All techniques are interchangeable, and you'll be surprised how the most advanced technique can be countered with a basic movement. Most of the time the solution to a big problem lies in a simple answer.

"All techniques are interchangeable, and you'll be surprised how the most advanced technique can be countered with a basic movement. Most of the time the solution to a big problem lies in a simple answer."

Mastering Brazilian Jiu Jitsu

Attacks from the Guard

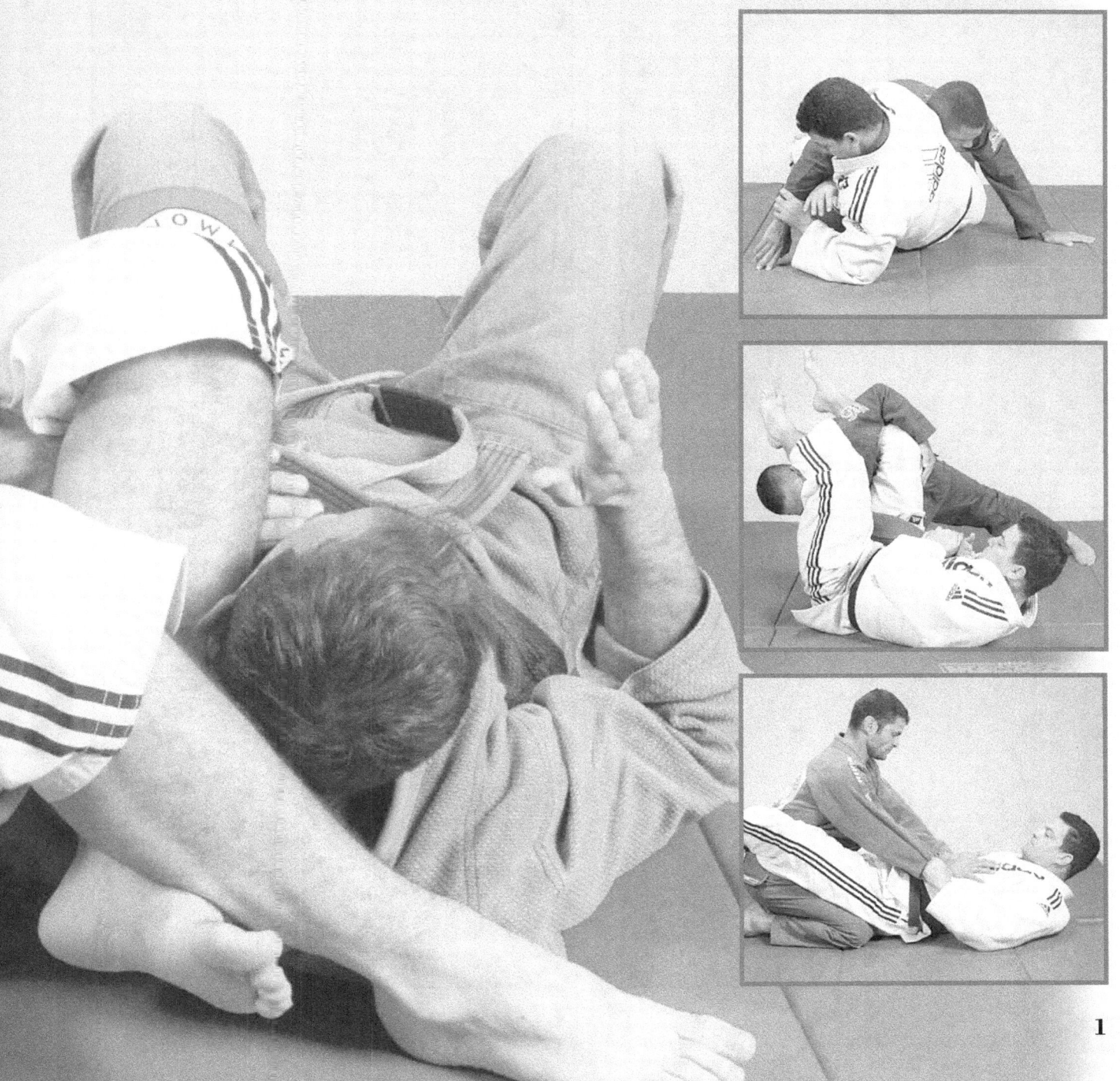

Attacks From The Guard   1

• Closed Guard

Rigan holds the opponent inside his guard and controls both sleeves (1). He then grabs his opponent's right sleeve with both hands (2) and pulls toward the opposite side, unbalancing him (3). Using his right elbow to support himself, Rigan turns to the right (4), reaches for his opponent's left armpit (5), hooks the opponent's left foot (6), and obtains a full back mount control with both hooks in (7).

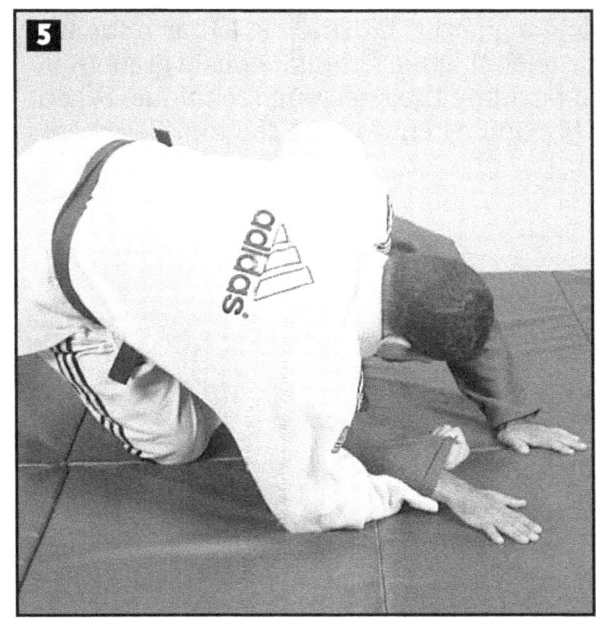
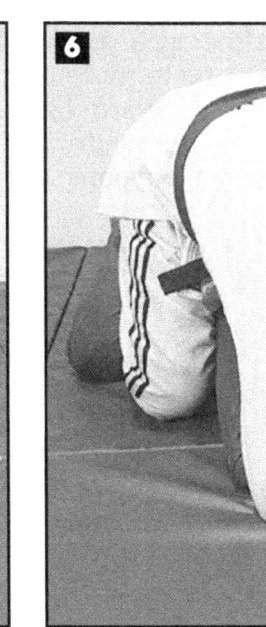

Mastering Brazilian Jiu-Jitsu 3

Attacks From The Guard 2

• Closed Guard

Rigan holds the opponent inside his guard (1). Using his left arm for support, Rigan starts to move to his left (2) while simultaneously grabbing his opponent's right arm (3). To facilitate the sweeping technique, Rigan puts his left leg on the ground (4), and he ends up on the top (5), where he can control his opponent (6).

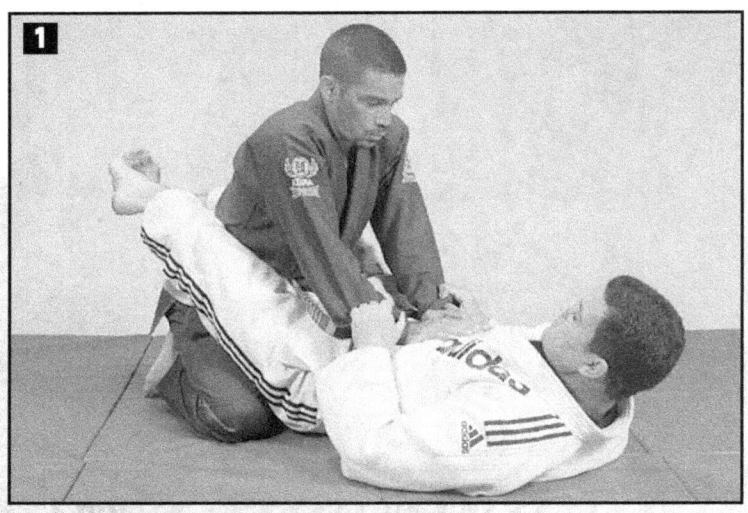

Attacks From The Guard 3

• Closed Guard

Rigan's opponent maintains control from the inside guard (1). To break the grip, Rigan uses both arms (2). Rigan then controls his opponent's right arm (3), grabs his adversary's wrist with his left hand and passes his right arm over (4) to secure a *kimura*. At the same time, Rigan lifts his left leg (5) to control his opponent on the ground, preventing him from escaping (6).

Attacks From The Guard 4

• **Closed Guard**

Rigan has his opponent inside his guard with full control of the collar (1). He opens the guard, drops his left leg to the floor (2), and simultaneously places his right shin on his opponent's stomach to apply a sweeping technique (3). Ultimately, Rigan ends up on top (4).

Attacks From The Guard 5

• Closed Guard

Rigan controls his opponent inside his guard with a light inside grip on the collar (1). While he moves his right hand all the way in to properly secure the grip (2), he slides his left hand under the right hand to get inside his opponent's collar (3). Note that his palm is up. Applying pressure and bringing his opponent's body closer, Rigan chokes him (4).

Attacks From The Guard 6

• **Closed Guard**

Rigan controls his opponent (1). As he did in the previous technique, Rigan moves his right hand all the way in (2), and then he slides his left hand under the right to reach the collar (3). Contrary to the previous technique, this time he grabs the collar from the top with the palm facing down (4). Then he pulls his opponent and applies pressure for the choke (5).

Attacks From The Guard 7

• **Closed Guard**

Rigan has his opponent inside his guard (1). He opens the guard, places his left foot on his opponent's right hip (2), and uses his right foot to push the opponent's arm (3-4). This creates space to place his right leg over the left shoulder. Meanwhile, he simultaneously pulls his opponent toward him using his left arm (5). Rigan then passes his left leg over the instep of the right foot, grabs his opponent's head, tilts the pelvis and applies a *triangle* choke (6).

Attacks From The Guard 8

• Closed Guard

Rigan has his opponent inside his guard (1). The opponent lifts his left leg to start passing the guard, but Rigan opens his guard and passes his right arm under the opponent's left leg (2). Using his left hand to pull and subsequently unbalance his opponent, Rigan uses his right leg to push the aggressor toward his left (3), bringing him down (4). He controls his opponent during the whole movement (5). Ultimately, Rigan mounts him so he can start the attack (6).

Attacks From The Guard 9

• Closed Guard

Rigan holds his opponent inside his guard (1). The opponent lifts his left leg to start passing the guard, but Rigan opens his guard and tries to pass his right arm under the opponent's left leg (2). To prevent the sweep, his opponent moves his left leg back. Rigan responds by pulling the opponent's right arm close to his body, swinging his left leg to get momentum (3). Then he brings his leg up front and finishes the opponent with a perfect armlock (4-5).

Mastering Brazilian Jiu-Jitsu

Attacks From The Guard 10

• Closed Guard

Rigan holds the opponent inside his guard (1). The opponent lifts his left leg to start passing the guard (2), but Rigan opens his guard and tries to pass his right arm under the opponent's left leg (3) to execute an armlock (4). The opponent manages to extricate his right arm (5). This forces Rigan to change grips and move to the left arm (6).

Rigan pulls his opponent toward him (7), twists his hips to the left and simultaneously passes his right leg over the opponent's triceps (8), finishing him off with an *omoplata* (9).

Attacks From The Guard   11

• Closed Guard

Rigan holds the opponent inside his guard (1). When the opponent lifts his left leg to start passing the guard (2), Rigan passes his right arm under the opponent's left leg and attempts an armlock (3-4). The opponent pulls his right arm out (5), nullifying the attack (6). Rigan reacts by pulling in the opponent's left leg and by moving his hips to the left to create momentum (7). He finishes with a straight kneebar (8).

Attacks From The Guard

Mastering Brazilian Jiu-Jitsu 15

Attacks From The Guard 12

• **Closed Guard**

Rigan holds his opponent inside his guard (1), and uses his left hand to initiate an attack (2). His opponent blocks the sweep attempt (3), and brings Rigan back to the floor. Rigan passes his arm around the opponent's neck (4), slides his left hand under the adversary's head, and grabs his own right wrist (5). He submits his opponent by pulling him back into the guard and applying pressure to the choke (6).

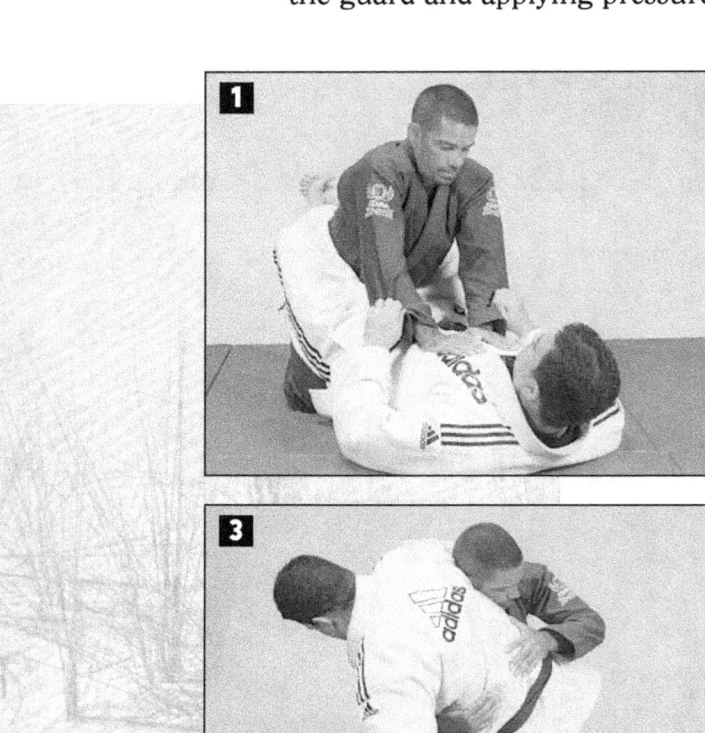

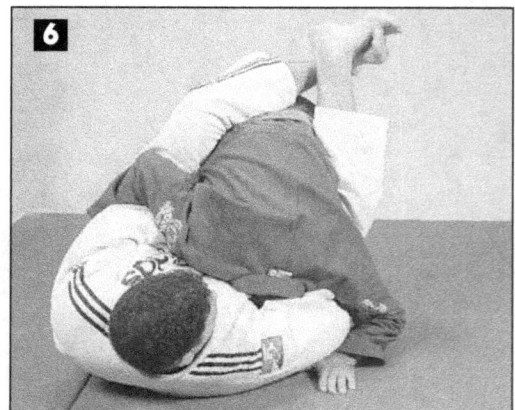

Attacks From The Guard 13

• Closed Guard

Rigan controls the opponent inside his guard (1). He uses his left hand to control his opponent's right arm and passes his right hand under the other arm to secure the opponent's right elbow (2). Then, he opens the guard, raises his right leg up close to the armpit (3), and pushes down to force the opponent's body to the right (4). He can now apply an armlock by closing his legs and pushing with his pelvis (5). It is important to not only maintain a tight grip but also to keep your opponent's elbow close to your body.

Attacks From The Guard   14

• **Closed Guard** Rigan holds his opponent inside his guard (1). He uses both hands to break the opponent's grip and create space (2-3). Rigan uses his left hand to move the collar close to his right hand (4).

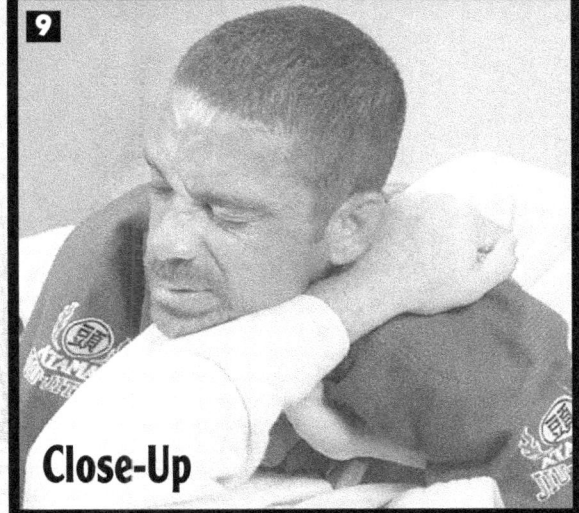

Next, he grabs the right side of the opponent's collar (5). He secures a tight grip with the right hand and simultaneously (6) passes his left hand around the neck to secure a grip on the left side of his opponent's gi (7). He closes the grip and applies pressure with his left forearm (8) to finalize the choke. A close-up (9).

Attacks From The Guard

Attacks From The Guard 15

• **Closed Guard**

Rigan has his opponent inside his full guard (1). He opens the guard and moves his left knee inside his opponent's left arm (2). Simultaneously, he uses his right hand to control his opponent's left arm and moves his hips to the left, which creates space to bring the right leg out (3),

and over his opponent's back (4). Then, he spins toward his left side. By keeping tight pressure on the opponent's arm (5), he applies an *omoplata*. He also applies additional pressure as he moves his body forward (6). To make this work, keep your right leg close to the opponent's left armpit and control the other side of his body. This prevents him from rolling and nullifying the technique.

Attacks From The Guard 16

• Closed Guard

Rigan controls his opponent inside his guard (1). He grabs the collar with both hands (2), and pulls his opponent close (3). Next, he passes his right arm around the neck and grabs the right side of the opponent's collar with his right hand (4). Using his right forearm to maintain pressure and control his opponent, Rigan grabs the sleeve of his own gi (5), and slides his left arm under his opponent's neck (6). Applying pressure with his left forearm, Rigan chokes his opponent with the *ezequiel* (7).

Attacks From The Guard

Mastering Brazilian Jiu-Jitsu 23

Attacks From The Guard   17

• **Closed Guard**   Rigan holds the opponent inside his guard (1). The opponent lifts his left leg to start passing the guard (2), but Rigan opens his guard and tries to pass his right arm under the opponent's left leg (3) so he can execute an armlock (4). The opponent manages to pull his right arm out, and escapes from the armlock (5-6).

The opponent then moves forward to improve his position, but Rigan pulls the left arm between his legs (7), moves his hips to the right side and passes his left leg over his opponent's neck. He grabs his own ankle (8), applies pressure and executes a *triangle* choke (9). While executing this, it is important to keep your opponent's arm tight, push your pelvis up consistently and pull your opponent's head down. And this must all be done simultaneously.

Attacks From The Guard 18

• **Closed Guard**

Rigan controls the opponent inside his guard (1). He grabs his opponent's left sleeve with both hands (2), and pulls toward the other side (3). He maintains the grip with his left hand but passes his right hand under the opponent's left arm (4). By applying pressure to bend the arm as he controls the wrist (5),

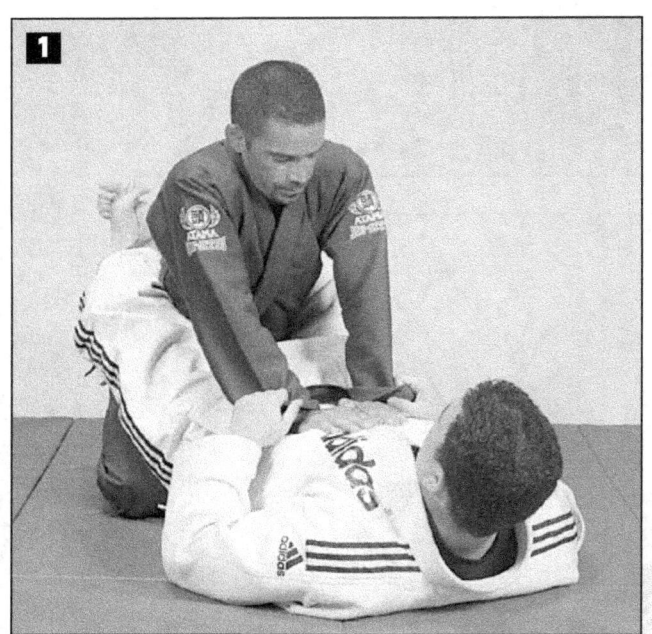

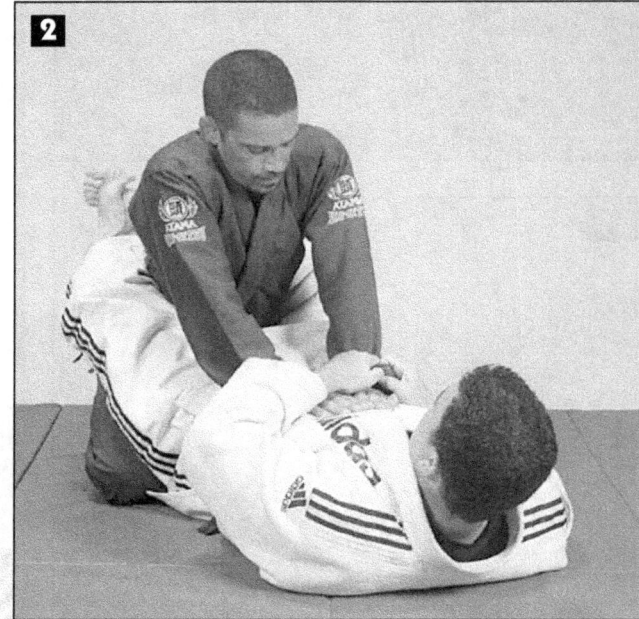

Rigan executes the wristlock (6). It is important to make sure the opponent's elbow is placed against your chest. This will create the necessary base to apply the wristlock and prevent the opponent from escaping.

Attacks From The Guard 19

• **Closed Guard**

Rigan holds the opponent inside his guard (1). He opens the guard, moves his hips back a little to create space, and brings his right knee inside his opponent's arms (2). He plants his left leg on the floor, creating a base, and simultaneously pushes the opponent's left arm away using his right foot at biceps level (3-4).

In this next sequence of moves, Rigan creates a situation in which force is simultaneously applied in different directions. Using his right hand, Rigan holds the opponent's sleeve. He uses his right foot to push the opponent away. Meanwhile, he uses his left hand to pull the opponent's right sleeve as the left leg creates a barrier (5). Rigan unbalances his opponent (6) and brings him down (7), where he is mounted and controlled (8).

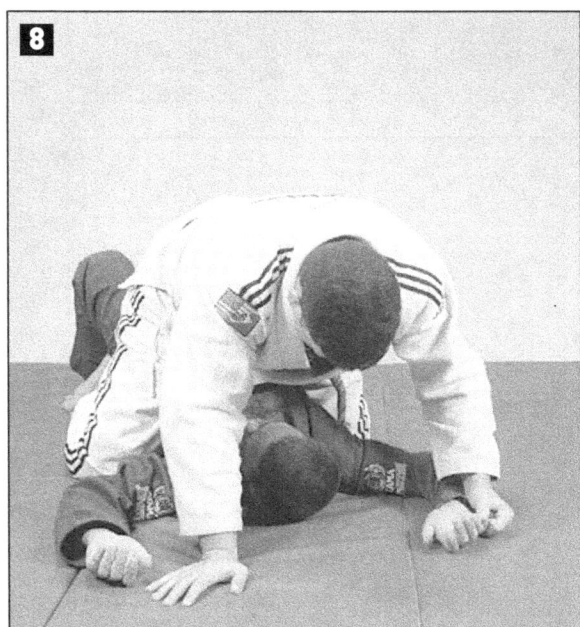

Attacks From The Guard 20

• **Closed Guard** Rigan controls his opponent in the full guard (1). With his right hand, he loosens his opponent's jacket (2) and brings the tip over (3), as he simultaneously pulls the opponent's head down (4).

Now he can pass a portion of the jacket over his opponent's head (5). He applies a front choke using the jacket and his left hand (6).

Attacks From The Guard 21

• Closed Guard

From the full guard (1), Rigan loosens the jacket, as he did in the previous technique (2). This time, however, he grabs it with his left hand (3), pulling it down and securing his opponent's left arm against his own body (4). Then, he uses his right hand to lower his opponent's body and moves his hips to the right (5-6), creating space to put his right leg over his opponent's head (7). He concludes with an armlock (8).

Attacks From The Guard

Mastering Brazilian Jiu-Jitsu 33

Attacks From The Guard 22

• Closed Guard

Rigan holds his opponent inside his guard (1). He controls both arms and moves his hip slightly out to bring his right knee inside his opponent's arm (2). He repeats this with his left knee (3). While maintaining control over the left sleeve, Rigan places his shin against the opponent's stomach (4). He then grabs the right leg on the outside of the knee and pulls. This is done in conjunction with pushing with his right leg (5). He sweeps his opponent (6), and finishes by placing his knee on the chest and pulling the right arm (7).

Attacks From The Guard 23

• Closed Guard

In this technique, Rigan maneuvers his hips to place both knees inside the opponent's arms (1-3). He uses his left foot to push the opponent's biceps (4). Swinging his body creates momentum and space to sweep, but his opponent stops the attempt (5). As soon as Rigan feels the sweep attempt has been stopped (6), he brings his right leg over, adapts the hip position and applies a perfect armlock (7).

Attacks From The Guard 24

• Closed Guard

Rigan holds his opponent inside his guard (1). He controls both arms and moves his hip slightly out so he can bring his left knee inside his opponent's arms (2). Then he does the same thing with his right knee (3). He places his left foot on his opponent's biceps and pushes (4). Using his left hand, Rigan pulls his opponent's right sleeve while he kicks his left leg out (5). This brings the opponent's head closer, which allows Rigan to bend his left leg over the opponent's neck, hooking it under the back of his right knee (6). He concludes with a *triangle* choke (7).

Attacks From The Guard 25

• Closed Guard

Rigan again maneuvers his hips to place both knees inside the opponent's arms (1-3). He then places his left foot on his opponent's biceps and pushes (4). However, this time he moves his hips to the right (5), so he can pass his right leg over his opponent's left arm (6) and apply an *omoplata* armlock (7). When moving forward to apply pressure in the armlock, it is important to control the opposite side of the opponent's body. Grab his belt or the side of his body to prevent him from rolling and escaping.

Attacks From The Guard 26

• Closed Guard

Rigan holds his opponent inside his guard (1). While he controls both arms, he moves his hip slightly out so he can bring his left knee inside his opponent's arm (2). Then he does the same thing with his right knee (3). He places his left foot on his opponent's right shoulder (4), and does the same with his right foot (5). Pulling up and out with both arms, Rigan brings his hips right under his opponent's center of gravity (6). This gives him leverage to throw his opponent over his head (7-8). Without releasing his grip (9), Rigan immediately obtains the mounted position (10).

Attacks From The Guard 27

- **Closed Guard** Rigan holds his opponent inside his guard (1). He controls both arms and moves his hip slightly out so he can bring his left knee inside the opponent's arms (2). He then does the same thing with his right knee (3). To create space, Rigan moves his hip slightly and moves his left leg to the outside (4), hooking the leg over his opponent's right arm (5).

To make room, he moves his right leg against his opponent's stomach and simultaneously grabs his opponent's pants at the knee (6). He synchronizes the push of the left leg with the pull of his right hand and the push of the right shin (7) to sweep his opponent. He controls him with the right knee on the chest (8). This technique can also be finished with a painful control of the opponent's trapped arm. This is done by applying pressure with the left shin over the opponent's right biceps.

Attacks From The Guard 28

• Closed Guard

Rigan performs the same movements that he did in the previous technique (1-4), but here he hooks his left leg over the opponent's right arm (5), and places his right leg against the stomach (6).

When the opponent blocks the attempt, Rigan reaches under the opponent's right arm (7), and pulls hard toward himself (8), applying an armlock (9).

Attacks From The Guard 29

• Closed Guard

Rigan holds his opponent inside his guard (1). While he controls both arms, he moves his hip slightly out to bring his left knee inside his opponent's arms (2). He does the same thing with his right knee (3). Rigan then brings his left leg over the opponent's right arm (4), but this time he hooks the opposite arm from under the biceps (5). He moves his hip out toward his right side and controls the opponent's left arm (6). By passing his right leg over the arm, he applies a straight armbar (7).

Attacks From The Guard 30

• Closed Guard

Rigan holds his opponent inside his guard (1). He controls both arms and moves his hip slightly out so he can bring his left knee inside his opponent's arms (2). He does the same thing with his right knee (3). Rigan starts to move his left leg over the opponent's right arm (4). He hooks the opposite arm from under the biceps (5). The opponent tries to create space, but Rigan maintains control of his left sleeve and the left side of the hip (6).

Next, Rigan brings the right leg over and across his opponent's left arm (7). Moving his hips to the right creates space (8) to apply an *omoplata*, which enables him to summit his opponent (9).

Attacks From The Guard 31

• **Closed Guard** Rigan holds his opponent inside his guard (1). He controls both arms and moves his hip slightly out to bring his left knee inside his opponent's arms (2). Then he does the same thing with his right knee (3). Rigan brings his left leg over the opponent's right arm (4),

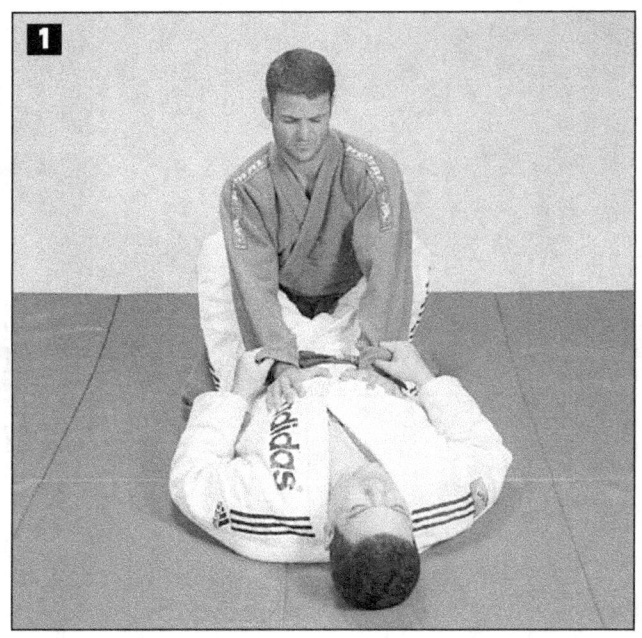

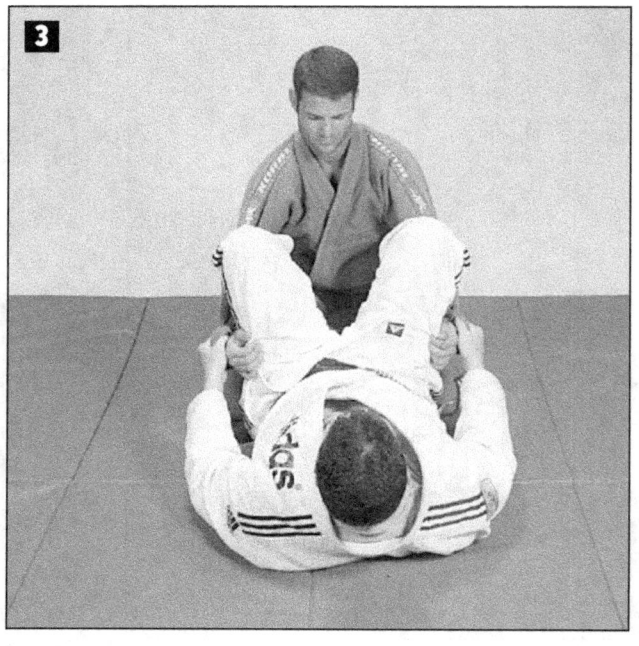

hooking the opposite arm from under the biceps (5). He moves his hip out toward his right side and tightly controls the opponent's left arm (6). He uses body momentum to sweep his opponent (7), and finishes with a full knee-on-the-chest control (8). It is very important in this technique to synchronize the sweeping motion of the left leg with the pulling action on the opponent's right arm.

Attacks From The Guard 32

• Closed Guard

Rigan holds his opponent inside his guard (1). He controls both arms and moves his hip slightly out to bring his left knee inside his opponent's arms (2). Then he does the same thing with his right knee (3). Rigan brings his left leg over the opponent's right arm (4), hooking the opposite arm from under the biceps (5). Then he releases the grip on the left arm, leans backward to create space (6), simultaneously grabs the opponent's left arm and places his left foot between the legs (7).

Rigan pulls the arm toward him (8) and allows his body to fall backward to sweep his opponent (9). He controls his opponent's body from a better position (10).

Attacks From The Guard 33

• **Closed Guard** — Rigan controls his opponent inside his guard (1), pulls the opponent's right sleeve toward his right side (2), moves his hip slightly to the outside and grabs the opponent by the belt (3). Rigan then falls backward and sweeps the opponent by lifting his left leg (4).

While executing this, he consistently controls all the grips (5) until the opponent falls to the ground (6). Rigan immediately turns and controls the opponent from the side (7).

Attacks From The Guard 34

• Closed Guard

Rigan has his opponent inside his full guard (1), grabs his opponent's sleeve with both hands (2), and swings his left leg to the right side (3-4). He uses momentum to pivot in the opposite direction (5) and brings his opponent down (6). He finishes by applying a full *omoplata* armlock (7).

Attacks From The Guard 35

• **Closed Guard**

Rigan controls his opponent inside the full guard (1). He grabs the opponent's left sleeve with his left hand and the pants at knee-level with his right hand (2). He swings his left leg over his opponent's head (3) and starts falling down on side right side (4). During this move, he uses his left foot for control (5). Rigan begins to stand up (6), but he suddenly pulls the opponent's pants and sleeve again, bringing him to the floor where he can control him by sitting on him (7).

Attacks From The Guard 36

• Closed Guard

Rigan holds the opponent inside his full guard (1). The opponent lifts his right leg (2) and then his left leg to start passing the guard (3). Rigan opens his guard and grabs both ankles at the same time that he moves his hips closer to his opponent (4). He pushes forward with his legs while simultaneously pulling both ankles (5-6).

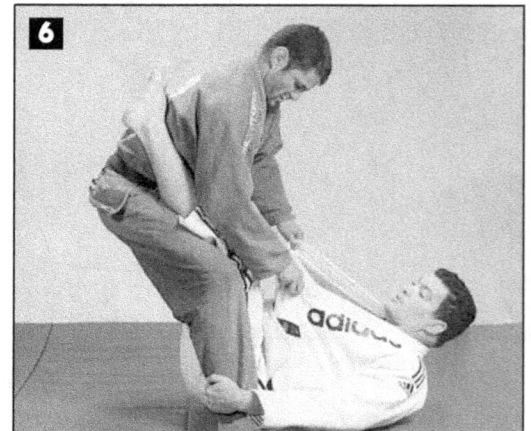

This brings the opponent to the ground (7-8) and allows Rigan to mount him for better control (9). In this last movement — when you try to mount the opponent — keep your hips as low and as close as possible to the opponent's body until you sit on him.

Attacks From The Guard 37a

• Closed Guard

Rigan holds the opponent inside his full guard (1). To start passing the guard, the opponent lifts his right leg (2) and then his left leg (3). Rigan opens his guard and grabs both ankles at the same time that he moves his hips closer to his opponent (4). He pushes forward with his legs while simultaneously pulling both ankles (5-6). This brings the opponent to the ground (7).

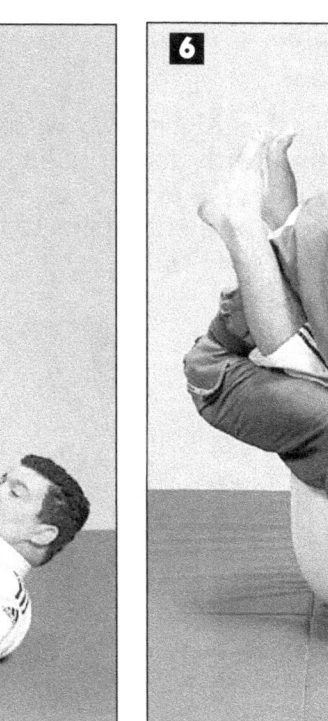

(Continued)

Attacks From The Guard **37b**

• **Closed Guard**

The opponent pushes Rigan away with his left arm (8). Rigan reacts by supporting himself with his left hand and lifting his hips (9). This enables him to pass his right leg over his opponent's head (10-11), and create enough leverage to bring him back to the ground (12), where Rigan can apply a tight armlock (13).

Attacks From The Guard 38a

• **Closed Guard**

Rigan holds the opponent inside his full guard (1). The opponent lifts his right leg (2), and then his left leg to start passing the guard (3). Rigan opens his guard and grabs both ankles at the same time that he moves his hips closer to his opponent (4).

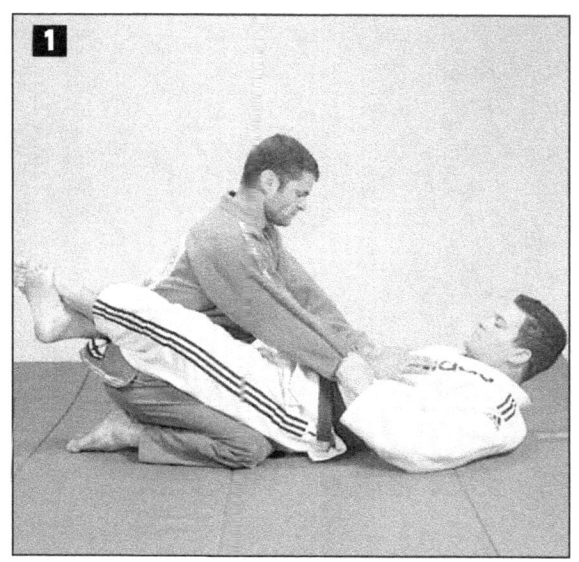

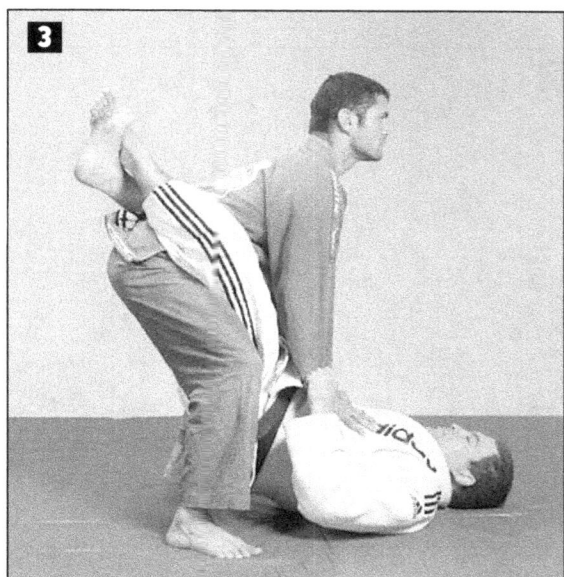

(Continued)

Attacks From The Guard 38b

• **Closed Guard**   He pushes forward with his legs while simultaneously pulling both ankles with his hands (5). This brings the opponent to the ground (6). Rigan finds himself close to his opponent (7), so he moves his hips forward (8)

and hooks his opponent's right arm with his right foot (9), blocking any defensive action that the opponent can attempt (10). With the right arm blocked, the opponent can't prevent Rigan from reaching his collar (11) and subsequently applying a devastating choke from the back (12).

Attacks From The Guard 39a

• Closed Guard

Rigan holds the opponent inside his full guard (1). The opponent lifts his right leg (2), and then his left leg to start passing the guard (3). Rigan opens his guard and grabs both ankles at the same time that he moves his hips closer to his opponent (4).

He pushes forward with his legs while simultaneously pulling both ankles with his hands (5). Again, this brings the opponent to the ground (6).

(Continued)

Attacks From The Guard 39b

• **Closed Guard**

The opponent moves his right arm and tries to create a base to prevent Rigan from following with a counterattack (7), but Rigan reaches with his right hand (8), and pulls the sleeve (9). At the same time, he keeps applying pressure with his hips forward (10) so he can mount the opponent (11).

Attacks From The Guard

Mastering Brazilian Jiu-Jitsu 73

Attacks From The Guard 40

• **Closed Guard**

Rigan holds the opponent inside his full guard (1). To start passing the guard, the opponent lifts his left leg (2), and then his right leg (3). Rigan opens his guard (4), and places both feet against his opponent's hips (5). Then, he pulls both of the sleeves and pushes the opponent into the air (6).

By slightly bending his left leg and pulling harder with his left hand (7), Rigan can make his opponent fall to the left side (8-9). Immediately, Rigan mounts him for better control (10).

Attacks From The Guard 41

• Closed Guard

Rigan holds the opponent inside his full guard (1). The opponent first lifts his left leg (2), and then his right to start passing the guard (3). Rigan opens his guard (4), and places both feet against his opponent's hips (5). Then, he pulls both of the sleeves and drops his hips down to lift the opponent into the air (6).

By slightly bending his left leg and pulling harder with his left hand (7), Rigan can force the opponent's body to fall to the left side (8). This time, however, Rigan pulls in with the left hand and opens his left leg, allowing the opponent to fall closer to him so he can apply an armlock (9).

Attacks From The Guard 42

• Closed Guard

Rigan has the opponent inside his full guard (1). Rigan grabs the opponent's left sleeve and pants just above the left knee (2). Using these points for leverage (3), Rigan spins around and starts an armlock (4-5). Suddenly, feeling the danger of an *omoplata*, the opponent starts to roll (6),

nullifying the attack (7). Maintaining his grip, Rigan pulls the opponent and forces him to accelerate the roll to the other side (8), where he finishes with arm control in a superior position (9).

Attacks From The Guard 43

• Closed Guard

The opponent tries to pass Rigan's open guard (1). As soon as Rigan feels the opponent is beginning to attack (2), he creates distance and stops the action by placing his right foot on the opponent's left hip and by grabbing the opponent's left sleeve (3). Once the action has been stopped, Rigan grabs the collar with his left hand and maintains control of the opponent's left hand (4).

Then, he moves his hip to the side and brings his right leg to the inside (5). By bending the leg and pulling from the sleeve with his right hand, he applies a bent armlock (6).

Attacks From The Guard 44

• **Closed Guard**

The opponent tries to pass Rigan's open guard (1). As soon as Rigan feels the opponent is beginning his attack (2), he creates distance and stops the action by placing his right foot on the opponent's hip (3). He puts his right foot against his opponent's inside left thigh (4), and starts moving to his right (5). Rigan raises his trunk and grabs the belt (6) as a supporting action to raise his hips (7).

He swings his right leg back (8), lifting his opponent's hips (9). After the sweep, Rigan adopts a full side control (10), which includes placing the right knee on his opponent's stomach (11).

Attacks From The Guard 45

• **Closed Guard** Rigan holds the opponent inside his full guard (1). The opponent lifts his left leg (2), and then his right leg to start passing the guard (3). This time, instead of opening his guard, Rigan keeps it closed, and grabs the opponent's gi with both hands (4). Then he pulls him toward his chest (5-6),

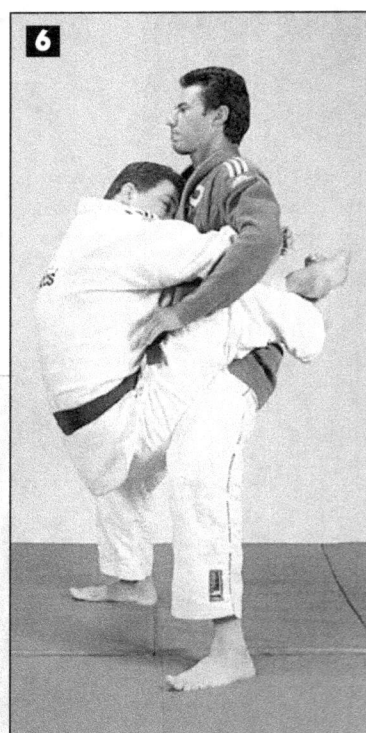

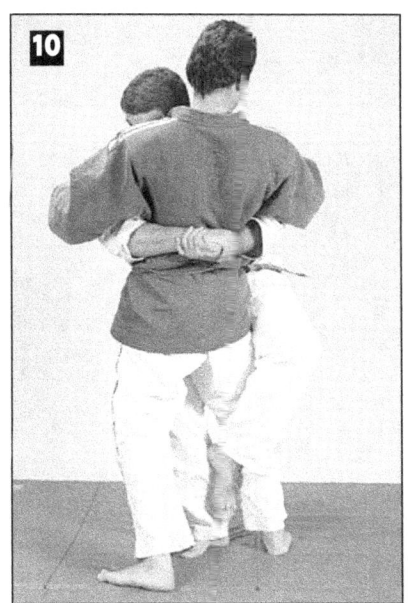

and adjusts his hips, keeping them close to his opponent's body (7). Immediately he lowers both feet to the floor (8). By keeping a tight grip behind the opponent's back, he unbalances him (9). He also hooks the left leg (10),

Attacks From The Guard

Mastering Brazilian Jiu-Jitsu

Attacks From The Guard 46

• Closed Guard

Rigan holds the opponent inside his full guard (1). The opponent lifts his left leg (2) and then his right leg to start passing the guard (3). This time, instead of opening his guard, Rigan keeps it closed and grabs the opponent's gi with both hands (4). Then he brings him close to his chest (5-6).

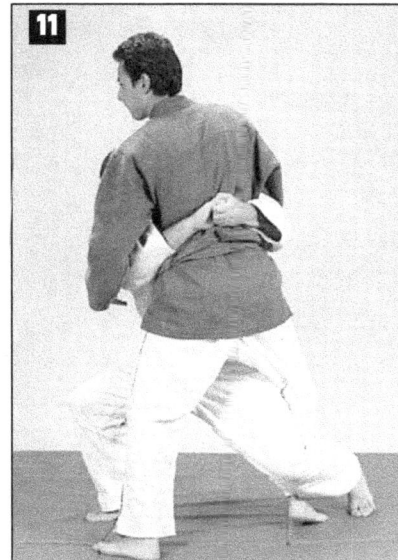

Now he adjusts his hips, keeping them close to his opponent's body, and Rigan starts to lower both feet to the floor (7). By keeping a tight grip behind the opponent's back, he unbalances him (8). Rigan moves his right foot back to create space (9) for an inside sweep with his left leg (10). This brings the opponent to the ground, where Rigan will start the offense (11-12).

Attacks From The Guard 47

• Closed Guard

Rigan holds the opponent inside his full guard (1). Attempting to pass the guard, the opponent lifts his left leg (2), and then his right (3). This time, instead of opening his guard, Rigan keeps it closed. Next, he grabs the opponent's gi with both hands (4), and pulls himself close to the opponent's chest (5-6).

Rigan adjusts his hips, keeping them close to his opponent's body, and lowers both feet to the floor (7). Rather than keeping his grip on the upper part of his opponent's body, Rigan bends and grabs both legs at thigh level (8). This unbalances the opponent (9), sending him to the floor (10), where Rigan controls him from the side (11).

Attacks From The Guard 48

• Closed Guard

Rigan holds the opponent inside his full guard (1). To start passing the guard, the opponent lifts his left leg (2), and then his right (3). Rigan uses his right hand to reach the opponent's left leg, and this prevents the opponent from stabilizing his position. Rigan then uses his left hand to grab the opponent's left sleeve, and he transfers the uniform to his right hand (4). This creates a tight trap and secures the opponent while Rigan reaches the inside collar with his left hand (5). He brings his left leg to the front (6), and pushes forward (7), bringing the opponent to the ground (8).

The opponent's momentum carries him to the other side (9). Rigan releases the grip and uses his right hand to support himself (10), and then he applies a bent arm control (11).

Attacks From The Guard   49

• Closed Guard

Rigan holds the opponent inside his guard (1). The opponent lifts his left leg (2) and then his right to start passing the guard (3). Rigan responds by releasing his grip on the opponent's sleeves (4). And then he reaches for his opponent's left ankle (5). Rigan uses this maneuver to get momentum (6) so he can bring his left leg to the right side (7). This enables him to escape from the attack (8).

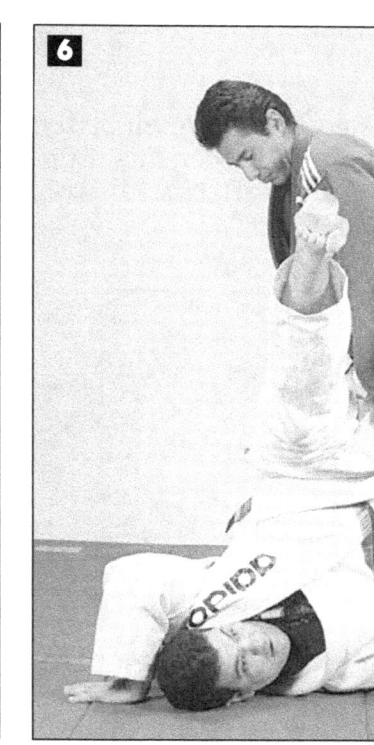
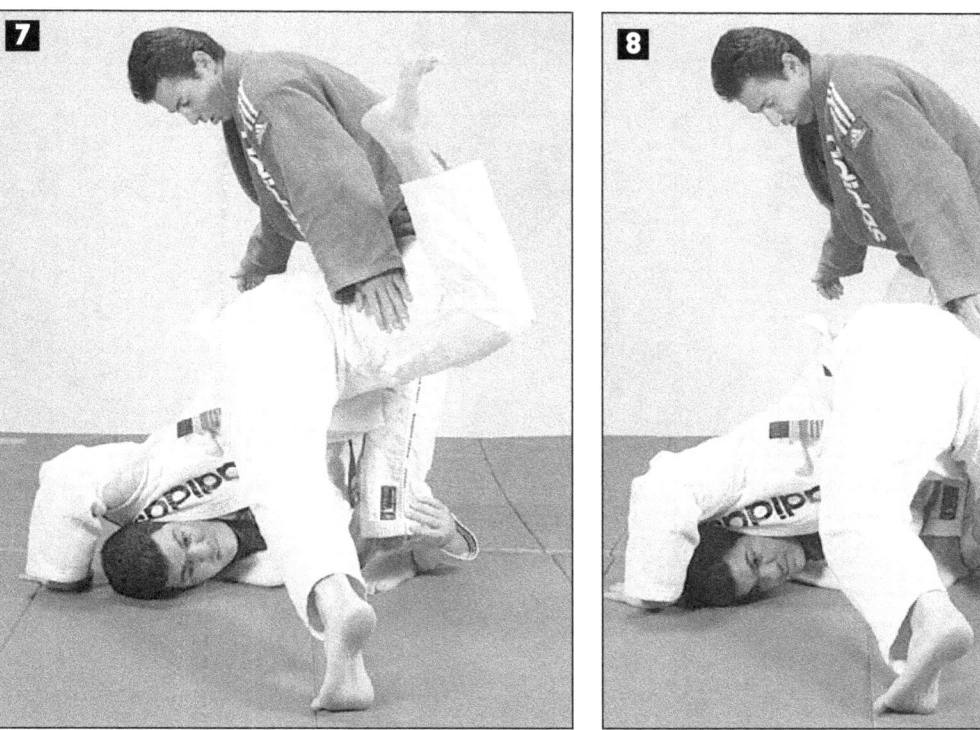

(Continued)

Attacks From The Guard 49

• **Closed Guard**

He positions himself better (9) so he can firmly grab his opponent's left leg (10). He then lifts it up (11-13), causing the opponent to fall. Now Rigan can attack with an anklelock (14).

Mastering Brazilian Jiu-Jitsu 95

Attacks From The Guard 50a

• Closed Guard

Rigan holds the opponent inside his full guard (1). The opponent lifts his left leg (2), and then his right leg to start passing the guard (3-4). To prevent the opponent from stabilizing himself, Rigan uses his right hand to reach the opponent's left leg and his left hand to grab the opponent's right sleeve (5). He then releases the grip and uses his left hand to (6) start turning his body to the side (7). This unbalances his opponent (8)

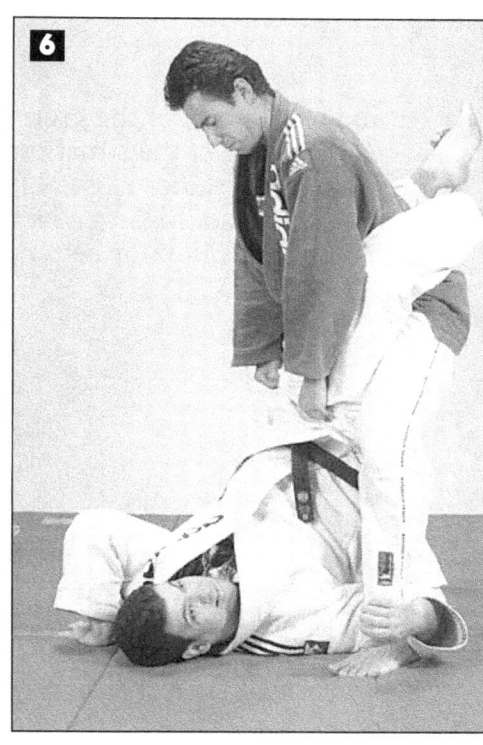

(Continued)

Attacks From The Guard 50b

• **Closed Guard**

and brings him to the ground (9). Once he's down, the opponent tries to gain control of the situation by moving backward (10). However, Rigan keeps the distance close (11). As soon as the opponent tries to use his left hand to stand, Rigan grabs it and pulls hard (12). This enables him to get a mount position for better control (13).

Attacks From The Guard

Mastering Brazilian Jiu-Jitsu

Attacks From The Guard 51

• **Closed Guard**

Rigan holds the opponent inside his full guard (1). The opponent lifts his left leg (2), and then his right leg to start passing the guard (3-4). To prevent the opponent from stabilizing himself, Rigan uses his right hand to reach the opponent's left leg (5), and his left hand to grab the opponent's right sleeve (6).

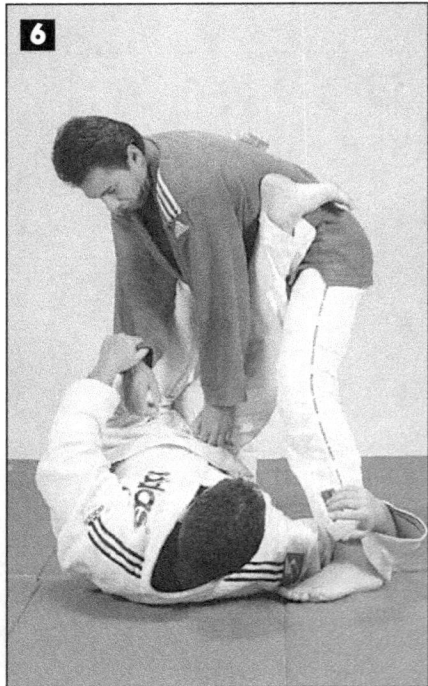

Rigan brings his left leg to the right side (7), over his opponent's left leg (8) and applies pressure, making the opponent fall (9). Rigan continues rolling to his right side (10), and applies a kneebar (11).

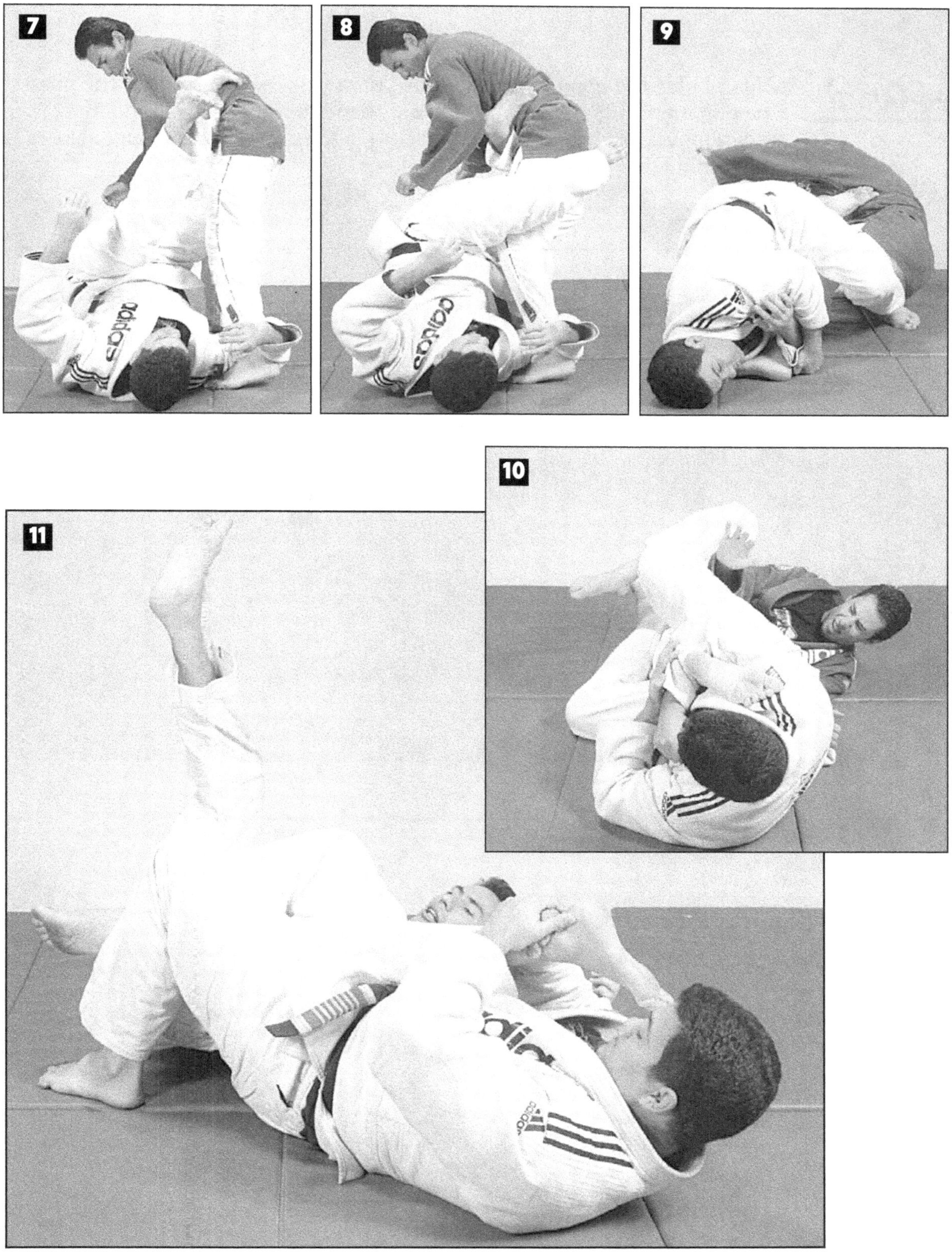

Attacks From The Guard

Attacks From The Guard 52

- **Closed Guard**

Rigan holds the opponent inside his guard (1). To start passing the guard, the opponent lifts his left leg (2), and then his right leg (3). This time, Rigan moves his hips to the left side (4), and reaches for the opponent's right ankle (5).

Then he pushes hard with his legs and pulls with his right hand (6), bringing the opponent to the floor (7). Rigan now controls him with firm grips to the arm and leg (8).

Attacks From The Guard 53

• **Closed Guard** Rigan holds the opponent inside his guard (1). The opponent lifts his left leg (2), and then his right leg to start passing the guard (3). Rigan moves his hips to the left side to reach the opponent's right ankle (4).

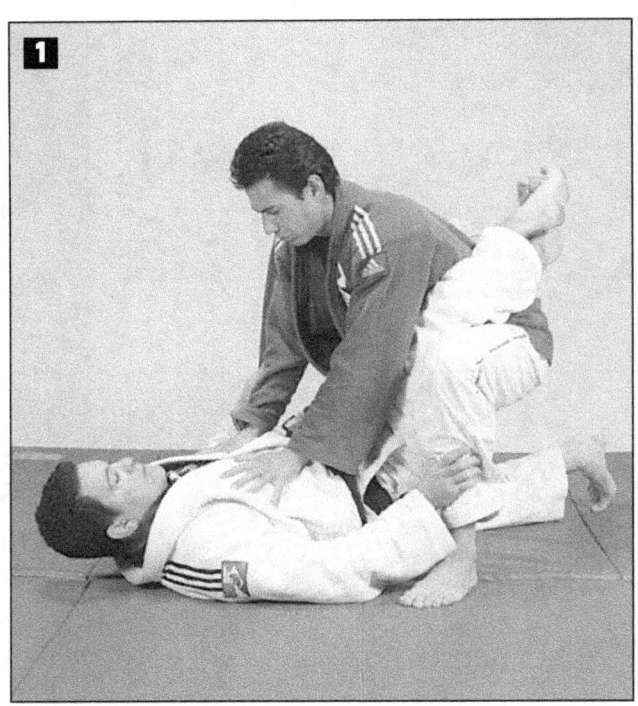

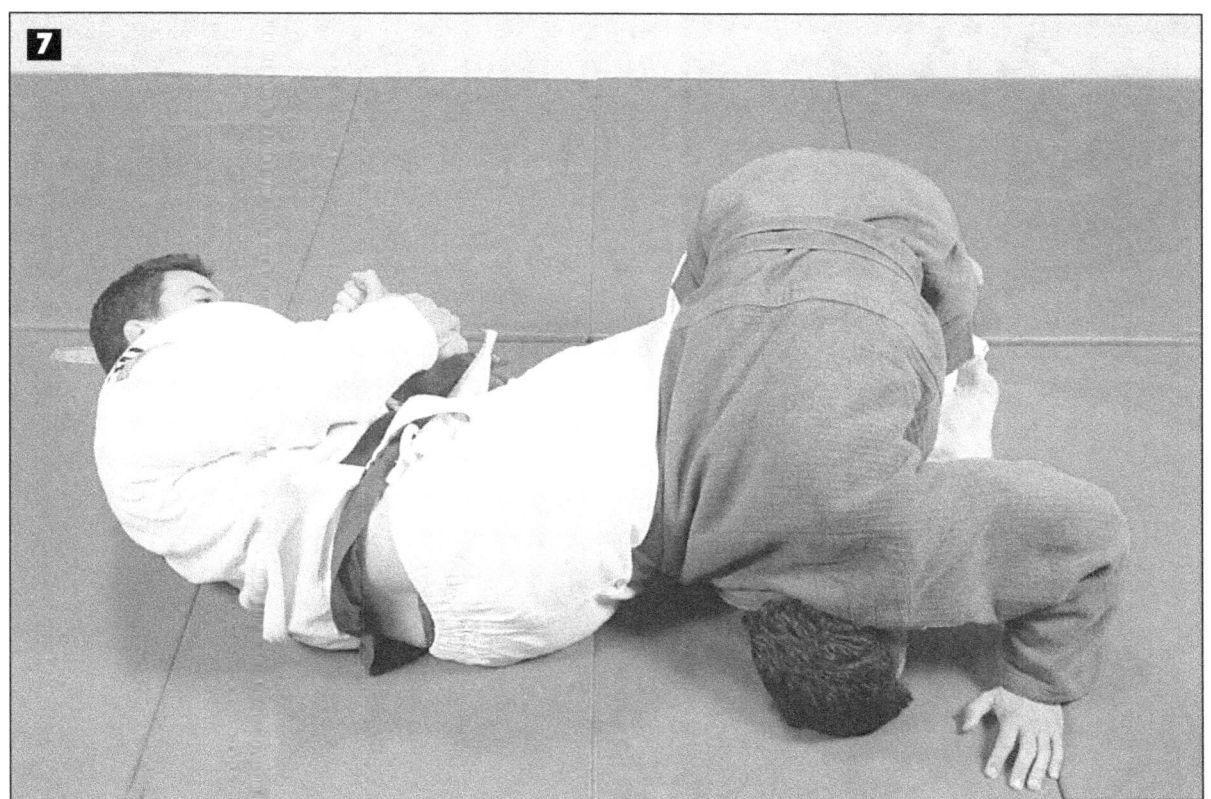

Using this as a supporting point (5), he rolls over his right shoulder, passing to the other side and getting an armlock (6). He finalizes this by turning his hips slightly to the left (7). It is important to maintain a tight grip on the opponent's right hand during all the movement because the arm that will be locked in the final stage has to be kept under control at all times.

Attacks From The Guard 54

• **Closed Guard**   Rigan holds the opponent inside his guard (1). The opponent lifts his left leg (2), and then his right leg to start passing the guard (3). Rigan reaches the opponent's left ankle with his right hand (4), and starts spinning to the left (5).

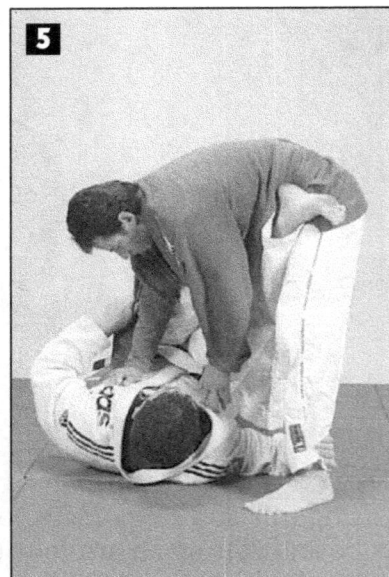

 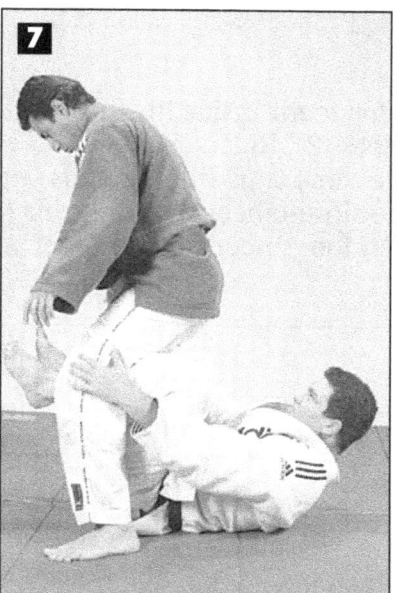

This creates momentum to reach the inside of his opponent's left ankle with his left hand, which replaces the right hand (6). After using the momentum to pass under the opponent's legs and get behind him (7), Rigan grabs the belt. Using his feet to create support (8), Rigan brings the opponent to the floor and between his legs (9-10). Then he applies a choke from the back (11).

Attacks From The Guard 55

• Closed Guard

Rigan has his opponent inside his full guard (1). From a normal double-grip to the sleeves (2), Rigan changes to a crossed-grip (3). He then opens his guard at the same time that he pulls with his left hand (4). This creates space as he simultaneously brings his left leg to the front (5) so he can hook his left foot under his opponent's left arm (6).

By pulling hard with his right hand, he unbalances his opponent (7), which makes the sweeping action of his left leg easier (8-9). The hooking motion of the right foot also helps (10). Once his opponent has been swept (11), Rigan moves to the mount position for better control (12).

Attacks From The Guard 56a

• **Closed Guard**

Rigan has his opponent inside his full guard (1). From a normal double-grip to the sleeves (2), Rigan changes to a crossed-grip (3), opens his guard, pulls with his left hand and pushes with his right hand (4). This creates space to bring his left leg (5) inside his opponent's right armpit (6).

Then he pulls hard with his left hand (7), and uses the momentum to swing his body to the left side (8). He simultaneously pushes with his right leg (9) without losing the grip on the opponent's right sleeve (10). He can then set the control for an *omoplata* (11). The opponent counters the *omoplata* by rolling (12)...

(Continued)

Attacks From The Guard 56b

- **Closed Guard**

over Rigan's body (13-15), but Rigan maintains full control of the grip and sits up (16). Then he can apply an armlock from the side (17).

Attacks From The Guard 57a

• **Closed Guard**

Rigan has the opponent inside his full guard (1). From a normal double-grip to the sleeves (2), Rigan changes to a crossed-grip (3), opens his guard, pulls with his left hand and pushes with his right hand (4). Using these grips as supporting points, Rigan starts to spin his body (5) and places his left foot over the opponent's left biceps (6).

(Continued)

Mastering Brazilian Jiu-Jitsu

Attacks From The Guard 57b

• Closed Guard

This creates space to bring his left leg in (7-8), and allows him to turn his body to the left (9). He then hooks his opponent's neck with his left leg (10) so he can apply a *triangle* choke (11-12). It is critical to keep control of the opponent's left arm at all times.

Attacks From The Guard 58a

• **Closed Guard**

Rigan has his opponent inside his full guard (1). From a normal double-grip to the sleeves (2), Rigan changes to a crossed-grip (3), and opens his guard at the same time that he pulls with his left hand and pushes with his right hand (4). Using these grips as supporting points, Rigan starts to spin his body (5). He then places both feet under his opponent's arms (6).

(Continued)

Attacks From The Guard 58b

• **Closed Guard** He pushes forward (7) and throws him over (8), immediately gaining control from the side (9-10).

Attacks From The Guard 59a

• Closed Guard

Rigan has his opponent inside his full guard (1). From a normal double-grip to the sleeves (2), Rigan changes to a crossed-grip (3), opens his guard, and pulls with his left hand and pushes with his right hand (4). This creates space to bring his left leg under his opponent's left arm (5). He simultaneously pushes with his right foot (6).

(Continued)

Attacks From The Guard 59b

• **Closed Guard**   To create distance so he can put his left leg inside both of his opponent's legs (7). Maintaining control over the opponent's left arm, Rigan allows himself to fall back without losing control of the right sleeve (8-9). Using his left leg, he then sweeps his opponent to the left side (10-11).

Rigan immediately turns around and, keeping himself close to the opponent (12), maintains control of the situation from the side (13).

Attacks From The Guard 60a

• **Closed Guard**

Rigan holds his opponent inside his guard with his left hand inside the opponent's collar (1). Using his right hand, Rigan reaches behind the opponent's back (2-4), grabs his belt and pulls him closer (5). Rigan leans back (6) and moves his hips to the left (7).

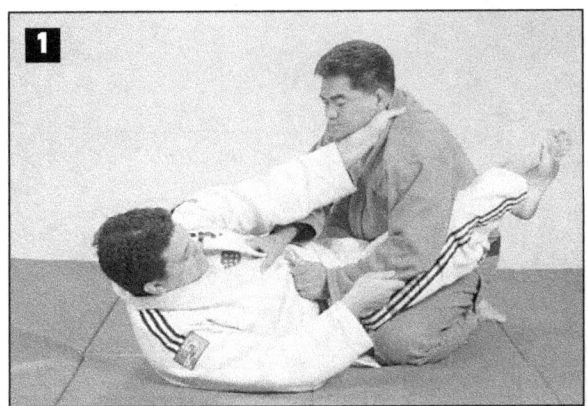

This creates space so he can get his legs out from under his opponent's body so he can begin to apply the *omoplata* (8-10). His opponent begins to feel the pressure. Before the attack is completed (11), the opponent begins to roll (12).

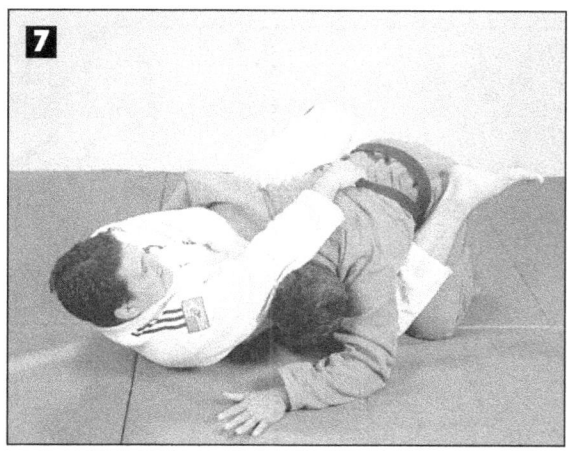

(Continued)

Attacks From The Guard 60b

• **Closed Guard** This action unbalances Rigan (13), and forces him to fall forward (14). Instead of losing control, Rigan keeps the pressure on the arm, follows the roll (15) and submits the opponent with the *omoplata* (16).

Attacks From The Guard 61

• Closed Guard

Rigan has the opponent inside his guard and his left hand inside the collar (1). He releases the opponent's left sleeve and inserts his right hand under his left (2). Feeling the attack, the opponent uses his left arm to nullify the pressure (3). Rigan moves his feet from the closed guard and places them on the opponent's hips (4). This enables him to control the body better and bring the opponent's body slightly down. This nullifies the opponent's left arm (5), and he applies a choke (6).

Attacks From The Guard 62

• Closed Guard

Rigan has the opponent inside his guard and his left hand inside the collar (1). He releases his grip from the opponent's left sleeve and inserts his right hand under his left (2). Feeling the attack, the opponent uses his left arm to nullify the pressure (3). He tries to stand up using his left leg (4), and then the right (5). Rigan doesn't release the choke attempt and puts his right foot on the opponent's left hip (6), and his left foot on the opponent's right hip (7).

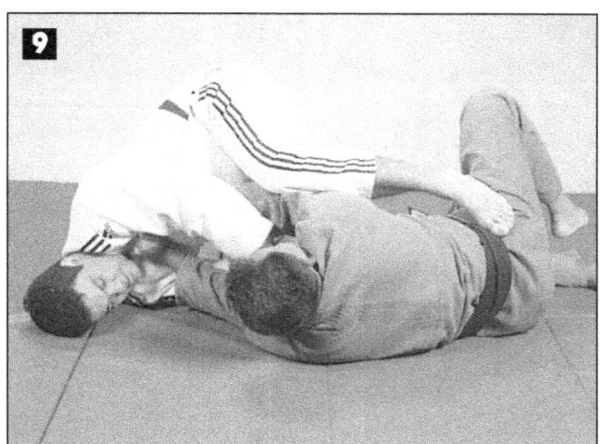

By bringing his hips forward, Rigan creates momentum to push the opponent up and over (8-9). Rigan then immediately mounts him (10). Because both hands were applying pressure during the complete movement, Rigan can easily choke his opponent out (11).

Attacks From The Guard 63

• **Closed Guard**

Rigan holds the opponent inside his guard (1). To start passing the guard, the opponent lifts his left leg (2) and then his right (3). Rigan hooks the opponent's left leg with his right hand (4). Then he pushes forward with his legs (5), making his opponent fall (6).

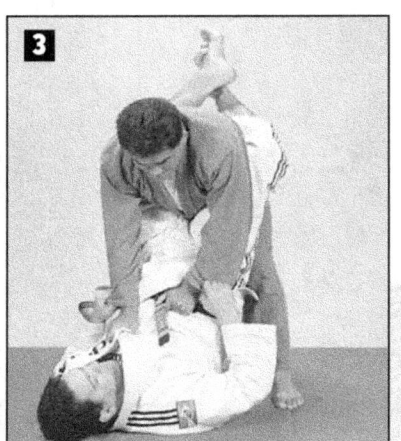

The opponent uses his right hand to prevent Rigan from standing up (7-8), so Rigan takes advantage of this and passes his left leg over while simultaneously keeping a tight grip on the opponent's arm (9). Then Rigan rolls him over (10). To assist in the move, notice how Rigan grabs his opponent's pants before finishing with the armlock (11).

Attacks From The Guard 64

• **Closed Guard**

Rigan has his opponent inside his guard with his hands firmly on his opponent's collar (1). By pulling with his right and and starts spinning to the left (5). pushing with his left, he's able to move his opponent's body to the right. Simultaneously, he opens his guard (2) and brings his left leg over to the front, hooking the opponent's neck with his instep (3). Using his left hand in conjunction with his left foot, he applies a finishing choke (4).

Attacks From The Guard 65a

• **Closed Guard**   While grabbing both sleeves, Rigan holds the opponent inside his full guard (1). Attempting to pass the guard, the opponent lifts his left leg (2), and then his right (3). Rigan opens his legs (4), pulls his opponent hard (5), and uses his legs to throw him over his own body (6).

(Continued)

Attacks From The Guard 65b

• **Closed Guard** — During the entire process Rigan controls the sleeve (7). Rigan then rolls over his back (8), and finishes the movement in the mount position (9).

Attacks From The Guard 66

• **Closed Guard**

Rigan holds his opponent inside his guard, and the opponent uses a double armpit control to prevent Rigan from coming closer (1). Rigan grabs the tip of his own gi with his right hand (2) and passes it over to his left hand (3), trapping the opponent's hand against his chest (4). By squeezing hard, he forces the hand to turn inside (5), which creates a perfect position to apply a painful lock (6).

Attacks From The Guard 67

• Closed Guard

Rigan has the opponent inside his guard (1). The opponent tries to control Rigan by putting his hands on the chest (2), but Rigan breaks the grip (3) and moves his hips simultaneously to the left. This unbalances his opponent (4). Note how Rigan keeps tight control of the right arm (5). He then brings his left knee close to the opponent's body (6), and applies a straight armlock (7).

Attacks From The Guard 68a

• Closed Guard

Rigan holds the opponent inside his guard. The opponent grabs both collars of Rigan's gi (1). He steps up with his left leg (2), and tries to pass the guard with his right leg (3). Rigan immediately opens his guard (4), pulls both sleeves and powerfully closes his legs behind the back of his opponent's knees (5).

(Continued)

Attacks From The Guard 68b

• **Closed Guard**

Then, Rigan turns his hips to the right, bringing the opponent to the floor (6-7). This enables Rigan to maintain better control and execute an attack (8).

Attacks From The Guard 69

• **Closed Guard**

Rigan holds the opponent inside his guard. The opponent grabs Rigan's collars (1), steps forward with his left leg (2), and tries to pass the guard with his right leg (3). Rigan reacts by keeping his legs closed and lifting his hips (4). Suddenly, Rigan drops his body and opens his legs (5).

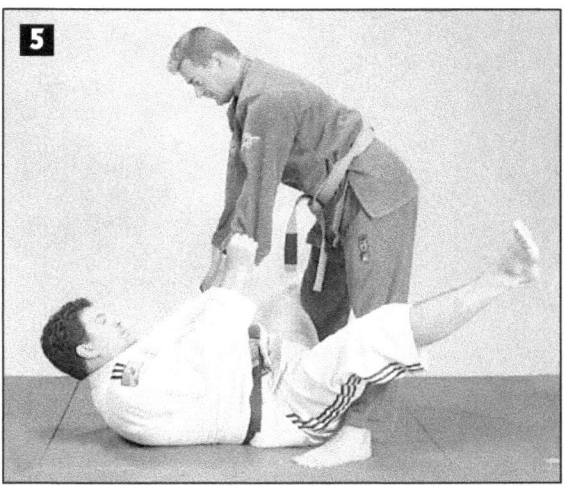

(Continued)

Attacks From The Guard 69b

• **Closed Guard**

Rigan closes them again as he gets close to the floor (6). Simultaneously, he grabs the opponent's legs (7). To initiate the counterattack, he turns his body to the right and brings the opponent to the ground (8).

Attacks From The Guard 70

• Open Guard

Rigan has his opponent in the open guard (1). Notice how he has both feet on the opponent's hips for control. Rigan moves his left foot and places it against the opponent's right biceps (2), which helps Rigan to spin and hook the opponent's left leg with his right foot (3). He simultaneously uses his right hand to grab the opponent's pants (4). Completing a turn to his left (5), Rigan sweeps the opponent to the ground (6-7). He follows him in the roll (8) to gain the side control (9).

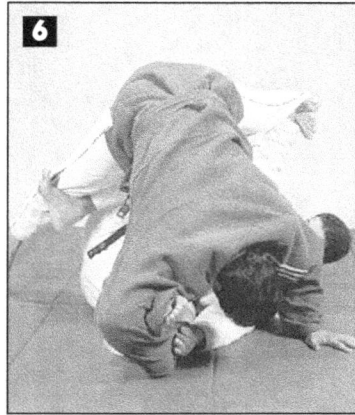
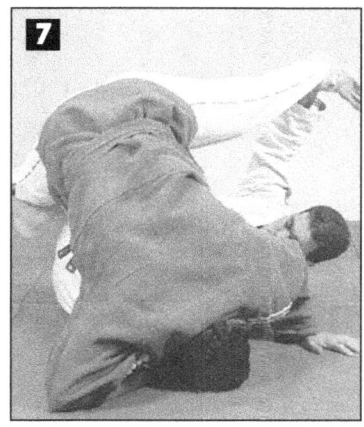

Attacks From The Guard 71

• Open Guard

Rigan has the opponent in the open guard, and he places both feet on the hips to control him (1). Rigan moves his left foot and places it against the opponent's right hip (2), which helps him to spin and put his right foot against the stomach (3). By pulling with his left hand and pushing with both legs, Rigan sends the opponent into the air (4). He throws him to the ground (5-6), where he maintains a tight grip on the left sleeve and the pants (7). This, along with his right knee, facilitates side control (8).

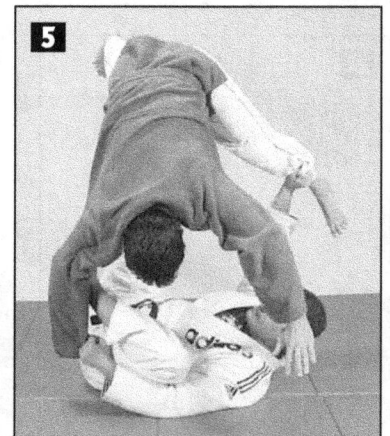

Attacks From The Guard 72

• Open Guard

Rigan gets his opponent in the open guard and controls him with both feet (1). He moves his left foot and passes it under the opponent's right arm (2-3). Meanwhile, he keeps a tight grip on the opponent's left sleeve as he grabs the left leg (4), and throws him to his left side (5-8). He finishes the move by getting side control (9).

Attacks From The Guard 73

• Open Guard

Rigan uses the open guard and places both feet on his opponent's hips to control him (1). He moves his left foot and passes it under the opponent's right arm (2-3). While keeping a tight grip on the opponent's left sleeve, Rigan grabs the left leg (4). The opponent pushes Rigan's right leg down and moves to the side (5-6). The opponent momentarily controls the situation by dropping his weight (7), and going for a full side control (8-9).

Still holding the opponent's pants and sleeve (10), Rigan turns to his left side and pulls hard (11), sweeping the opponent (12), and sending him to the ground (13). Rigan reverses the position and now controls from the side (14).

Attacks From The Guard 74

• Open Guard

Rigan has his left hand inside the opponent's collar (1). Rigan releases his left hand and double grabs the opponent's left sleeve (2). Using his right hand, he then grabs the opponent's left ankle (3). By hooking the opponent's right leg with his left foot and pulling from the ankle and left sleeve (4), Rigan brings the opponent to the ground (5). He can now maintain control (6), and begin the counterattack (7).

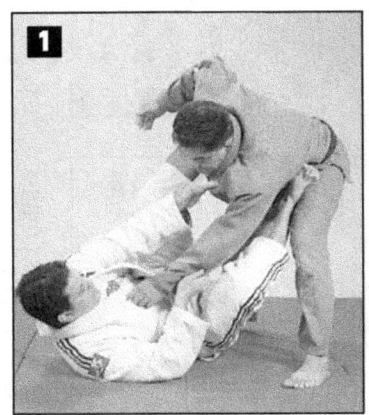

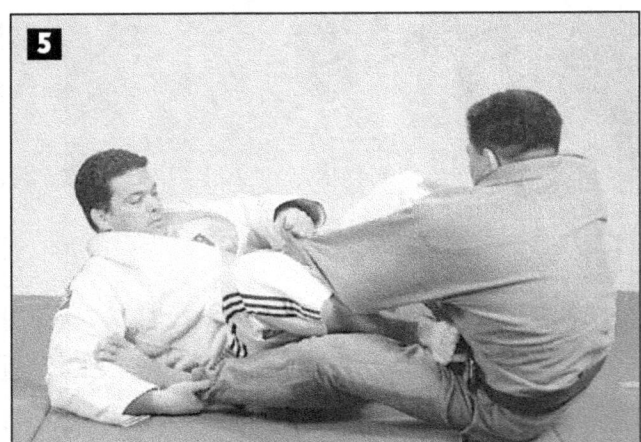

Attacks From The Guard 75

• Open Guard

Rigan uses the open guard, places his left hand inside the collar (1) and uses his right hand to grab the opponent's left ankle (2). When he brings his right leg to the floor (3), he creates momentum (4) to sweep the opponent. This is done in conjunction with pushing with his left leg (5-6). Once they are both on the ground, Rigan controls the opponent's arm and leg (7), and goes for the offensive (8).

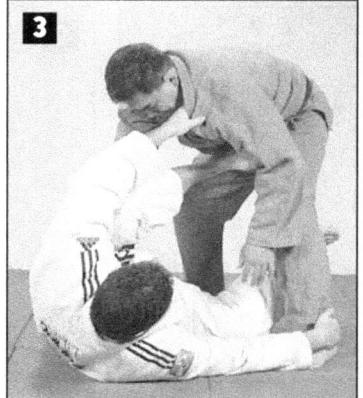

Attacks From The Guard 76

• Open Guard

Rigan is in good position to execute a *triangle* choke (1). Realizing the threat, the opponent comes closer, nullifying the attack. In response, Rigan spins 180 degrees (2), reversing the position (3-4). Now he's able to grab his opponent's legs (5). By using his weight (6), and putting more pressure on the side of the leg he is pulling inward (7), Rigan is able to obtain full side control (8).

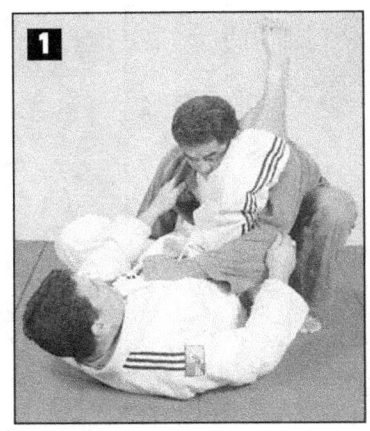

Attacks From The Guard 77

• Open Guard

Rigan is in a good position to attack with a *triangle* (1), but the opponent starts to pass the guard (2). Rigan reacts by moving to the side (3), and reaching for the collar with his left hand (4). He rolls the opponent on his back (5-6), and brings him to the other side (7), where he applies a final choke (8). It is important to maintain full control of the collar with your left hand during the entire rolling motion.

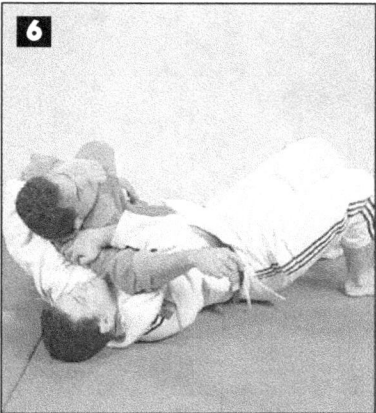

Attacks From The Guard — 78

• Open Guard

Using the open guard, Rigan faces his opponent (1). He brings his left leg over the opponent's right hand (2), and sits down (3). Rigan then passes his left hand under the opponent's right leg (4), reaching for the opponent's left sleeve. Rigan places his right hand on the left side of the collar, and his right foot on the knee to prevent him from moving (5), and sweeps the opponent (6). He's now able to fully control him from the side (7).

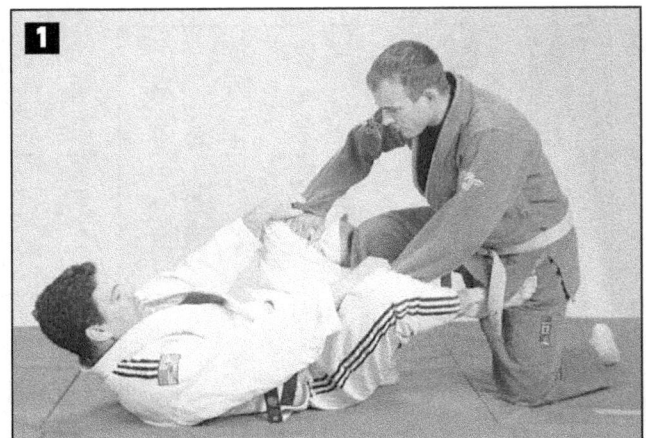

Attacks From The Guard 79

• **Open Guard**

Rigan, using the open guard, faces his opponent (1). He brings his left leg over the opponent's right hand (2), and sits down (3) so he can pass his left hand behind the opponent's right leg (4), reaching for the opponent's left sleeve. He places his right hand on the left side of the collar and pushes away with his right leg (5). He then sweeps his opponent to the right side (6-7), and gains full side control (8).

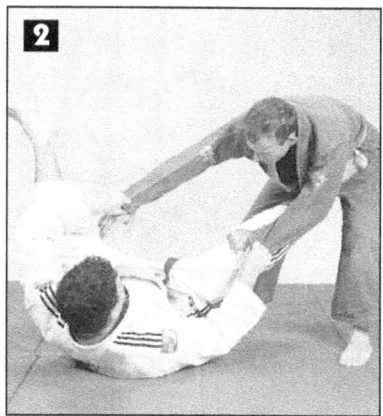

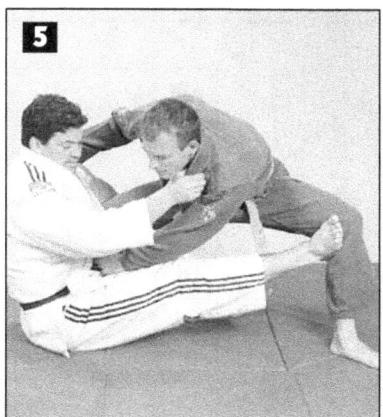

Attacks From The Guard 80

• Open Guard

Rigan starts on his back (1). He sits up and reaches for the tip of the opponent's jacket (2). He passes the tip of the gi to his left hand (3) and begins to stand (4). While doing this, he grabs the opponent's right leg (5), pulling up (6) and then forward (7-8).

The opponent ends up on the ground, where Rigan can now initiate the offensive (9).

Attacks From The Guard 81

• Open Guard

Rigan begins on his back (1). He moves forward, sits and reaches for the tip of the opponent's jacket (2). He takes the tip of the gi in his left hand (3), and grabs the opponent's left leg (4). He turns to the right (5), and throws the opponent to the ground (6), where he controls him and begins the counterattack (7-8).

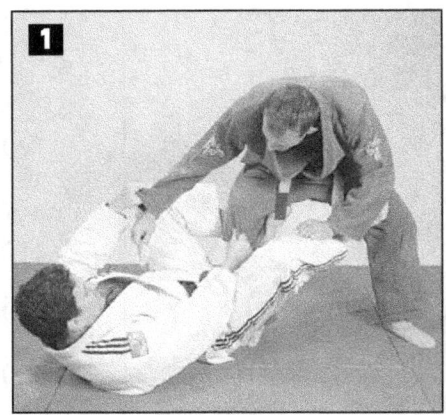

Attacks From The Guard 82

• Open Guard

Rigan begins on his back, facing his opponent (1). He uses his right leg to prevent the opponent from coming closer (2), and he utilizes his left foot to control the opponent's left hip (3). Immediately, he spins and positions himself behind the opponent's back (4), which gives him better control to pull him down (5) between his legs, where he can finish with a submission technique (6-7).

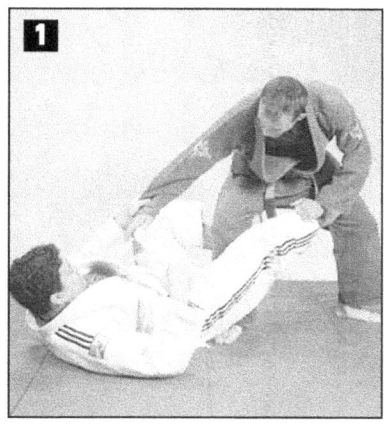
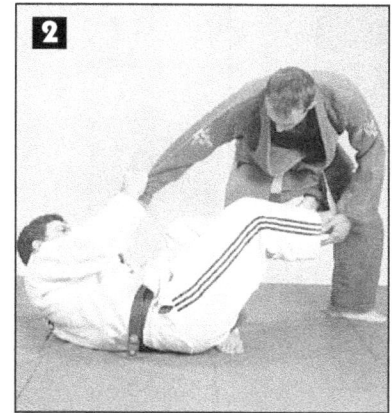

Attacks From The Guard 83

• Open Guard

Rigan is on his back, facing his opponent (1). As soon as the opponent tries to pass the guard (2), Rigan moves his hips forward and places his leg between the opponent's (3). This position enables Rigan to sweep the opponent (4), and start the offensive (5).

Attacks From The Guard 84

• **Open Guard**

Rigan is on his back, facing his opponent (1). As soon as the opponent tries to pass the guard (2), Rigan moves his hips forward, places his right leg inside the opponent's left leg and grabs the ankle (3). Rigan hooks his leg around and pushes hard, turning the opponent sideways (4). He takes him to the ground and applies an anklelock (5).

Attacks From The Guard 85

• Open Guard

Rigan controls his opponent with the open guard (1). He sits and grabs the opponent's right arm (2-3) to bring him closer (4). Rigan immediately turns and places his left hand on the opponent's hip for better control (5). Then he mounts him from the back (6).

Attacks From The Guard 86

• Open Guard

Rigan has the opponent in his open guard, and his right hand is firmly on the collar (1). As soon as the opponent tries to force Rigan's right leg down (2), Rigan slides back and creates some distance between them (3). Meanwhile, using his left hand, Rigan simultaneously pulls the opponent's right sleeve (4), bringing him to the ground (5). Rigan moves to the back (6), where he will start his offensive (7).

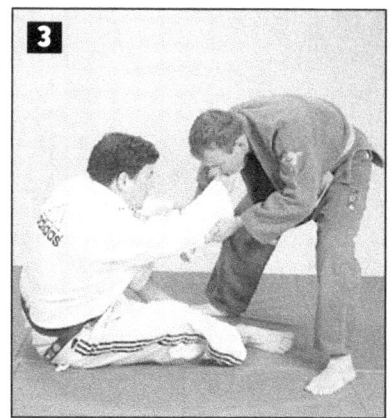

Attacks From The Guard 87

• Open Guard

Rigan controls his opponent, who tries to pass the guard (1). With his right hand under Rigan's left leg and left hand over Rigan's right leg, the opponent keeps himself tight (2). Rigan slides his hips back (3), and turns to his right (4), hooking the opponent's right arm with his right leg as he rolls over (5-6). By adding a choke and a control to the left arm, he fully submits his opponent (7).

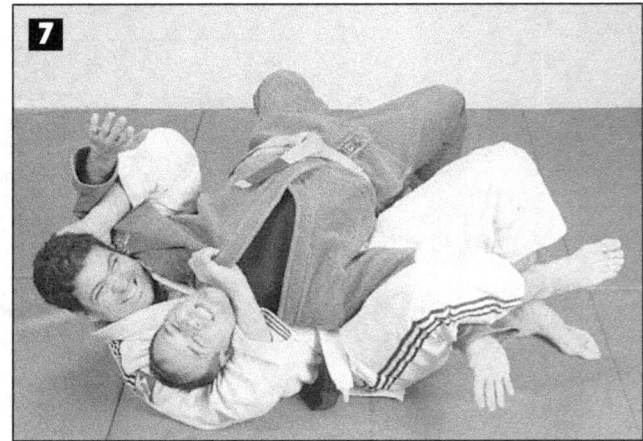

Attacks From The Guard 88

• Open Guard

Rigan controls his opponent, who tries to pass the guard (1). With his right hand under Rigan's left leg and the left over Rigan's right leg, the opponent keeps himself tight. Rigan slides his hips back and turns to his right (2-4), hooking the opponent's right arm with his right leg as he rolls over (5-6). This time he keeps himself on the same side after the roll and applies an armlock (7). He also adds an additional control to the right leg to prevent the opponent from rolling over to escape.

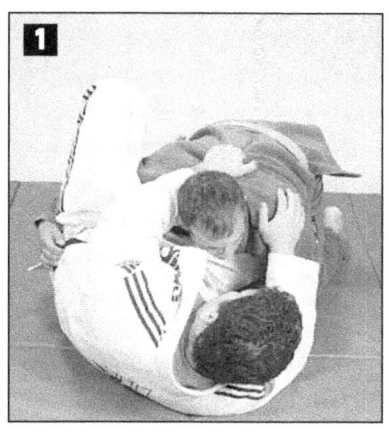

Attacks From The Guard 89

• Open Guard

Rigan has the opponent in his open guard (1). He brings his right knee up to pass the opponent's arm (2), twists his hips slightly to put the leg over the left shoulder (3), and grabs the belt to start applying the *omoplata* (4). As soon as the opponent feels he is being trapped, he tries to move away. Rigan, however, grabs the back of his collar and brings him down (5-6). Rigan immediately turns around, and keeping a tight grip with his legs (7-8), mounts the opponent, who has no chance of escaping (9).

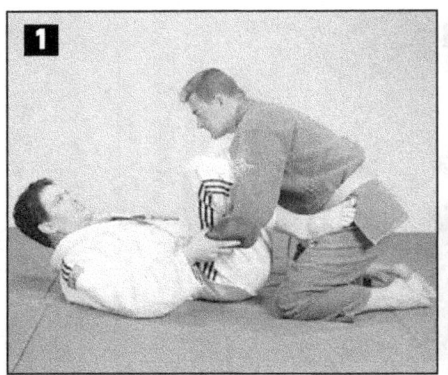

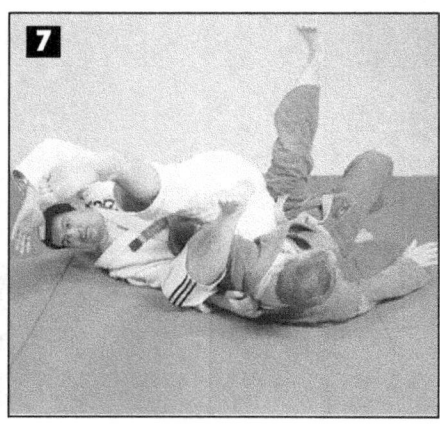

Attacks From The Guard 90

• **Open Guard**

Rigan faces his opponent, who has his right knee up (1). Rigan moves his left leg under his right and grabs the left side of the opponent's collar (2). Using his hands to bring the opponent closer (3), Rigan pushes the opponent's left hip, sending him into the air (4). Next, Rigan slightly pushes to the left and pulls hard with his left hand (5-6), which makes the opponent fall next to him (7). Here he can obtain side control.

Attacks From The Guard 91

• Open Guard

Rigan faces his opponent, who again has the right knee up (1). Rigan brings his left leg under his right and grabs the left side of the opponent's collar (2). Using his hands to bring the opponent closer (3) and his left leg to push the left thigh, Rigan pushes the opponent's left hip, sending him airborne (4-5). This time he allows the opponent's body to fall diagonally (6-7). Rigan can now apply a straight armlock (8).

Attacks From The Guard 92

• Half Guard

Rigan has the opponent in his half-guard (1). Note that the opponent's body is crossed to the left side and Rigan has a tight grip on the opponent's pants. Rigan releases the right leg (2), hooks the opponent's leg with his left foot (3), and lifts him up (4). Simultaneously, he opens the legs (5) to put him inside his closed guard (6-7). Between the push and the opening of the legs, the timing has to be good. Otherwise, the opponent will fall on you, and it will be easy for him to mount you.

 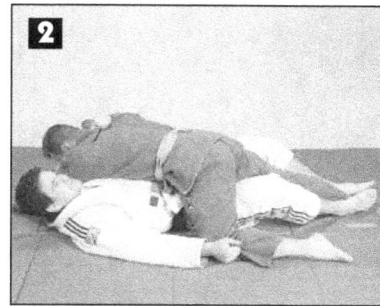 

Attacks From The Guard 93

• Half Guard

Rigan, who has the opponent in his half-guard, maintains a tight grip on the left wrist (1). Rigan then moves his body to the right and reaches over the opponent's left arm (2). He immediately turns to the other side, and using his right leg (3), sweeps his opponent (4-5). While doing this, he maintains side control (6) so he can apply a bent armlock (7).

Attacks From The Guard 94

• Half Guard

Rigan has the opponent in his half-guard, and he keeps a tight grip on the left wrist and collar (1). Rigan moves to the right and reaches with his left hand over the opponent's left arm (2). He immediately turns to the other side and applies a *kimura* (3).

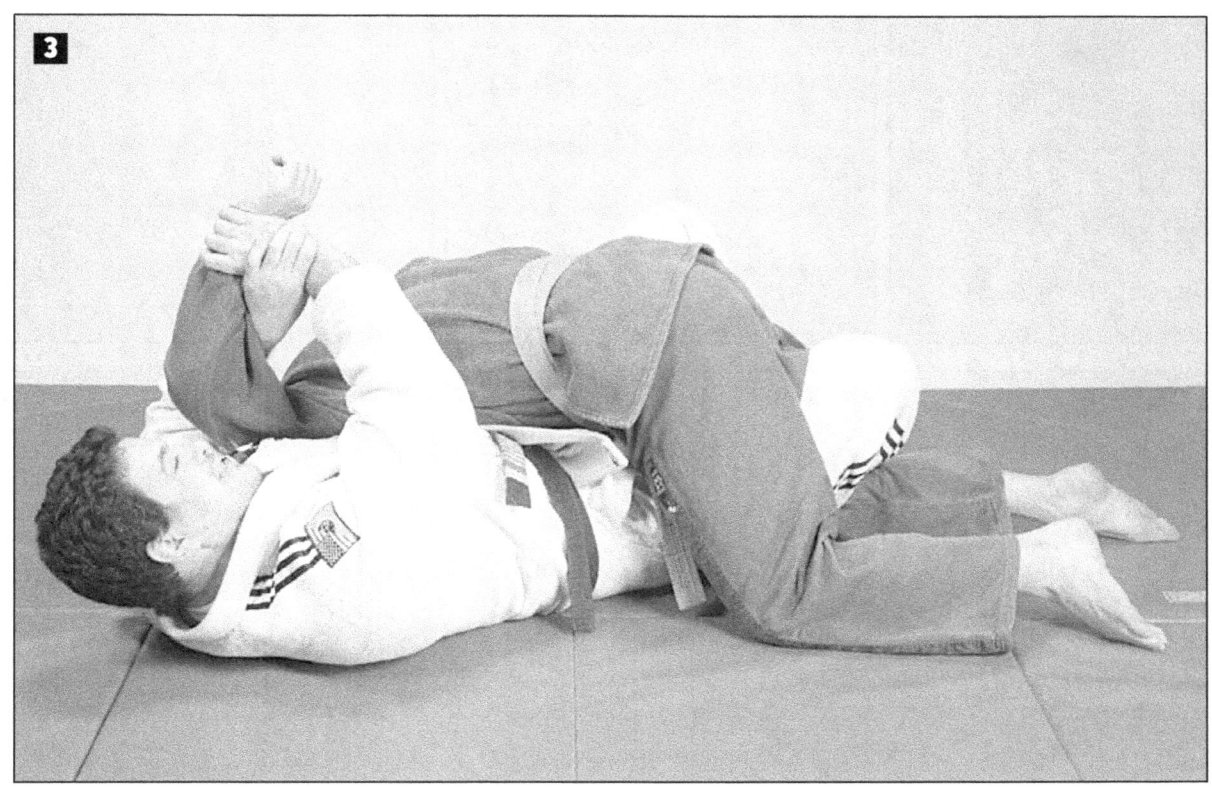

Attacks From The Guard 95

• **Half Guard**

Rigan holds the opponent in his half-guard (1). He reaches the opponent's left sleeve and changes the grip to his left hand as he uses his right hand to grab the left leg (2-3). He then pulls and sweeps with the left leg (4-5), bringing the opponent to the ground (6). Here he starts the offensive from a side control (7-8).

 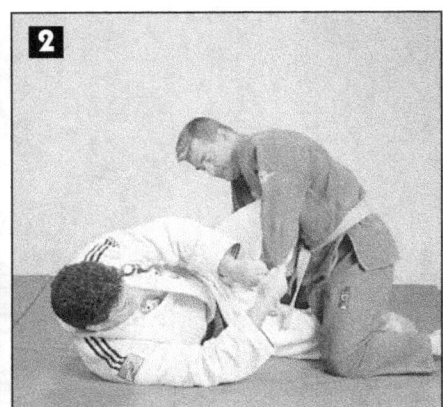 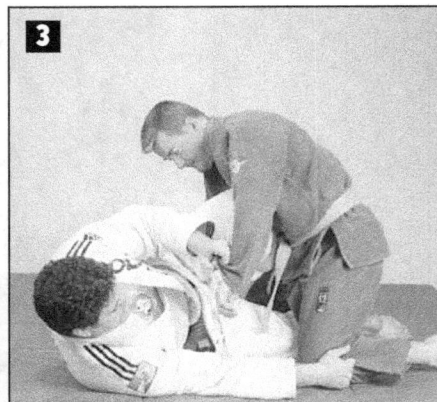

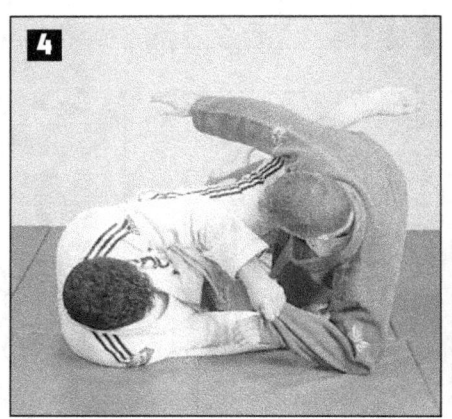  

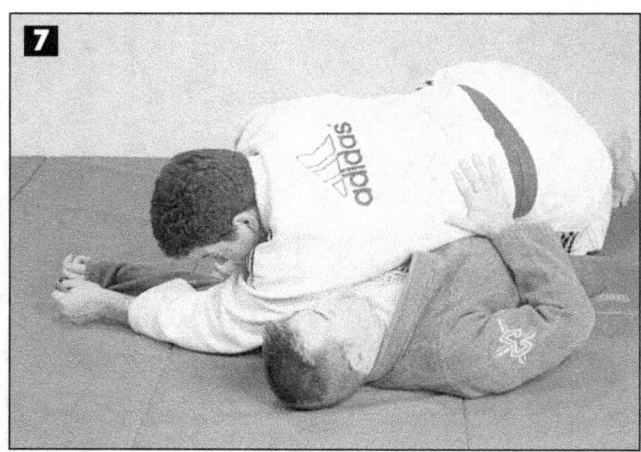 

Attacks From The Guard 96

• Half Guard

Rigan holds the opponent in his half-guard (1). He reaches the opponent's left sleeve and changes the grip to his left hand as he again uses his right hand to grab the left leg (2-3). He pulls and tries to sweep with the left leg (4-5). The opponent reacts by expanding his base and nullifying the sweep (6). Rigan then changes directions and moves to the left rapidly (7). He grabs the opponent's right leg (8), and pushes him to the ground with his body weight (9).

Attacks From The Guard 97

• Half Guard

Rigan holds the opponent in his half-guard (1). He passes his right hand under the opponent's left leg (2), and creates space for (3) his left leg to swing to the right (4). From here, he can get better leverage (5) to push the opponent forward (6), and to the ground (7). Then he can apply a finishing footlock (8).

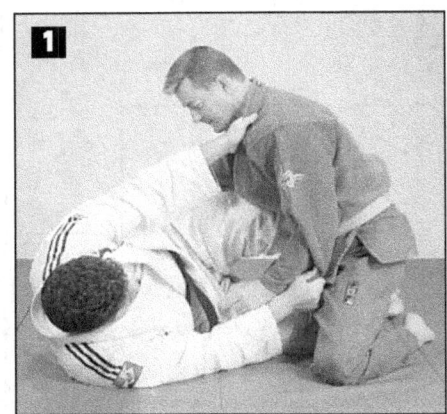

Attacks From The Guard 98

• Half Guard

Rigan has the opponent in his half-guard (1). He moves his hips to the left and simultaneously starts to grab his opponent's right foot (2), as his right hand hooks under the left leg (3). He starts moving to the right and slightly turns (4). This brings his opponent to the ground (5-6), where Rigan can launch his attack (7).

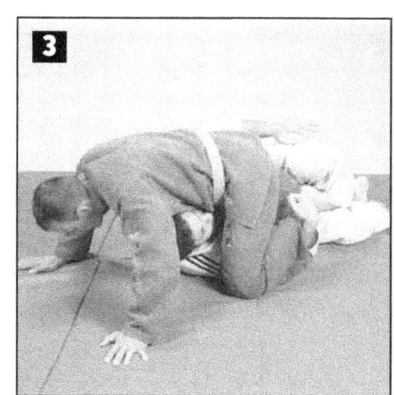

Attacks From The Guard 99

• Half Guard

Rigan has his opponent in his half-guard (1). He moves his hips to the left (2), and simultaneously grabs his opponent's right foot (3), as he hooks his right hand under the left leg (4). As soon as he feels his opponent's right hand under his head (5), Rigan starts turning to the left (6), so he can take full control of the action (7).

Attacks From The Guard 100a

• **Half Guard**

Rigan has his opponent in his half-guard (1). He grabs the tip of the opponent's gi with his right hand (2), and then puts it in his left hand (3-4). To add force to the sweep, he uses his left leg (5) and right leg (6-7).

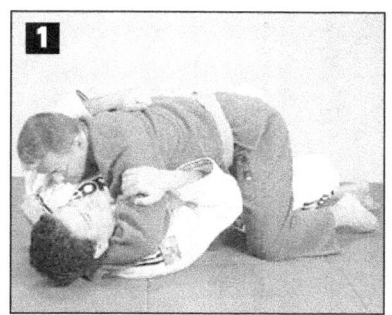

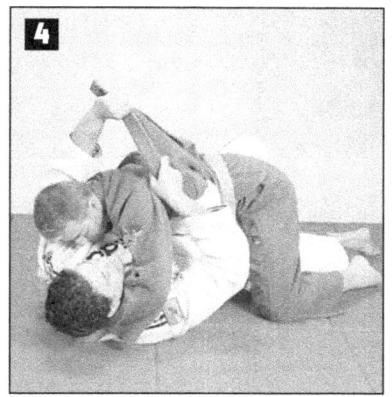

(Continued)

Attacks From The Guard 100b

• **Half Guard**

Once the opponent is on the ground (8), Rigan maintains tight control on the left arm and the right knee (9). Thus, he's able to mount his opponent (10).

Attacks From The Guard 101

• **Half Guard**

Rigan has his opponent inside his half-guard (1). While he uses his left arm to push up hard (2), he brings his hips down (3). This simultaneous action allows him to escape, and he rapidly uses his left arm to grab the other side of the opponent's body. This provides better control (4). Rigan finishes by taking the back (5).

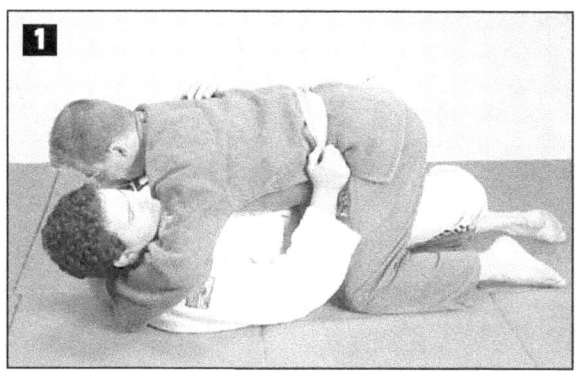

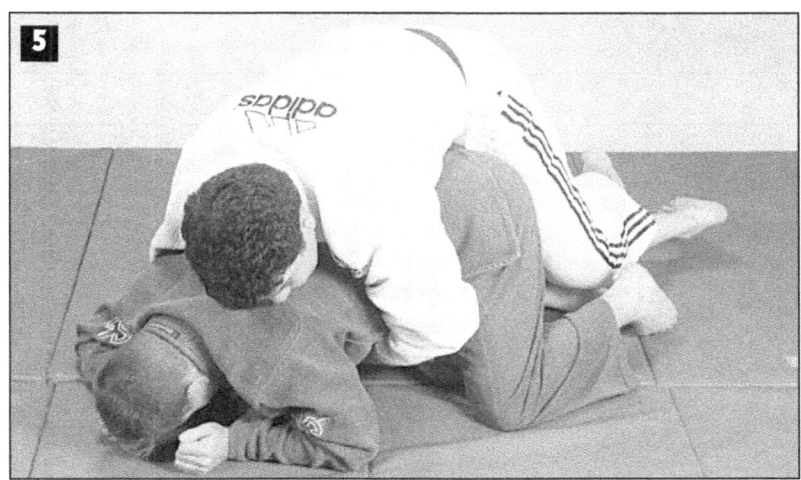

Attacks From The Guard 102

• Half Guard

Rigan has his opponent inside his half-guard, but this time the opponent's body is crossed (1). Rigan maintains tight control with his left hand, grabs the opponent's left knee (2), passes his left foot under the adversary's right leg (3), and pushes him into the air (4). Rigan opens his right leg (5) to receive him inside his full guard (6-7). It is important to create momentum with your leg and hand when pushing the opponent. Keep in mind that the opponent has to be pushed into the air just far enough for you to open your leg and put him inside the full guard.

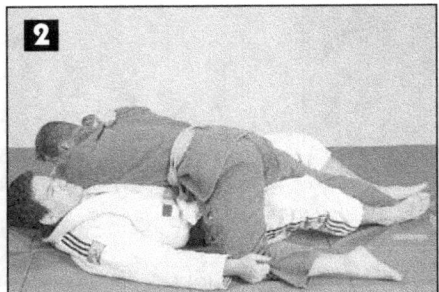
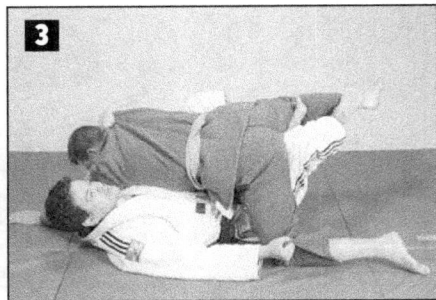

Attacks From The Guard 103

• Half Guard

Rigan has his opponent inside his half-guard, and the opponent's body is crossed (1). Rigan maintains tight control with his left hand, grabs his opponent's left knee (2), passes his left foot under the opponent's right leg (3), and pushes him toward the left (4). Rigan moves his body to the right as his opponent lands on the floor (5). He immediately turns around (6), and takes control from the back (7).

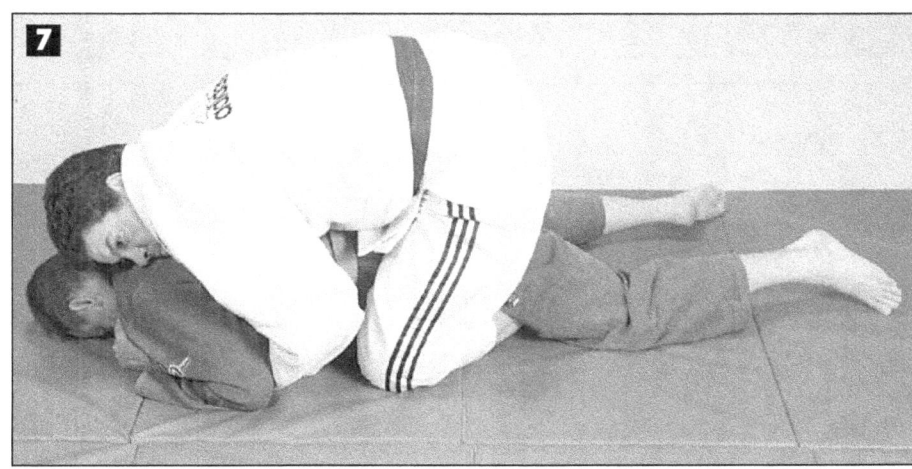

Attacks From The Guard 104

• Half Guard

Rigan has his opponent inside his half-guard with the opponent's body crossed (1). Rigan maintains tight control with his left hand, grabs his opponent's left leg (2), passes his left foot under the right leg (3), and pushes him into the air (4). Rigan brings his right leg out, but he uses it as a hook (5) to make the opponent turn his body in the air (6). This enables him to redirect the opponent to his right (7), where he mounts him as soon as he hits the ground (8).

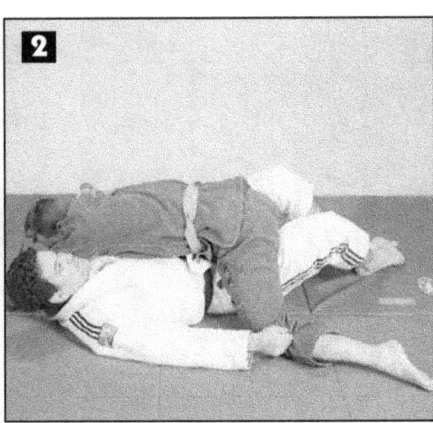
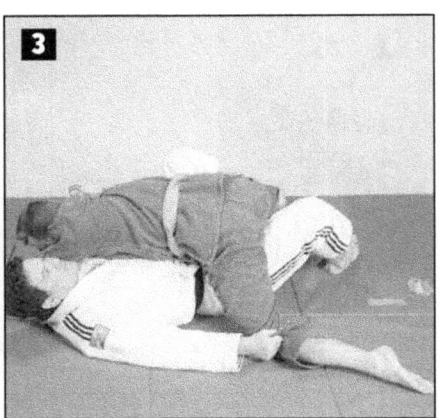

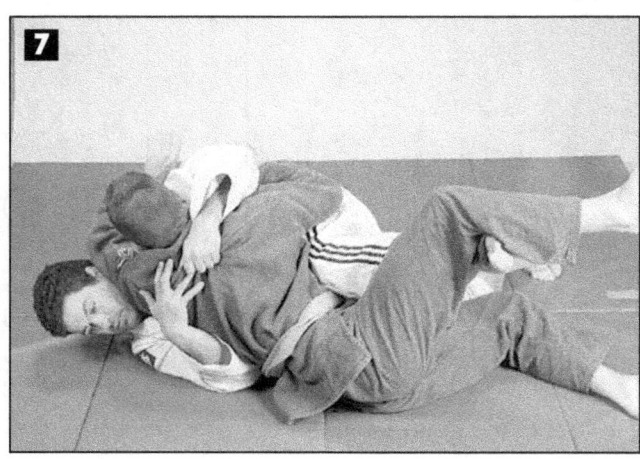

Attacks From The Guard 105

• **Half Guard**

Rigan has his opponent inside his half-guard with the opponent's body crossed (1). Rigan uses his right elbow on the opponent's left leg to create space (2). This enables him to bring his knee up (3). Creating additional room by moving his hips to the front (4), Rigan easily brings his right leg out and puts the opponent inside his full guard (5).

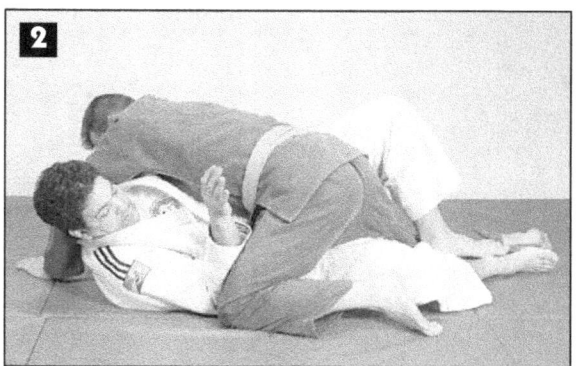
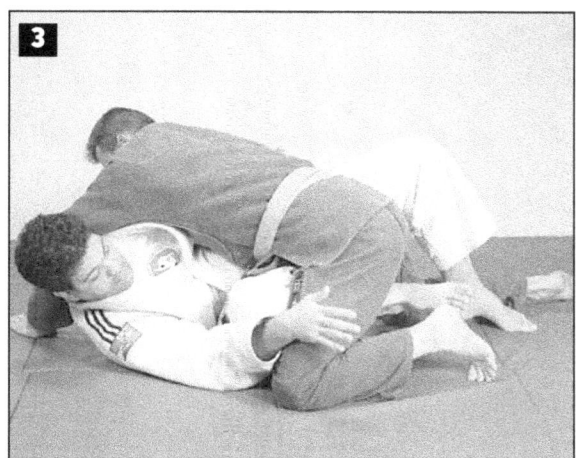

Attacks From The Guard — 106

• Half Guard

Rigan has his opponent inside his half-guard, and the opponent's body is crossed (1). Rigan uses a right grip on the belt and a left grip under the armpit (2) to push the opponent away (3). This creates more space and enables him to escape because he can move his hips out (4.) Before the opponent falls to the other side, Rigan controls his left leg (5), passes his right leg over (6), and applies an anklelock (7).

Attacks From The Guard 107

• **_Seated Position_** Rigan has his right hand inside his opponent's collar while he starts to pass the guard (1). Using his left hand, Rigan forces the opponent's head down and circles to the right with his right elbow (2). This will allocate space to insert his left hand over the back of the neck and apply a choke (3).

Attacks From The Guard   108

- **Seated Position**

The opponent tries to pass Rigan's guard (1). Rigan moves his hips slightly to the right and brings his left hand over the opponent's neck (2). Rigan begins to squeeze (3). He leans back to bring the opponent to the floor, where he can apply a front choke (4).

Attacks From The Guard 109

• **Seated Position**

From a seated position, Rigan faces his opponent (1). As his opponent straightens up (2), Rigan releases his hold on the sleeve and grabs the opponent's right ankle (3). As Rigan starts to stand, he moves his leg back and pulls the opponent's ankle forward (4). Rigan stands and begins to circle to the right (5-6), unbalancing his opponent (7) and sending him to the floor (8).

Attacks From The Guard 110

• **Seated Position**   From a seated position, Rigan faces his opponent (1). He then moves his left hand from his opponent's sleeve to his pants (2), and starts to stand (3). This knocks his opponent off balance (4). Rigan then employs an inside sweep (5), and throws his opponent to the floor (6).

Attacks From The Guard 111a

• Seated Position

While seated, Rigan faces his opponent (1). As soon as the opponent straightens up (2), Rigan releases the sleeve, grabs the pants (3), starts to stand (4), and pulls his opponent off balance (5). Rigan moves in a clockwise motion 180 degrees (6).

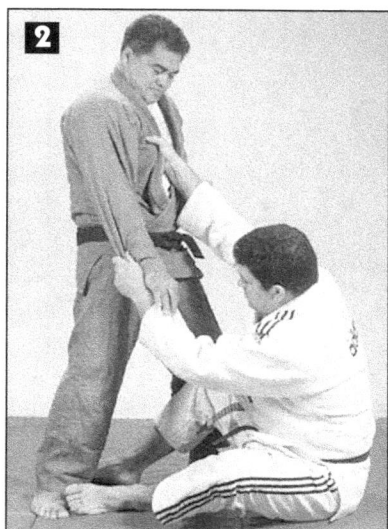

(Continued)

Attacks From The Guard 111b

• **Seated Position**

then, he applies an outside sweep at ankle level (7), bringing the opponent to the ground (8-9). Once his opponent is down, Rigan uses his left knee (10) to apply full control from the side (11).

Attacks From The Guard 112a

• **Seated Position**

Rigan controls the opponent with his left hand inside the collar and his right hand on the left sleeve (1). He moves his right leg (2) and places it against the opponent's left hip (3-4). The opponent tries to escape by pulling away (5). Rigan slides his hips forward and passes his right leg over the left arm (6),

(Continued)

Attacks From The Guard   112b

• **Seated Position**

as he simultaneously controls the left sleeve (7) so he can start applying an *omoplata* (8). This will enable him to submit the opponent (9).

Attacks From The Guard 113

• **Seated Position**

The seated opponents face each other (1). To gather momentum, Rigan leans forward (2), and grabs his opponent's pants at the left knee (3). Rigan moves his hips to the left (4), and turns to the right. The opponent starts to fall back (5). This enables him to fully control the opponent from the top (6).

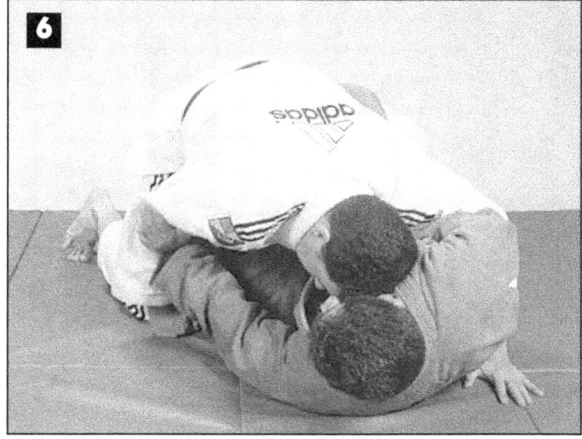

Attacks From The Guard 114

• Seated Position

Rigan grabs his opponent's pants at the knee (1). The opponent moves his left leg away (2), and Rigan immediately moves back to create distance (3), and stand (4). The better position will enable him to throw (5) his opponent onto the floor (6), where he can take the offensive (7).

Attacks From The Guard 115

• Seated Position

Rigan faces his opponent, who is grabbing his pants (1). Rigan, who is controlling his opponent by securing his feet, inserts his right arm (2) to grab his opponent's left arm (3). He then pulls inward (4), as he simultaneously places his right foot on the opponent's left hip (5). By pulling hard on the arm, he forces the opponent to come down to the ground (6), where he applies a final armlock (7).

Attacks From The Guard 116

• Seated Position

Rigan faces his opponent, who is grabbing his left leg to try to pass the guard (1). Rigan shoots his right arm under his opponent's left arm (2), and reaches over with his left hand (3). Simultaneously, he brings his left leg over the shoulder and puts it inside the opponent's left thigh (4). He rolls to the right (5), using his left leg to create momentum (6). To conclude, he pulls the opponent's head with his right leg (7), and brings his opponent to the other side (8), where he applies an armlock (9).

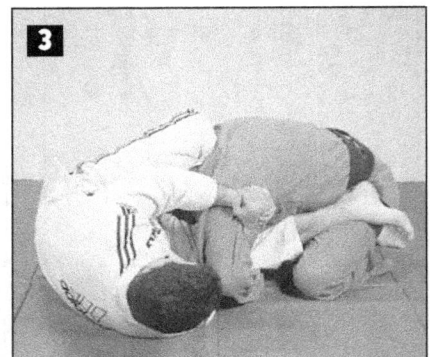

Attacks From The Guard — 117

• Seated Position

Rigan secures his left hand inside the opponent's collar (1). He moves his left leg inside the opponent's left thigh as he simultaneously moves his right knee back (2), to create space. This also enables him to roll to the side (3), and sweep his opponent onto the ground (4). From this position, he can apply a straight kneebar by passing his left leg over the prone opponent (5).

Mastering Brazilian Jiu-Jitsu

Attacks From The Guard 118

• Seated Position

Rigan places his left hand inside the opponent's collar (1), and then moves his left leg inside the opponent's left thigh. The opponent blocks the action (2), grabs Rigan's left leg (3), and tries to take him to the ground (4). Rigan, feeling the momentum, grabs the opponent's right sleeve (5), and allows himself to roll (6), trapping the opponent's right arm (7). He finishes with an *omoplata* (8).

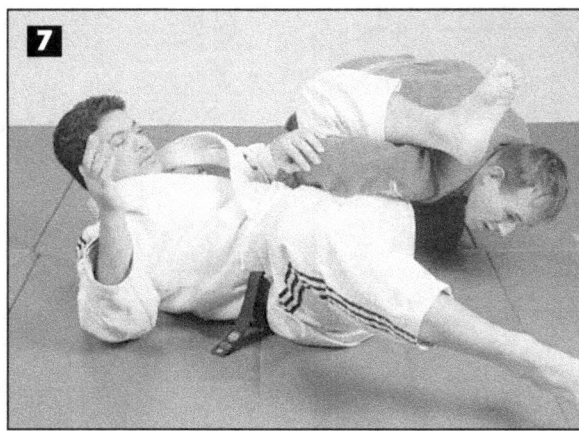 

Attacks From The Guard — 119

• Seated Position

While seated, Rigan faces the opponent (1). He moves his right leg back to create space (2), and stands (3). Now he can bring his right hand over his opponent's neck (4). He rolls to his right side (5), turns 360 degrees without releasing the grip (6), and applies a choke to his opponent (7-8).

Attacks From The Guard 120

• Seated Position

Rigan faces the opponent (1). To stand, Rigan moves his right leg back. The opponent tries to grab his left leg (2), so Rigan uses his right hand to break the grip (3). Rigan grabs the opponent's belt from behind (4), and simultaneously places his left leg between the opponent's (5) so he can execute a throw (6). The opponent ends up on his back (7). Rigan then moves his right leg to the outside (8). This gives him a more established position and better control (9) to initiate his offense (10).

Attacks From The Guard **121**

- ### *Seated Position*

From a seated position, Rigan faces the opponent (1). When Rigan moves his right leg back to create space and stand, the opponent tries to grab his left leg (2). Using his right hand, Rigan, unsuccessfully tries to prevent that from happening (3-4). As soon as he feels the opponent bringing him down (5), Rigan rolls backwards and uses his feet as hooks (6-7) to throw the opponent to the ground (8). Once there, Rigan controls him from the side (9).

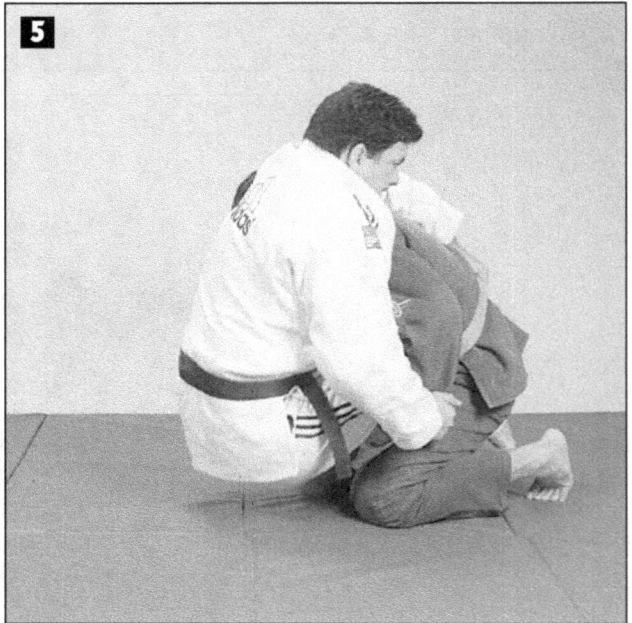

Attacks From The Guard — 122

• Seated Position

Rigan faces the opponent (1), who tries to pass the guard by pushing both legs to the side (2). Rigan reacts by pulling his left leg back — which unbalances the opponent — (3), and by putting his right hand over the opponent's neck (4). Rigan turns (5), and applies a choke from the reverse position (6).

Attacks From The Guard 123a

• Seated Position

Rigan faces his opponent (1). When the opponent tries to open Rigan's legs to initiate an attack (2), Rigan pulls him on top of him (3-4). Because he already has the hooks inside the opponent's legs (5), Rigan uses them to push his opponent (6).

(Continued)

Attacks From The Guard 123b

- **Seated Position**

He then moves both feet to the hips (7), from where he spins his legs (8), and throws the opponent (9) to the right side (10). He now controls him from the mount position (11).

Attacks From The Guard 124

• Seated Position

Rigan faces the opponent and grabs the left sleeve (1). Rigan goes on the offensive by moving to the right (2), but the opponent counters by establishing his base and bringing the left leg out for support (3-4). Rigan immediately releases the grip on the opponent's left sleeve and grabs the leg (5), using this as a sweep (6) to bring the opponent to the other side (7-8). Here he will start his offensive (9).

Attacks From The Guard 125

• **Seated Position** Rigan grabs the opponent's left sleeve (1). The opponent establishes his base by bringing his left leg out and extending it for support (2). Rigan reacts by releasing the grip on the left sleeve and grabbing the opponent's leg, bringing it close to his body (3-4).

Maintaining the grip on the opponent's collar with his left hand, Rigan starts to sweep him (5-6). This time the opponent falls face down (7). Rigan reacts immediately by mounting him from behind so he can proceed with his offensive techniques (8).

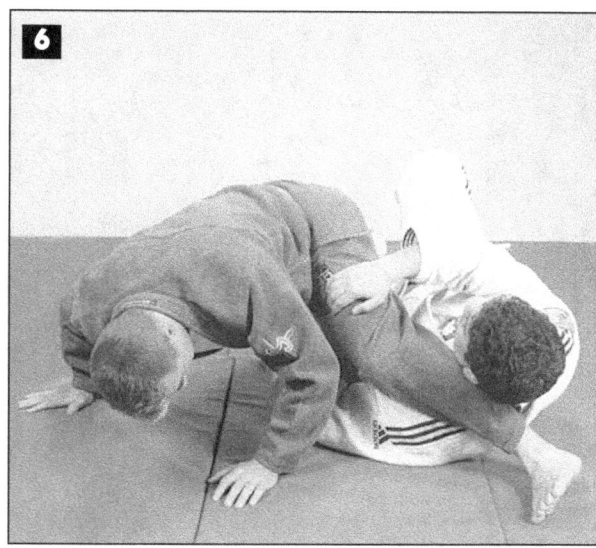

Mastering Brazilian Jiu Jitsu

Passing the Guard

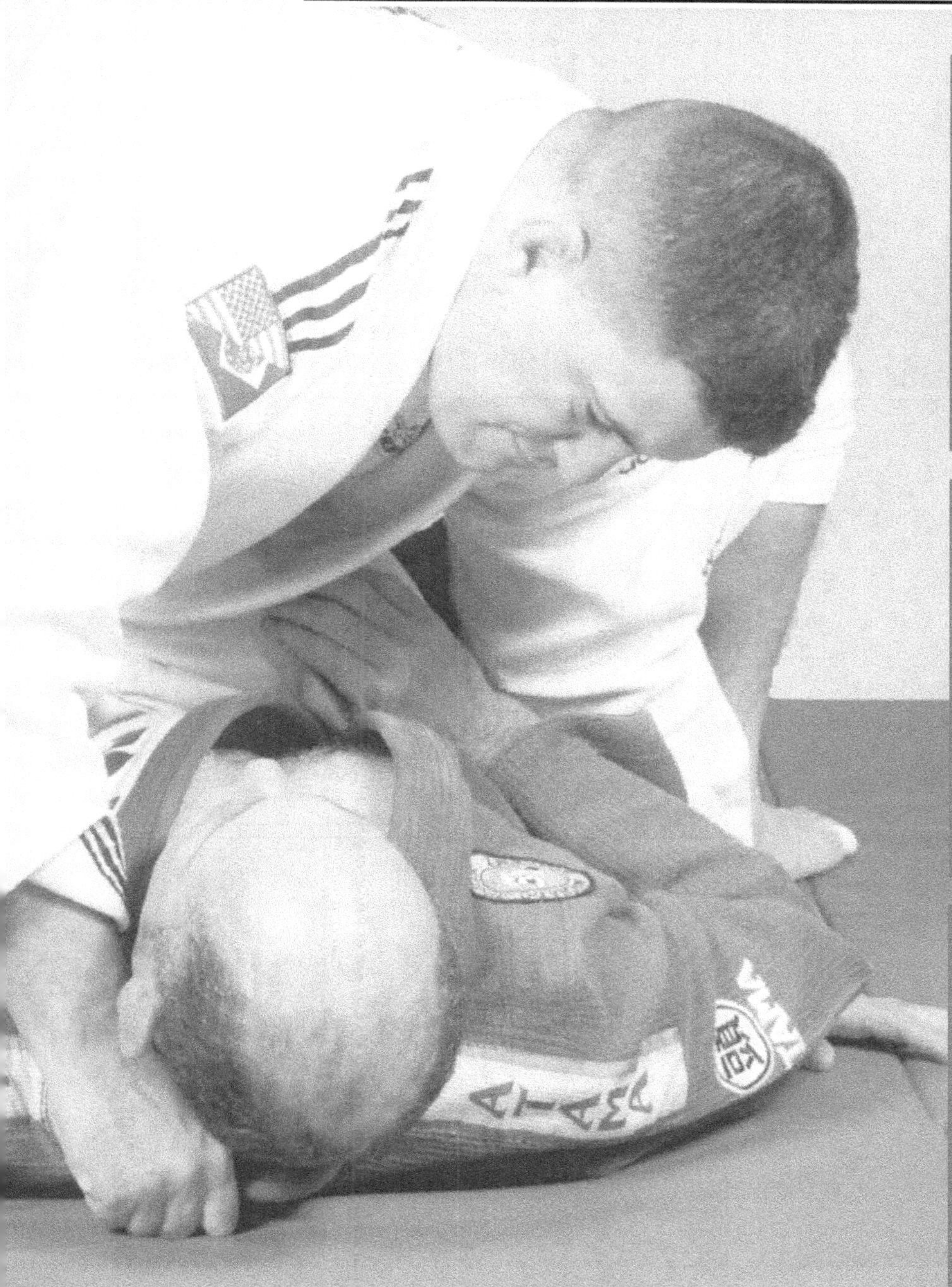

Passing The Guard 1

Rigan begins against the opponent's open guard (1). Keeping his left hand on the opponent's gi, Rigan passes his right hand around the outside of the opponent's left leg (2), reaches the upper part of the jacket on the opposite side (3), leans forward and creates pressure (4). Now the opponent's left leg is an awkward and uncomfortable position. Rigan twists his body, while maintaining a firm hold (5), and controls the opponent from the side (6).

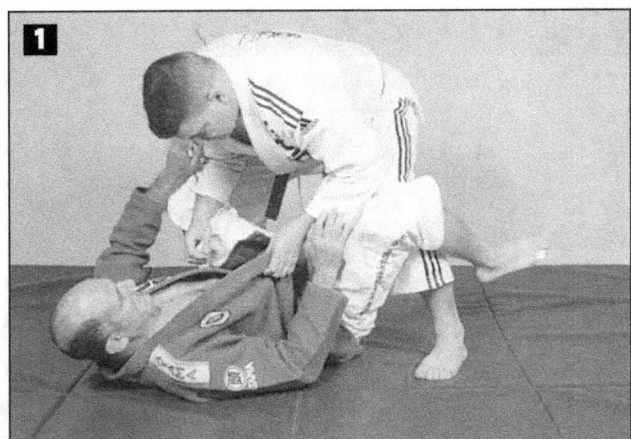

Passing The Guard 2

Rigan faces the opponent's open guard (1). Keeping his left hand firmly on the opponent's gi, Rigan first passes his right hand around the outside of the opponent's left leg and holds on (2). He does the same thing on the other side with his left hand. Now he has both legs (3). Rigan starts leaning forward and clutches his hands together (4). He continues leaning forward until he feels the opportunity to twist his body (5-6). This enables him to pass the guard and assume the side control position for taking the offensive (7).

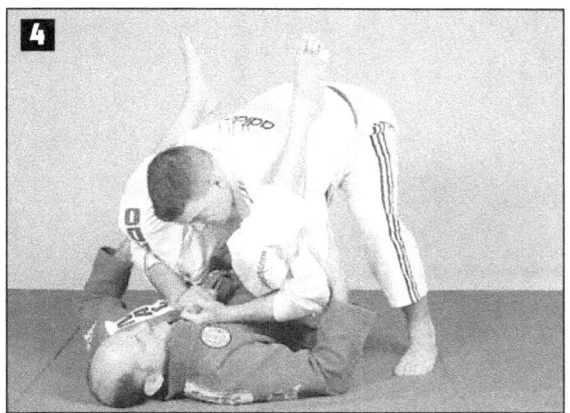

Passing The Guard 3

Rigan begins against the opponent's open guard (1). Keeping his left hand securely on the opponent's gi, Rigan passes his right hand around the outside of the left leg, grabs on and simultaneously puts pressure on the opponent's right leg with his left elbow (2). Note how that opens the leg. Next, Rigan simply uses his left hand to push the leg down (3) and then passes his left knee over the opponent's right leg (4). To establish himself, Rigan uses his left hand to reach the back of the opponent's collar (5). He then brings his right leg all the way back to pass the guard (6). Finally, Rigan switches the positions of his legs to gain side control (7).

Passing The Guard 4

Rigan faces the opponent's open guard (1). While grabbing the gi with his left hand, Rigan uses his right hand to grab the opponent's right pants leg (2). He then immediately does the same thing with his left hand (3). Rigan moves to the right and pushes both of the opponent's legs to the left side (4). He slides his left leg close to the opponent's left side (5) and takes the offensive from a side control (6).

Passing The Guard 5

Rigan faces the opponent's open guard (1). While keeping his left hand on the opponent's gi, Rigan uses his right hand to grab the lower part of the opponent's pants (2). Rigan then immediately does the same thing with the left hand (3). Rigan pushes both legs to the floor (4), and rolls to the right (5). By keeping constant pressure (6), Rigan assumes full side control (7).

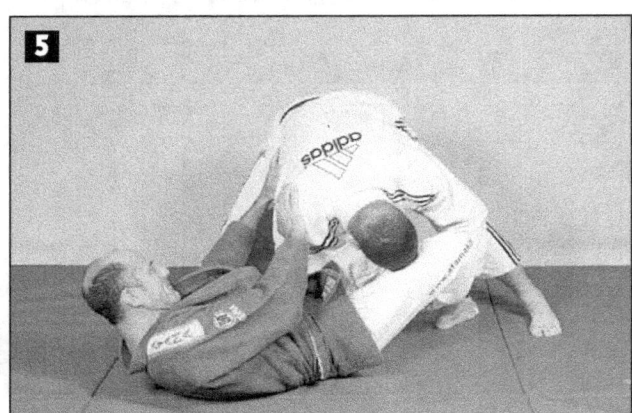

Passing The Guard 6a

Rigan faces the opponent's open guard (1). Keeping his left hand firmly on the opponent's gi, Rigan grabs his opponent's pants with his right hand (2). Rigan pushes the right leg down (3), and moves his right leg to the side so he can circle around the opponent's left leg (4). Using his left leg to help to control the opponent's left leg (5), Rigan moves carefully to the side (6), where he brings his knees up to control the position (7). Now he can start his offensive from the side (8).

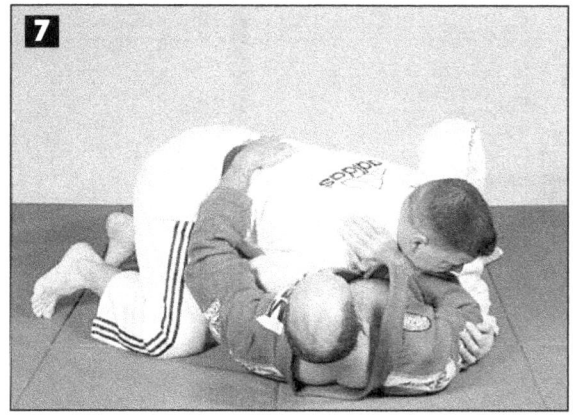
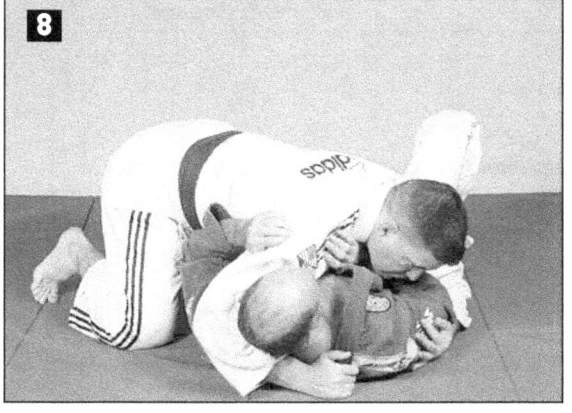

(Continued)

Passing The Guard 6b

Side View of Previous Technique

From this angle, we can see how Rigan pushes his opponent's leg all the way to the floor (9-10). By moving his hips to the right, Rigan avoids the opponent's guard (11-12). Note that Rigan's right hand is in full control of the opponent's left leg until Rigan brings his knee forward (13). This allows him to move into side control (14).

Passing The Guard 7

Rigan faces the opponent's open guard. Keeping his left hand firmly on the opponent's gi, Rigan uses his right hand to grab the lower part of the opponent's pants. He immediately does the same thing with the left hand (1-2). Rigan then pushes both legs directly to the floor (3). Next he rolls over the opponent (4-5). This allows him to rotate 360 degrees (6) until he assumes side control (7).

Passing The Guard 8

Rigan faces the opponent's open guard (1). Keeping his left hand on the opponent's gi, Rigan uses his right hand to grab the opponent's left ankle (2). Using his left hand, he clamps onto the opponent's right ankle (3). Rigan pushes both ankles down (4) until they reach the point in which he can bring his hips forward (5), and trap both legs by lowering his body to the ground (6). Now inside the opponent's guard (7), Rigan controls the opponent's left leg with his right arm (8), and moves his hips to the outside, securing the leg with his right hand (9). When he feels comfortable and confident (10), he releases the grip and secures the position with his left knee from the side (11).

Passing the Guard

Mastering Brazilian Jiu-Jitsu

Passing The Guard 9

Rigan faces the opponent's open guard (1). Keeping his left hand on the opponent's gi, Rigan lowers his body while permitting his opponent to keep his left knee up (2). Rigan uses this to his advantage because he can apply pressure to the left leg (3). Rigan then passes over the opponent's right leg (4). Once comfortable with the control, Rigan uses his right knee to pass the guard (5). He quickly assumes side control so he can initiate the attack (6). When you use your right knee to pass over the opponent's right leg, use your left foot to hook his leg. This will prevent him from reversing the movement and putting you inside his guard. The left foot secures the move until the right knee takes over the control and completely passes the opponent's right leg.

Passing The Guard 10

Rigan encounters the opponent's open guard (1). Rigan grabs his opponent's pants with his left hand, applies pressure and moves to the left (2). Then he pulls the left leg all the way up, unbalancing the opponent and preventing him from countering (3). Rigan pushes the leg away from him while keeping his left leg close to the opponent (4). He immediately releases the leg and places his right knee on the opponent's chest for a knee side control (5).

Passing The Guard 11

Rigan faces the opponent's open guard (1). Keeping his left hand on the opponent's gi, Rigan passes his right hand around the left leg (2). He then does the same thing on the other side with his left hand (3). Rigan pulls both legs up (4), and pushes forward with his hips to completely unbalance the opponent (5). Rigan pushes the legs to the left (6). Next, Rigan tries to establish better control (7), but the opponent rolls and tries to escape (8). Rigan reacts by controlling him from the back (9).

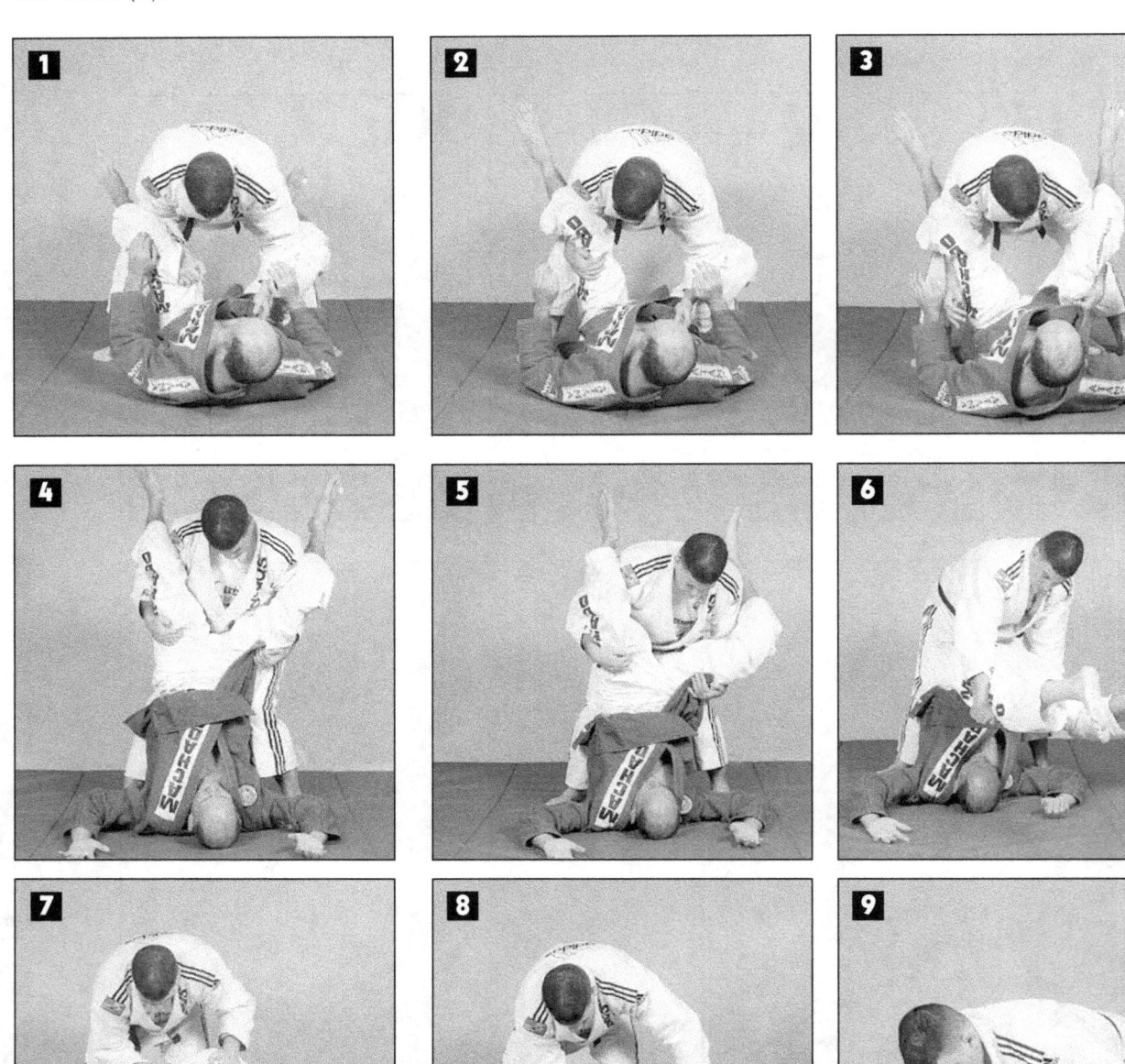

Passing The Guard 12

Rigan faces the opponent's open guard (1). He releases the opponent's gi and quickly grabs the pants (2). Rigan pulls hard with both hands to nullify the opponent's guard (3). Rigan turns 360 degrees (4-5), and assumes the knee side control (6).

Passing The Guard 13

Rigan faces the opponent's open guard (1). He changes grips and moves his left hand to the opponent's pants (2). Once both hands are controlling the opponent's pants (3), Rigan opens the legs by pushing them out (4). Rigan immediately turns and moves to his left (5), using his left elbow to keep the pressure on and pass the guard (6). Maintaining control by adding pressure with his left hand (7), Rigan drops to the ground and uses his left side for initial control (8). Then he completes the movement (9).

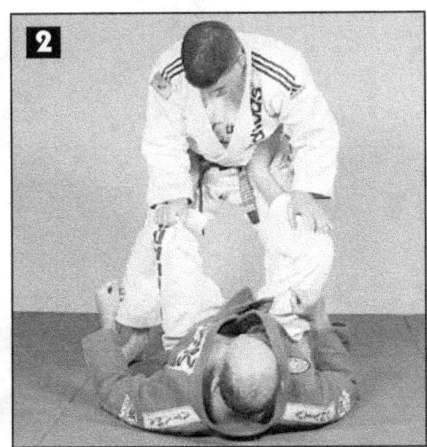
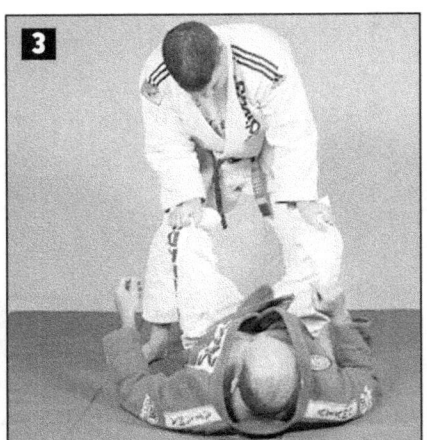

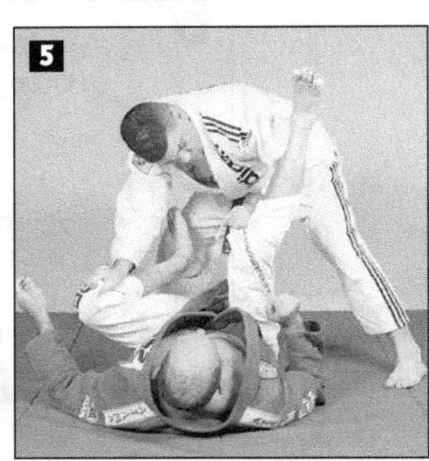

Passing The Guard   14

Rigan faces the opponent's open guard (1). He again changes grips and moves his left hand to the opponent's pants (2). Once both hands are controlling the opponent's pants (3), Rigan releases his grip, pushes down (4-5), leans forward (6), and mounts the opponent (7).

Passing The Guard   15

Rigan faces the opponent's open guard (1). He releases his opponent's gi and puts his left hand on the ground (2). This creates support to push himself up (3), and spin in the air (4). He lands on the other side, where he controls the opponent from the side (5).

Passing The Guard   16

Rigan faces the opponent's open guard (1). He moves his left leg slightly backward to create space (2), and then he places it between the opponent's legs (3), putting pressure over the left thigh (4). By sliding his hips down to the right side (5), Rigan passes the guard (6), and assumes full side control (7).

Passing The Guard 17

Rigan faces the opponent's open guard (1). By moving his body backward, he creates space (2) to circle around with his right leg (3). Rigan sits on the ground, but he maintains tight control on the opponent's left leg (4-5) until he feels comfortable to move his hips (6), and left leg out (7). He then assumes full side control (8).

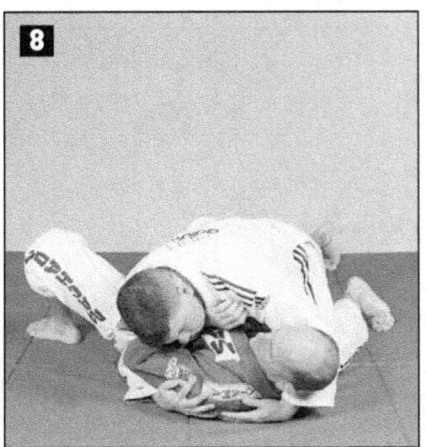

Passing The Guard 18a

Rigan faces the opponent's open guard (1). Keeping his left hand firmly on the opponent's gi, he uses his right hand to grab the opponent's left ankle (2). He then releases the gi and grabs the opponent's right ankle (3). Rigan pushes both ankles down (4) until they reach the point in which he can bring his hips forward (5). He then traps both legs by lowering his own body to the ground (6). Now inside the opponent's guard (7), Rigan moves to the left and uses both hands to support himself (8).

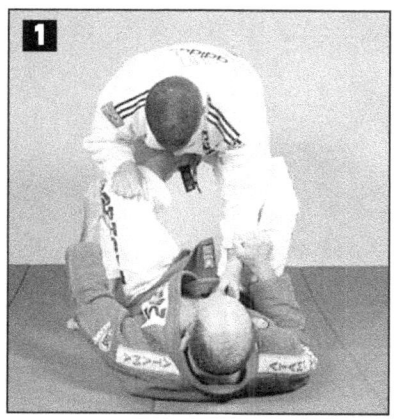
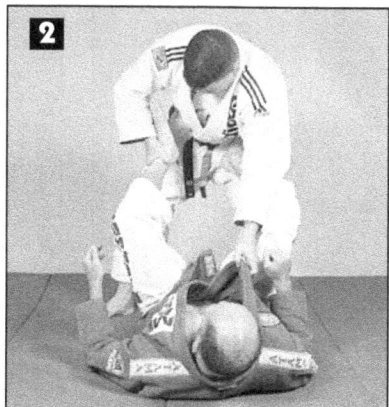

(Continued)

Passing The Guard 18b

He pushes up (9) and thrusts his body into the air (10). He spins and lands with both feet on the opponent's left (11). Reversing his position (12), Rigan assumes side control so he can take the offensive (13).

Passing The Guard 19a

Rigan faces the opponent's open guard (1). Keeping his left hand on the gi, Rigan uses his right hand to grab the opponent's left ankle (2). He releases the gi with his left hand and grabs the opponent's right ankle (3). Rigan pushes both ankles down (4), until they reach the point that he can bring his hips forward (5). He traps both legs by lowering his body to the ground (6). Now inside the opponent's guard (7), Rigan moves to the left and uses both hands to support himself (8).

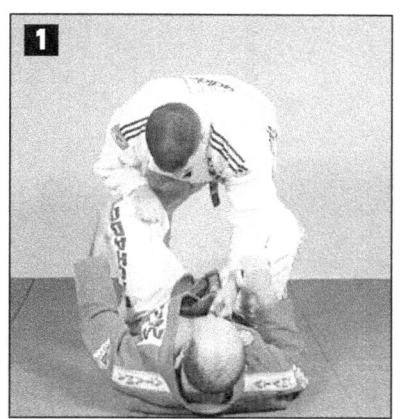

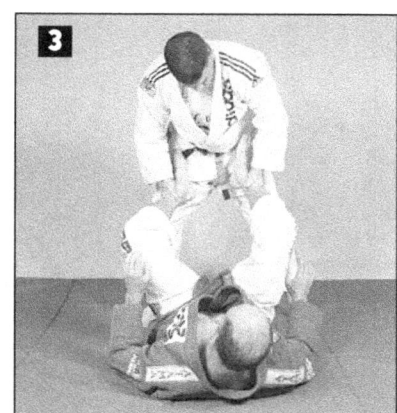

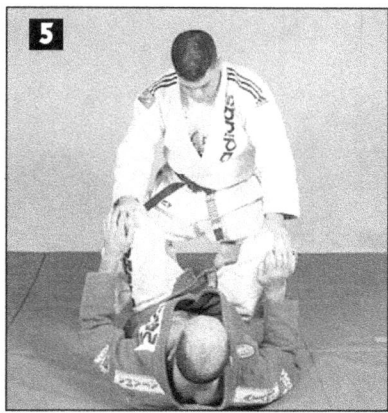

(Continued)

Passing The Guard 19b

Rigan uses his right hand to prevent the opponent from using his left leg to put him back in the guard (9-10). Rigan gathers momentum and pushes himself to the opposite side (11-12). Here he switches his position (13), and goes for the final side control (14-15).

Passing The Guard 20

While facing his opponent's open guard, Rigan grabs his opponent's gi (1). Then he moves his grip to the opponent's right sleeve (2), as his right hand moves to the right leg (3). Rigan pulls hard and moves around the opponent (4), which enables him to avoid the guard (5). Rigan then places his right knee on the chest for a full side control (6). It is critical to maintain control of the opponent's right leg and sleeve during these moves because this will enable you to avoid the guard or an attack.

Mastering Brazilian Jiu-Jitsu

Passing The Guard 21

Rigan faces the opponent's open guard with his left hand securely on the gi (1). He passes his right hand under the opponent's left leg so he can grab the opponent's right leg (2). He does the same thing on the other side with his left hand (3). He lowers both legs (4-5), rolls to the right and passes the guard (6-7). Now he can control the opponent completely (8-9).

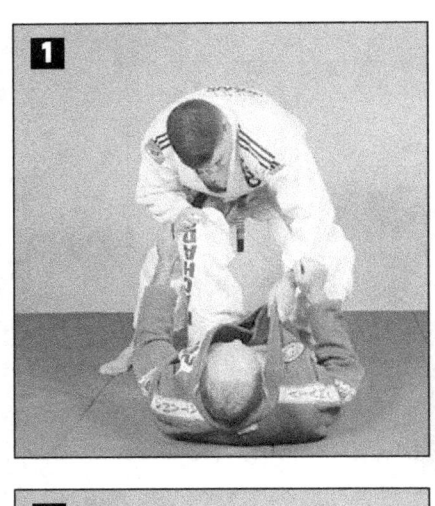

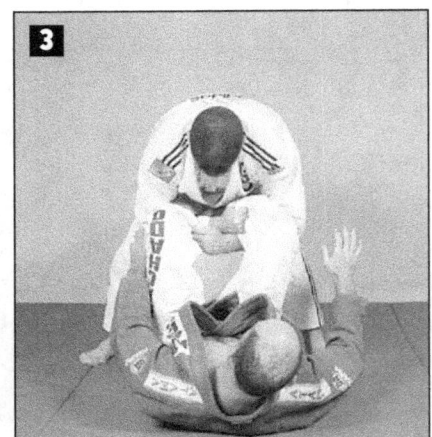

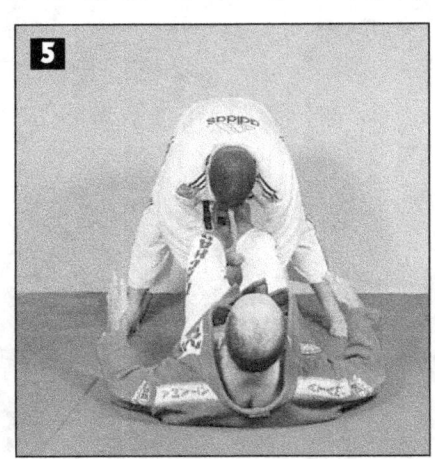

Passing The Guard 22a

Rigan faces the opponent's open guard (1). Keeping his left hand firmly on the gi, Rigan uses his right hand to grab the opponent's left ankle (2). He does the same with his left hand on the opponent's right ankle (3). Rigan pushes both legs down (4). When they reach the point where he can bring his hips forward (5), he traps both legs with his body (6).

(Continued)

Passing The Guard 22b

He swings his left leg to his right side (7) and then reverses the position of his legs (8) to pass his right leg outside the opponent's left side (9). For better positioning, he again switches the position of his legs (10), turns and assumes side control (11).

Passing The Guard 23

Rigan grabs both of his opponent's legs (1). By pushing forward with his hips and hands, Rigan adds pressure to the opponent's back, preventing him from escaping (2-3). Rigan maintains the pressure by continuing to push forward (4). As soon as he feels the opportunity, Rigan grabs the opponent's collar under the neck with his right hand (5) and starts passing the guard (6). He ends up with side control (7).

Mastering Brazilian Jiu-Jitsu 231

Passing The Guard 24

Rigan faces the opponent's open guard (1). He uses his right hand to grab the opponent's left ankle and his left hand to grab the opponent's right ankle (2). Rigan pushes both ankles down (3), until they reach the point where he can bring his hips forward (4) and trap both legs by lowering his body to the ground (5). Now he "opens" his right leg to the side as he traps the opponent's right leg with his left arm (6). Using the right leg for support, Rigan swings to the other side (7) and now uses his left leg to control the opponent's right leg. This allows him to move his left hand to the back of the collar (8). For better control, he again switches the position of his legs. Note how his right leg is over the opponent's right hip. Rigan then assumes side control (9).

Passing The Guard 25a

Rigan faces the opponent's open guard (1). He passes his right hand under the opponent's left leg (2), and starts leaning forward (3) until his knees touch the ground (4). Keeping firm control on the opponent's left hip with his right hand (5).

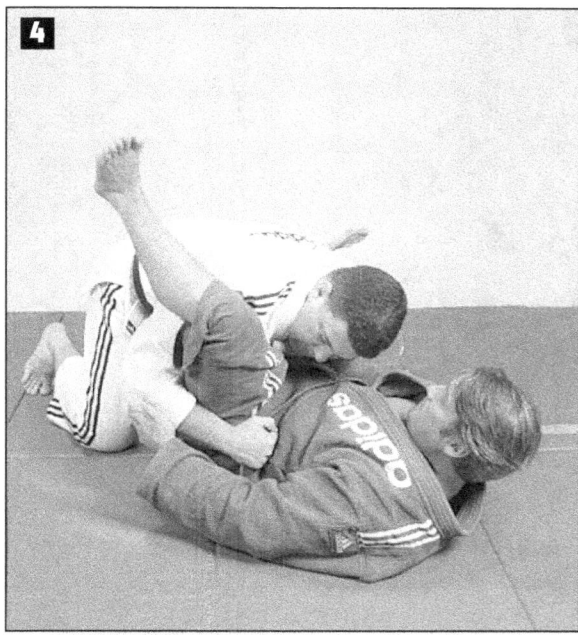

(Continued)

Passing The Guard 25b

Rigan starts moving to his left so he can pass the guard. Notice how he keeps a tight grip on the opponent's collar with his left hand (6). The opponent tries to counter by lifting his left leg up and bringing it to the front (7-8), but Rigan reacts by pulling the opponent's left hip hard with his right hand (9), and moving fast to the left. He then assumes side control (10).

Passing The Guard 26a

Rigan faces the opponent's open guard (1). He passes his right hand under the opponent's left leg (2), and he starts leaning forward (3). He grabs the opponent's belt with both hands (4), and pulls hard.

(Continued)

Passing The Guard 26b

This places the opponent in a disadvantageous position (5) to counter Rigan when he moves to his right (6-8), and passes the guard. Ultimately, Rigan assumes side control (9).

Passing The Guard 27a

Rigan faces the opponent's open guard (1). He passes his right hand under the opponent's left leg (2), and starts leaning forward (3). Rigan then grabs the opponent's hips with both hands (4), and applies pressure with his body (5) until he finds the right opportunity to pass his right leg over (6) his opponent.

(Continued)

Passing The Guard 27b

Meanwhile, he keeps tight control with his right arm on the opponent's left leg (7). Using this control as a support, he pushes himself in the air (8), and fully passes the opponent's guard (9). From here he assumes side control, where he can then initiate the offensive (10).

Passing The Guard 28a

Rigan faces the opponent's open guard and grabs the opponent's pants right above the knee (1). He twists the grip to the inside (2), and begins to push the opponent's left leg with his forearm (3). He immediately releases the grip and grabs the collar (4), which gives him superior position to maintain pressure (5-6).

(Continued)

Passing The Guard 28b

Then, he moves to the right side (7). Here he can pass the guard (8), and assume side control (9).

Passing The Guard 29

Rigan faces the open guard and grabs the opponent's pants at the knee (1). He twists the grip to the inside and begins to push the opponent's left leg with his forearm (2). He immediately releases the grip and grabs the collar (3), providing him with superior position to keep the pressure on and move to the left (4). He passes his right leg by lifting it up all the way (5) to the opponent's right side (6). He wraps up the move by taking control from the side (7). It is important to keep a tight grip over the opponent's left leg during the complete movement. This will ensure that he can't bring it up to your head and prevent you from passing to the side.

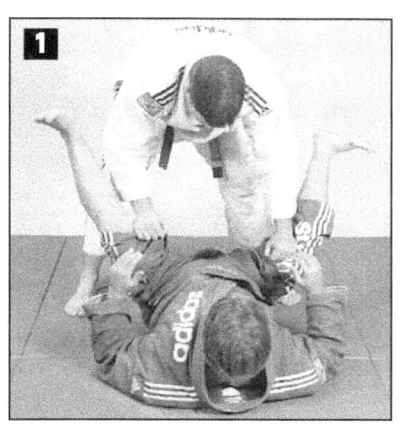

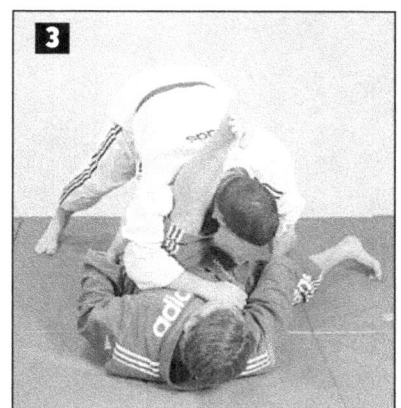

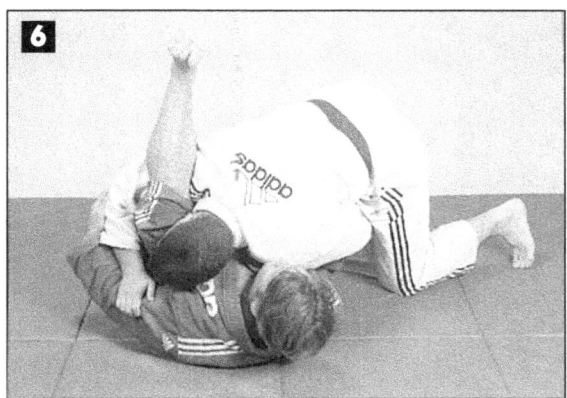

Passing The Guard 30

Rigan faces the opponent's open guard (1). He uses his right hand to grab the opponent's left ankle and his left hand to grab the opponent's right ankle (2). Rigan pushes both legs down until they reach the point where he can bring his hips forward (3), and get full control of the opponent's legs (4). He reaches under both legs (5), and grabs the opponent's left pant's leg with his left hand (6). Meanwhile, he maintains a firm grip on the opponent's left knee with his right hand (7). This keeps the opponent's leg still while Rigan passes the guard (8).

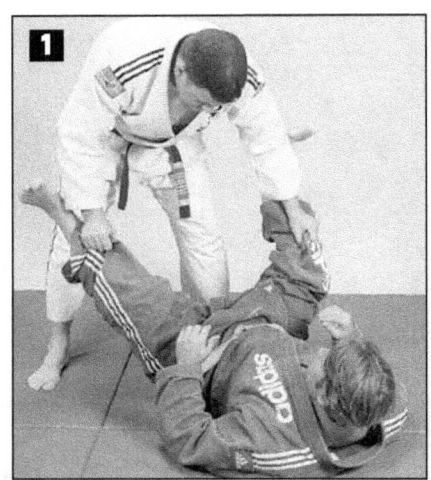

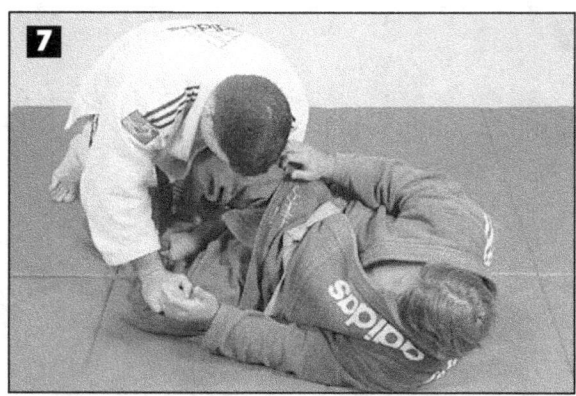

Once his right leg has passed the guard (9), Rigan switches grips and moves his right hand to the collar (10). He can use this hold to support himself (11), move upward, and shift his left leg to the right (12). He can now control the opponent's actions (13) before he finally brings his left knee close to the opponent's left hip (14) for full side control (15).

Passing The Guard 31

Rigan grabs his opponent's ankles (1), and he pushes them down (2) until they reach the point where he can bring his hips forward (3). This permits him to obtain full control of the opponent's legs (4). He then grabs the legs (5) and latches firmly onto the left pant leg (6). This enables him to pass his right leg to the side (7). Rigan lifts his hips and grabs the opponent's collar (8). This gives him momentum (9), and he pushes his body into the air (10-11), landing on the opponent's right side (12). Here he assumes the final side control (13).

Passing The Guard 32

Rigan faces his opponent (1). He grabs both of the opponent's sleeves (2), steps forward with his left leg (3), and places his leg next to the opponent's left hip (4). By pushing with his hips (5), Rigan forces the opponent to the ground, where he controls him with the knee on his chest (6). While maintaining a tight grip on the opponent's left arm (7), Rigan then grabs the collar (8). This confuses his opponent (9), which gives Rigan the opportunity to submit him with a straight arm-lock (10).

Passing the Guard

Mastering Brazilian Jiu-Jitsu 247

Passing The Guard 33

Rigan faces a seated opponent (1). He grabs the opponent's right sleeve with his left hand and uses his right hand to push the opponent's head down (2). This maneuver helps Rigan lift his right leg over (3) the opponent's left shoulder (4). Pushing with his hips forward forces the opponent toward the ground (5-6). Before the opponent's back touches the ground, Rigan moves his right leg behind the opponent's neck (7). Rigan rolls to his right (8), bringing the opponent with him. He then reaches his right ankle with his left hand (9), choking his opponent with a *triangle* (10).

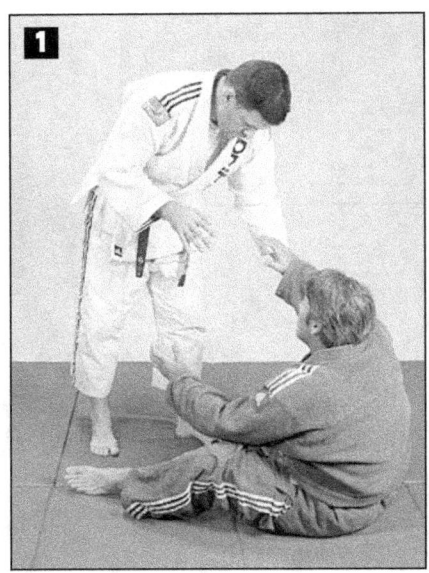

Passing The Guard 34

Rigan faces his seated opponent (1), and uses his right hand to grab the back of the opponent's collar (2). Meanwhile, he lowers his left hand to the ground (3), and pushes himself into the air (4-5). He lands on the opponent's left (6), and finalizes the move with a side control (7).

Passing The Guard 35

Rigan faces his seated opponent (1). Using his right hand, he grabs the back of the opponent's head (2), and forces him slightly down (3). Rigan slides his arm around the front of the opponent's neck and raises his hips (4). This takes his hips out of the opponent's reach (5-6), and prevents the opponent from controlling him. Rigan moves to the right (7), and assumes full side control (8).

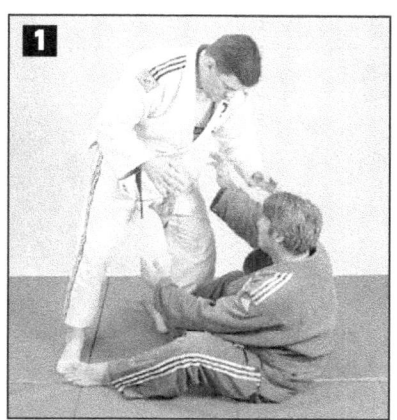
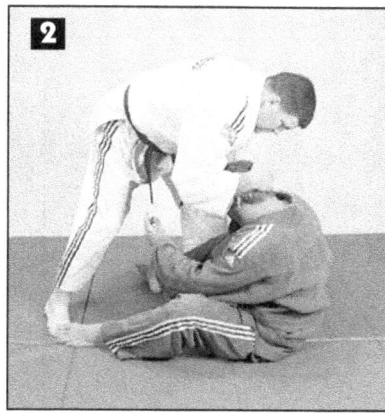

Mastering Brazilian Jiu-Jitsu

Passing The Guard 36

Rigan starts by grabbing both of the opponent's ankles (1). He first releases the ankle with his left hand and grabs the jacket (2), and then he does the same with his right hand (3). Putting his head onto the opponent's chest (4), Rigan gets momentum to push himself into the air (5-6). He lands on the opponent's left (7), passes the guard (8) and assumes a knee side control (9). To establish that momentum to push yourself into the air, it is important to keep a tight grip and put lots of pressure onto the opponent's chest with your head.

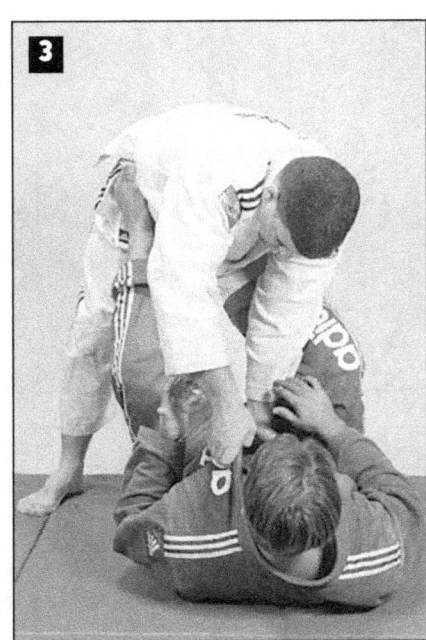
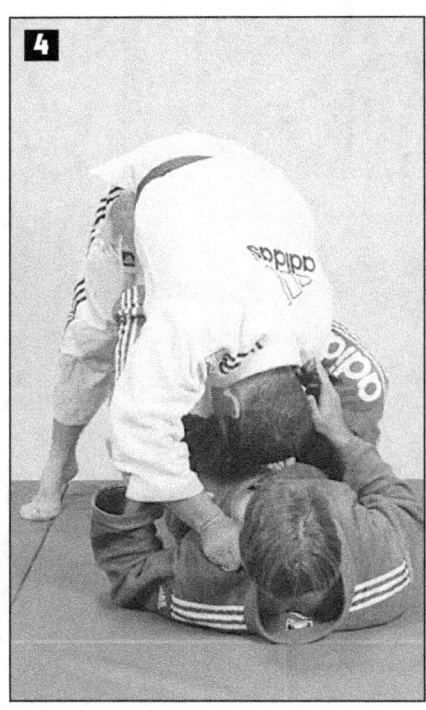

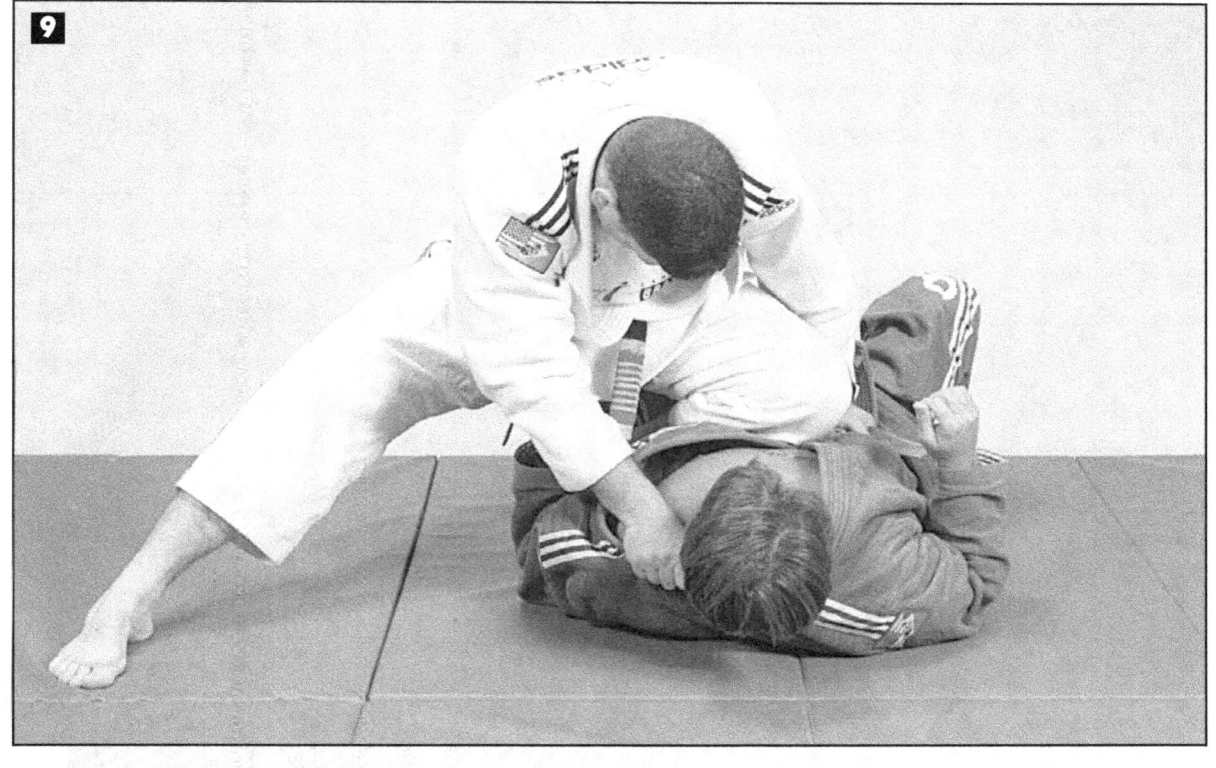

Passing the Guard

Mastering Brazilian Jiu-Jitsu 253

Passing The Guard 37

Rigan faces the opponent's open guard (1). He grabs both ankles (2), and pushes them to the floor (3-4). He puts his head on the opponent's abdomen (5), pushes himself into the air (6) and lands on the other side (7). He immediately starts to roll to the left (8). Using his right hand, Rigan grabs the opponent's collar (9), and then assumes full side control (10).

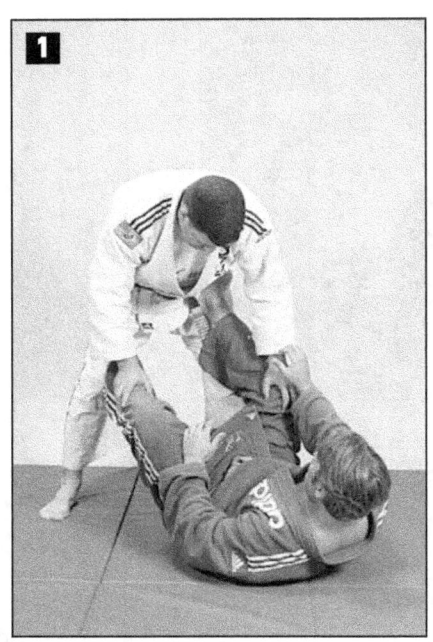
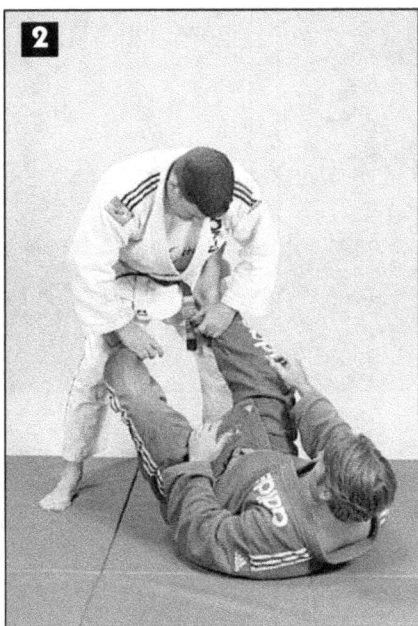
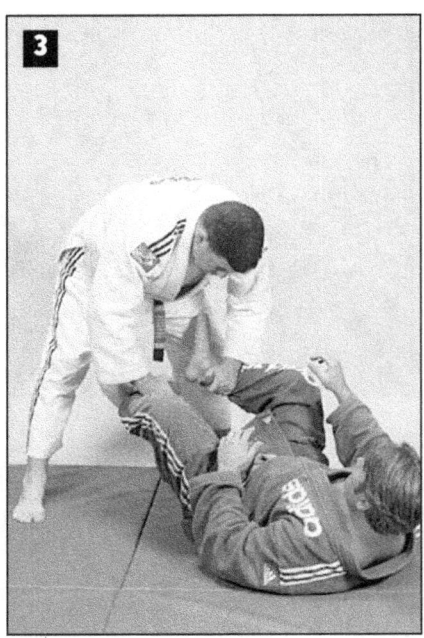
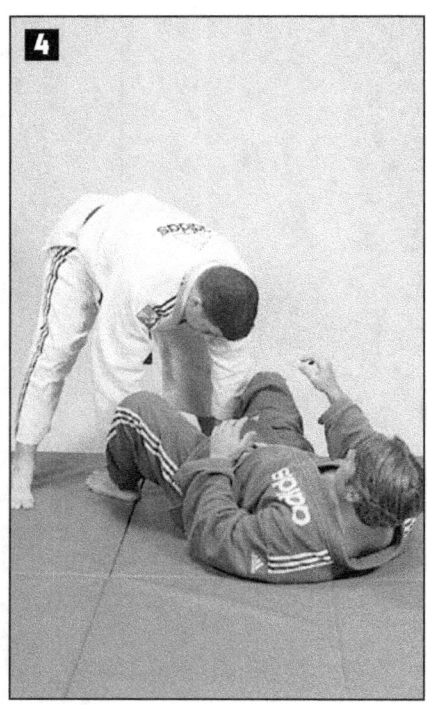
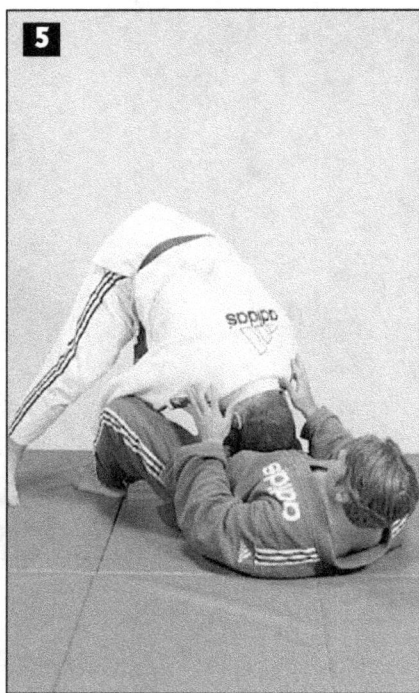

Passing The Guard 38

Rigan faces the opponent's open guard (1). He moves his right leg to the side as he pushes the opponent's left leg down (2). Next, Rigan grabs the opponent's left ankle with his right arm (3), and leans back, bringing his right leg over the opponent's left leg (4). Rigan places his left hand over the opponent's left leg, reaches under the opponent's left leg with his right hand, grabs his left wrist and pushes forward with his hips (5). The result is a devastating anklelock (6).

Passing The Guard 39

Rigan controls the opponent's left leg with his right arm (1). Rigan lowers his left knee to the opponent's left hip (2), moves to the opponent's left (3), and sits on the floor adjacent to the opponent's left side (4). Note that he still has control of the opponent's left leg. Allowing himself to lean backward to the ground, Rigan pushes his hips forward and applies a kneebar (5).

Passing The Guard 40

Using his right arm, Rigan again controls the opponent's left leg (1). Rigan twists his body to the right (2), brings his right leg over the opponent's left hip (3), and prepares to sit (4). Rigan leans all the way back (5), and applies a painful kneebar (6).

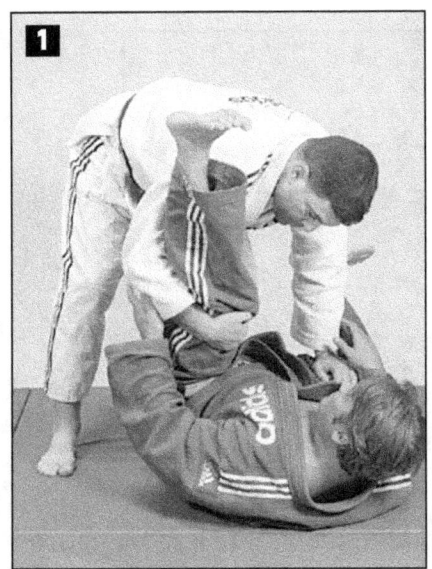
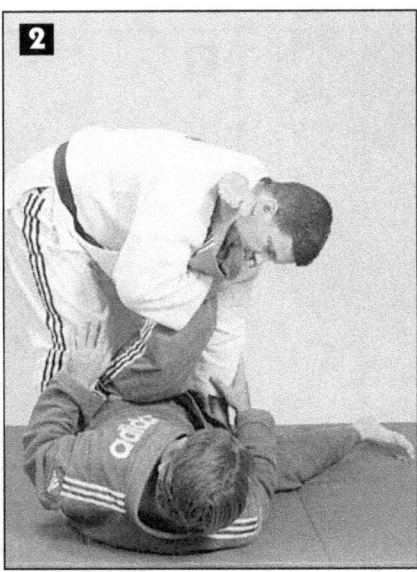
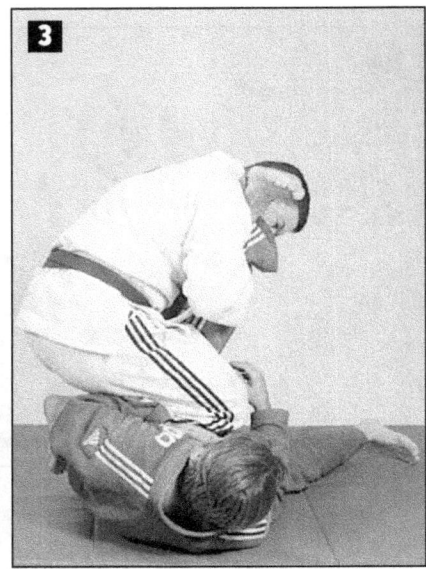
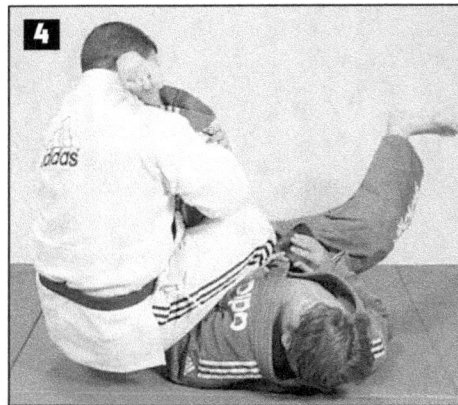

Passing The Guard 41

Rigan faces the seated opponent (1). Using his left hand, Rigan grabs the left side of the opponent's collar (2). He brings his left arm around the opponent's neck (3-5), and moves his hips to the right (6). From there, he spins until he's on his back (7). Rigan turns slightly, wraps his right arm around the opponent's left arm, maintains the hold on the opponent's neck (8), and applies a choke (9).

Passing The Guard 42

Rigan's opponent places his left leg over Rigan's right hip (1). Rigan pushes the opponent's right leg with his left hand (2), and maintains control of the left leg as he leans backward (3). Once on the ground, Rigan passes his right leg over the opponent's left leg (4-5). Rigan hooks his right instep under his left leg (6), joins his hands, cranks the opponent's ankle and applies the painful lock (7-8).

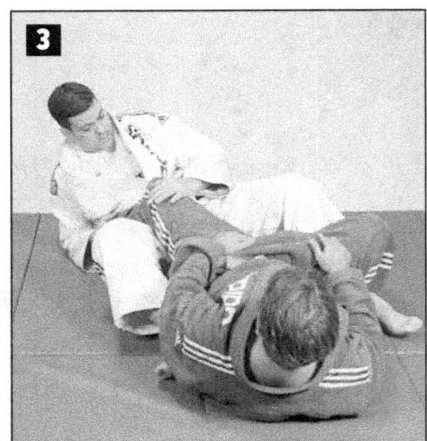
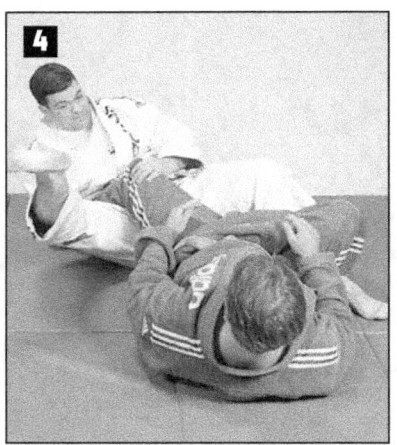

Passing The Guard 43

Rigan faces the opponent (1). He leans forward (2), and places his left hand under the opponent's right armpit as he maintains a safe distance by keeping his hips away (3). Rigan uses his right hand to control the opponent's left arm (4). The opponent cannot stop Rigan from passing his right leg to the left side (5). Rigan can now finalize the move by taking the opponent to his back and controlling him from the side (6).

Passing The Guard 44

Rigan initiates the passing of the guard (1) by moving his right arm under the opponent's left leg. Next, he lowers his hips to keep the center of gravity low (2-3). Using his right knee as a pivot point (4), Rigan moves his left leg around (5), and ultimately brings it to the other side (6). Rigan releases the opponent's left leg and controls him from the mount position (7).

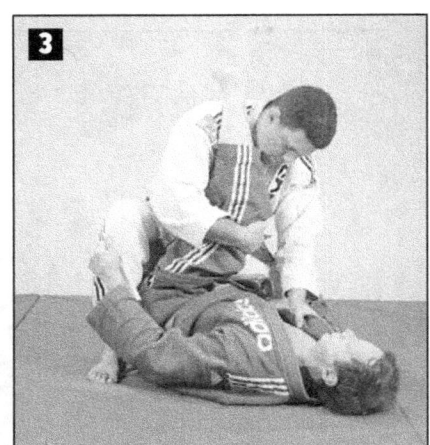

Passing The Guard 45

Rigan tries to pass the opponent's guard (1), but he is countered with a sweeping technique (2). Rigan prevents himself from falling by placing both hands on the ground (3), and he immediately turns to his right (4). He controls the opponent's body (5), close and tight (6). He assumes side control, where he can now initiate the counterattack (7).

Passing The Guard 46

Rigan tries to pass the opponent's open guard (1). He moves his right leg to the side as he pulls the opponent's left leg (2). This allows him to move his right leg to the other side (3). Having full control of both of the opponent's legs, Rigan sits (4) and slides to the left (5). While doing this, he uses his right hand to control one side of the opponent's collar (6), and his left hand to grab the other side of the collar (7). Finally, he applies pressure from the side (8).

Passing The Guard 47

Rigan tries to pass the open guard (1), but the opponent maintains tight control of his movements, which forces Rigan to place his left knee on the opponent's chest (2). Rigan now focuses on getting a submission by controlling the opponent's left foot (3). Ultimately, he applies an anklelock (4).

Passing The Guard 48

Rigan faces his opponent's open guard (1). As he controls both of the opponent's legs, Rigan circles to the left (2). Using his right hand, he grabs his opponent's left ankle (3). He lowers his left knee onto the chest (4). Rigan rolls over the opponent (5), and applies an anklelock (6).

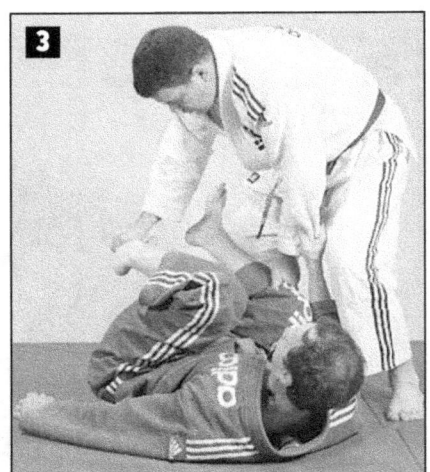

Passing The Guard 49

Rigan is in the opponent's closed guard (1). He lowers his body (2), passes his left hand behind the opponent's neck (3), and grabs his own sleeve (4). He raises the edge of his right forearm to the front of the opponent's neck (5), and chokes him with an *ezequiel* (6).

Passing The Guard 50

Rigan is inside the opponent's closed guard (1). Rigan grabs the opponent's left wrist (2), lifts his hips and "walks" forward (3-4). Notice the space between the opponent's back and the floor. Rigan passes the opponent's left wrist under the upraised back (5), and grabs the arm on the other side (6). Rigan uses his right hand to push the opponent's left knee down (7-8).

Note: As you "walk" forward in the beginning of the technique, remember to keep strong pressure on the opponent's body. It is also important to make sure the opponent's arm gets trapped between his back and the floor as you move to the side. When his hands are trapped, it will be impossible for him to prevent you from passing the guard. This enables him to pass his right leg (9) and then his body over the opponent (10). Now he can obtain side control and initiate the attack (11).

Passing The Guard 51

Rigan is in the opponent's closed guard (1). He reaches the back of the opponent's neck with his right hand (2), and then his left hand (3). Keeping his elbows close and tight to the opponent's body (4), Rigan applies pressure and executes a neck crunch to submit him (5).

Passing The Guard 52a

Rigan is inside the opponent's guard (1). He brings his right leg up and grabs the opponent's gi (2). Rigan quickly rips the uniform off his opponent's shoulder, trapping the left arm (3-4). He reinforces the hold by grabbing the jacket with his left hand, which is under the opponent's back (5-6).

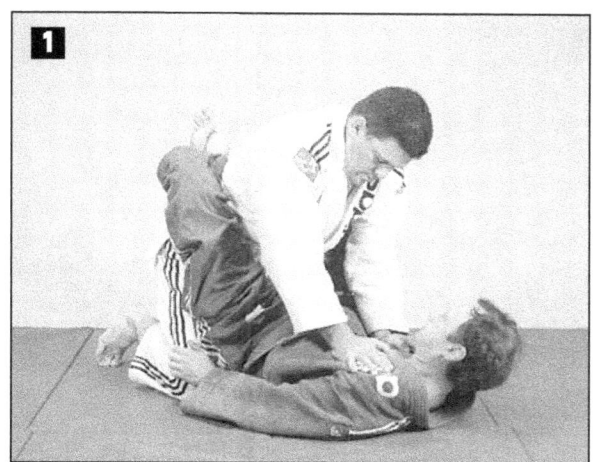

(Continued)

Passing The Guard 52b

Once the arm has been trapped, Rigan uses his right hand (7), to push the opponent's left knee down (8-9). He passes his right knee over his opponent (10), and then his entire body (11). Now he can start an offensive action (12).

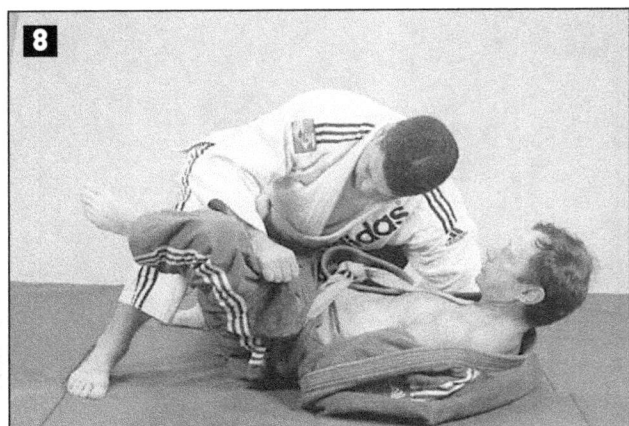

Passing The Guard 53

Rigan tries to pass the guard (1), but his opponent counters with a sweeping technique. Rigan prevents himself from falling with both hands (2-3), immediately turns to his right, controls the opponent's right leg close and tight, and executes a reverse anklelock (4).

Passing The Guard 54

Rigan tries to pass the opponent's guard from the left side (1). As he feels the opponent controlling the situation, Rigan grabs the left leg with his left hand (2), pushes the opponent's hips to the left and "walks" to the right (3). With his right hand, Rigan reaches around the back of the opponent's neck and grabs the collar (4). He shifts over and assumes side control (5).

Passing The Guard 55

Rigan tries to pass the opponent's guard (1). Using his left leg, the opponent blocks Rigan's move and slides his hips to the right (2-3). Rigan counters by controlling the opponent's belt (4), raising his hips (5), and pulling the opponent's right leg and right arm (6). Rigan then releases the leg (7), and gains better control of the right arm before going for the armlock (8).

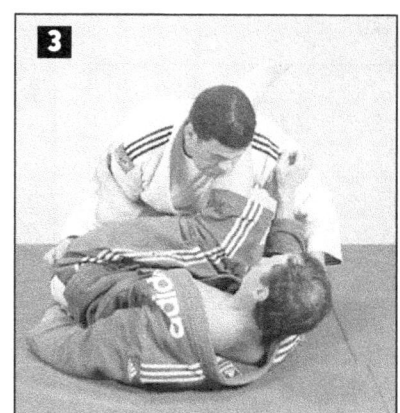

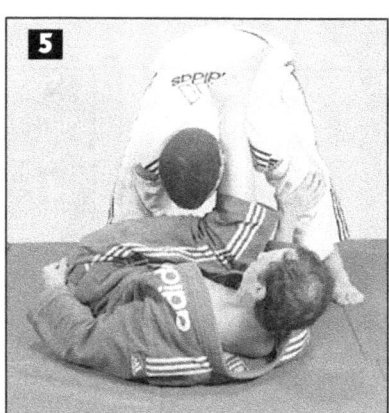

Passing The Guard 56

Rigan tries to pass the guard (1), but the opponent prevents him from doing this by placing his foot on Rigan's right hip. Rigan grabs the collar of his own gi with his left hand (2), and uses his right hand to grab the opponent's left wrist (3). With his opponent's right leg still up, Rigan starts "walking" forward (4). This puts pressure on the opponent. Rigan circles to the right, avoiding contact with the opponent's hips (5). Rigan immediately leans backwards and places his left knee at the opponent's left armpit (6). He slightly moves his hips to the right (7), and applies a finishing armlock (8).

Passing The Guard 57

Rigan begins inside the opponent's guard (1). He then moves his hips back to create space (2), which enables him to move his left knee to the opponent's coccyx (3). With both hands firmly on the opponent's belt, Rigan applies pressure and increases the space between them (4). He then immediately brings his left knee up to start the offensive action (5).

Passing The Guard 58

Rigan is inside the opponent's guard (1). He grabs the opponent's jacket with his right hand (2), applying pressure to the left armpit. He does the same thing with his left hand and leans forward (3-4). Maintaining pressure with his hips, Rigan "walks" forward until his opponent's hips are off the ground (5).

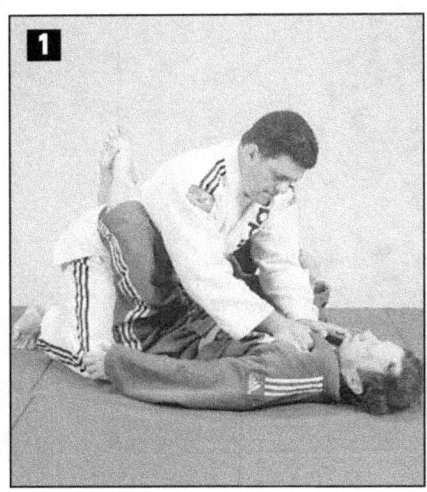

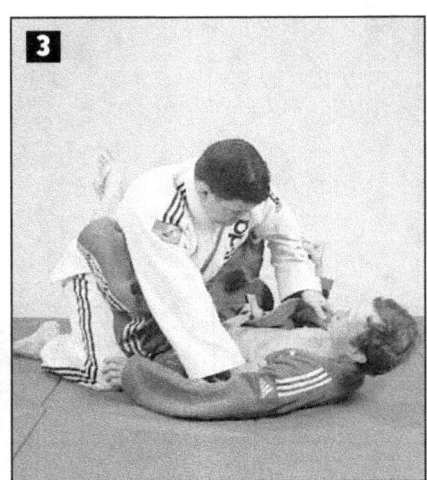

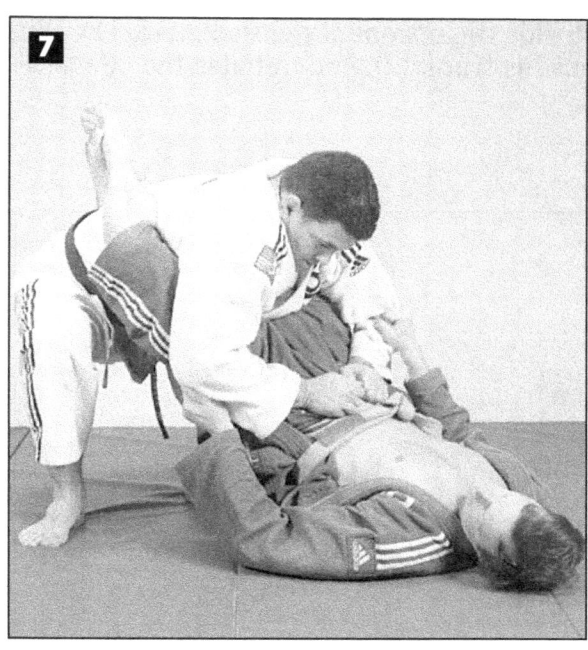
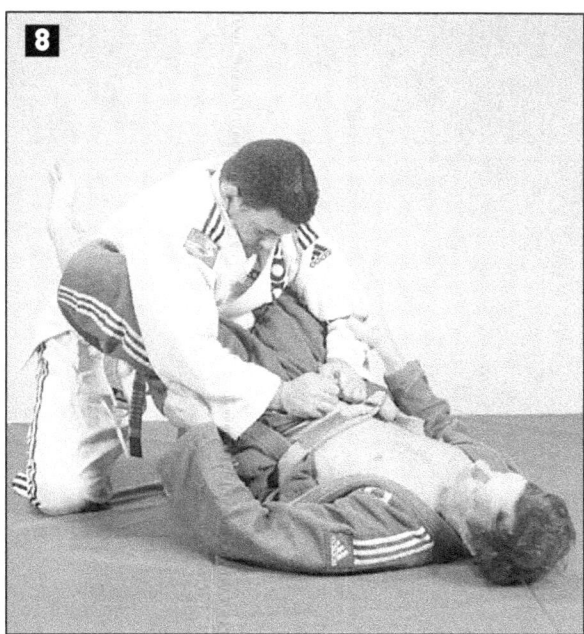

He then brings his left knee forward to the middle of the opponent's lower back or coccyx (6), and starts to sit (7). The pressure on the opponent's lower back forces him to open his legs (8). This allows Rigan to bring his left knee up so he can begin passing the guard (9).

Passing The Guard 59

Rigan is inside the opponent's closed guard (1). While holding onto the opponent's gi, Rigan straightens his trunk (2), and initiates the offensive (3) by bringing his left leg up (4).

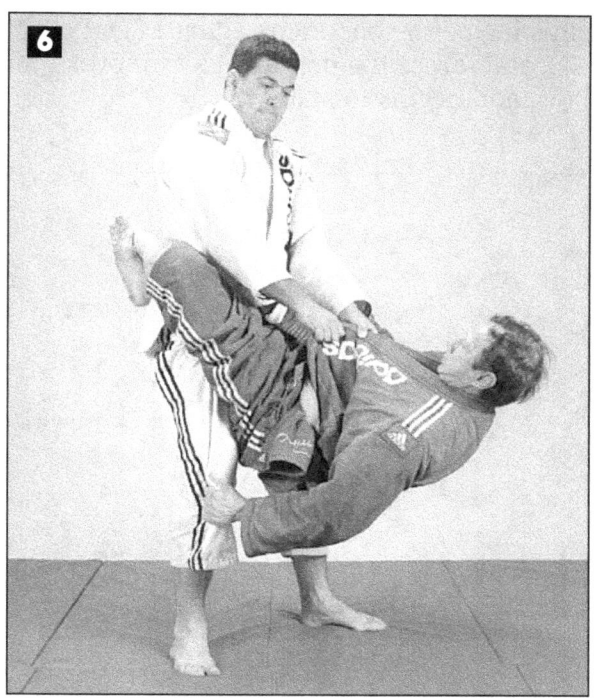
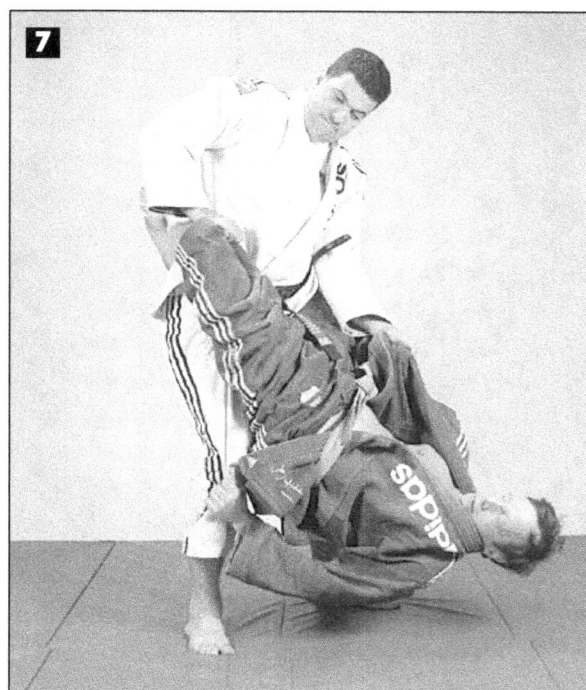

He then does the same thing with the right leg (5). Without releasing his grip on the opponent's gi, Rigan stands (6), and uses his right hand to push the opponent's left knee down (7). This opens the guard (8).

Passing The Guard 60

Rigan begins inside the opponent's guard (1). Using his right hand, Rigan grabs the opponent's left sleeve (2-3), and forces the opponent's arm over the stomach (4). Rigan maintains control with the left hand (5), and begins to stand (6).

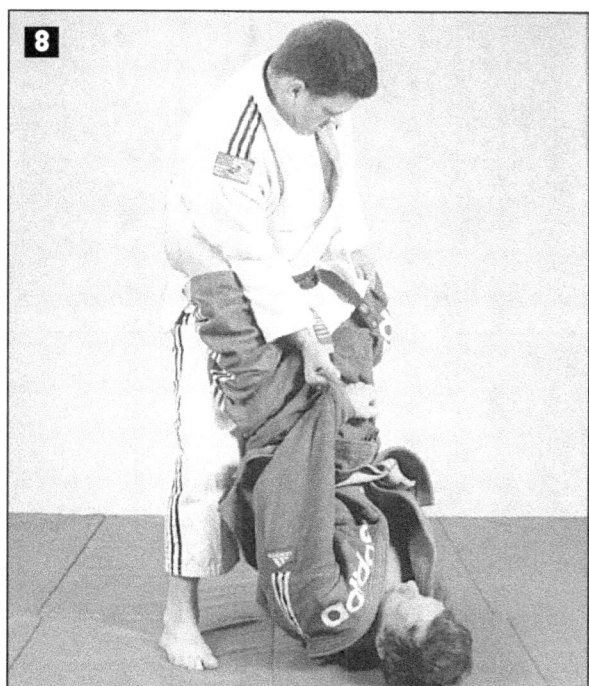 

Once he is up (7), Rigan uses his left hand to push the opponent's right knee down (8) to open the guard (9).

Passing The Guard 61

Rigan begins inside the opponent's guard (1). Using his right hand, Rigan grabs the gi (2), and moves it across the opponent's neck (3-4). He uses his left hand to grab the other side of the collar (5). By pulling with his left hand and pushing with his right, Rigan chokes his opponent (6).

Passing The Guard 62

Keeping both hands inside, Rigan tries to pass the opponent's open guard (1). He squats and uses his left knee to put pressure on the opponent's right thigh (2). When he reaches the ground (3), Rigan moves to the side, uses his right knee to block the opponent's attempt to put him back into the guard and assumes side control (4).

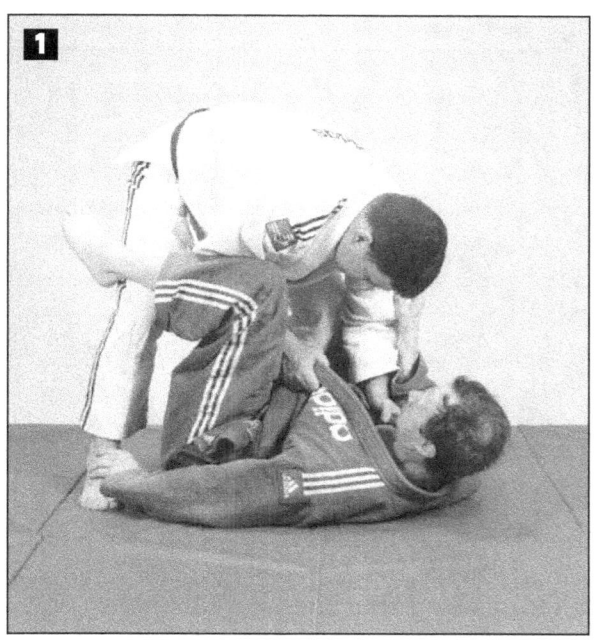

Passing The Guard 63

While keeping both hands inside, Rigan tries to pass the opponent's open guard (1). He lowers his body and uses his left knee to put pressure on the opponent's right thigh (2). Now that he's even lower, Rigan can reach around to the back of the opponent's collar (3). Rigan rolls across the opponent and grabs the fighter's left wrist with his right hand (4). He lifts the opponent's arm (5), slides his left arm under (6), and applies a painful *kimura* (7).

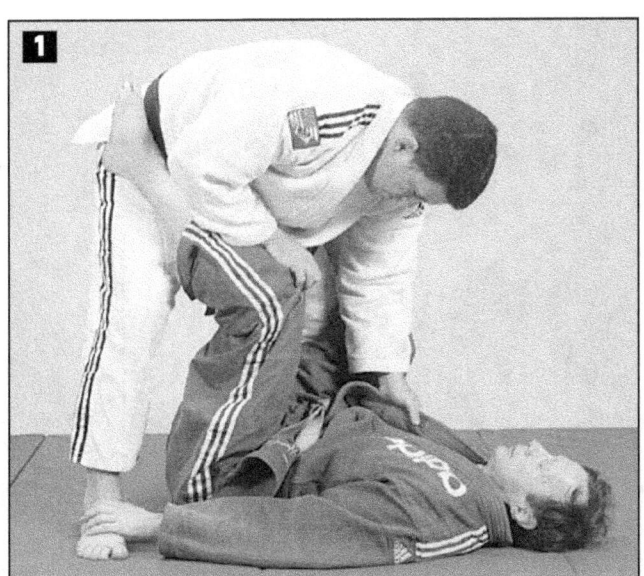

Mastering Brazilian Jiu-Jitsu 287

Mastering Brazilian Jiu Jitsu

Side Control

Side Control 1

Rigan controls his opponent from the side (1). He uses his right hand to grab the opponent's collar and his left hand to grab the belt (2). Rigan starts to stand and places his left knee on the opponent's stomach (3). Immediately, he switches grips and moves his right hand to the opponent's left sleeve and his left to the left side of the collar (4). Rigan pushes the opponent's left arm to the opposite side (5), and moves his right leg over the opponent's head (6). Keeping tight control over the left arm, Rigan leans back (7), and applies a straight armlock (8). During the whole movement, it is important to keep a tight grip on the opponent's arm and make sure your left knee stays close to the his left armpit.

Side Control 2

Rigan controls the opponent from the side (1). Then he uses his right arm to trap the opponent's right arm (2). Keeping a tight grip on that arm, Rigan circles around the other side (3-4), leans back (5), and finishes his opponent off with an armlock (6).

Side Control 3

While controlling the opponent from the side (1), Rigan pushes himself up (2). Next, he puts his right knee on the opponent's chest (3) as he grabs the left arm (4). He passes his right arm under the opponent's left arm (5), stands and circles around. (6-7) until he reaches the other side. He sits (8) and applies a finishing armlock (9).

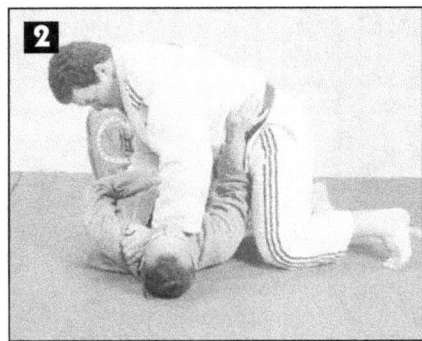

Side Control 4

The opponent reacts to Rigan's side control by turning his body away (1). Using his left hand, Rigan loosens the opponent's gi (2). Using his right hand, Rigan reaches around the opponent's neck and grabs the jacket (3). To apply the finishing choke, Rigan tightens the grip with his right hand and puts his left hand over the opposite side of the opponent's neck (4).

Side Control 5

Rigan establishes side control over his opponent (1). While maintaining contact with the adversary, Rigan switches the position of his hips (2), and then grabs the opponent's right wrist (3). He switches his hips again, passes his left hand under the opponent's arm (4), and applies a bent armlock (5).

Side Control 6

Rigan partially controls the opponent from the side (1). To prevent Rigan from gaining full control, the opponent pushes Rigan's right knee (2). Rigan uses his right hand to grab the opponent's left arm (3). He pulls the arm up, switches his hips and adopts a side control with his left arm under the opponent's head (4). He grabs the trapped arm with his right hand (5), and forces it down (6), trapping it with his left leg (7). Rigan grabs his left hand and pulls back, subjecting his opponent to a painful neck crank (8).

Side Control 7

Rigan controls the opponent from the side (1). When the opponent tries to stop Rigan's right knee, Rigan pulls the opponent's arm up (2), and switches his hips for better position (3). He can now control the opponent's left arm (4). Rigan passes his left arm under the opponent's head and grabs his own leg just inside the knee (5). Next, he leans forward and grabs his left wrist (6). Pulling back, Rigan applies a neck crank (7).

Side Control 8

Rigan establishes control from the side (1), but the opponent keeps pushing Rigan's right knee to prevent full control. Using his right hand, Rigan grabs the opponent's arm (2). While pulling the arm up, Rigan switches his hips (3), and adopts side control with his left arm under the opponent's head (4). Notice that Rigan is grabbing his left leg just inside the knee. Next, Rigan controls the opponent's left leg with his right hand (5). For better control, Rigan also grabs his right thigh (6). Rigan applies pressure and executes a painful crank to his opponent's body and neck (7).

Side Control 9

Rigan maintains control from the side, but the opponent uses his right knee to prevent Rigan from mounting him (1). Rigan moves his right hand over the opponent's right shin, which forces the right foot forward (2). Using his left hand (3), Rigan grabs the opponent's instep (4). He then reaches under with his right hand and applies an ankle-lock (5).

Side Control 10

Rigan establishes control from the side, but the opponent uses his right knee to prevent Rigan from mounting him (1). Rigan moves his hips back slightly (2), and grabs the opponent's right calf (3). He moves his hips forward, slides his left knee onto the opponent's pelvis (4), leans back and applies a painful kneebar (5).

Side Control 11

Rigan maintains control from the side, but the opponent again uses his right knee to prevent Rigan from mounting him (1). This time Rigan changes his strategy. First, using both hands, he grabs the opponent's left arm (2). This forces the opponent to roll to the opposite side to avoid the control (3). Rigan then brings his left leg over the opponent's head (4). When the opponent tries to use his right hand to release Rigan's grip (5), Rigan switches the grip and grabs the opponent's right arm as he simultaneously sits (6) to apply a finishing armlock (7).

Side Control 12

Controlling the altercation from the side (1), Rigan pushes his body up (2), and puts his right knee on the opponent's chest (3). Notice that he maintains his left hand on the opponent's collar. With the palm up (4), Rigan slides his right hand under his left (5), and applies a front choke (6).

Side Control 13

Rigan controls the opponent from the side (1). He puts his left hand on the opponent's collar (2) and his right hand on the opponent's belt (3). He raises himself and puts his right knee on the opponent's chest (4). While maintaining his grip on the collar, he moves his hand to the other side of the neck (5). Rigan places his right hand exactly where his left hand was (6-7). Without releasing his grip, Rigan circles around the opponent's head (8). This enables him to make the grip even tighter. By leaning forward, Rigan creates additional pressure and executes a finishing choke (9).

Side Control 14

Rigan establishes control from the side, but the opponent is grabbing his own belt, which prevents Rigan from getting an armlock (1). Rigan slides his right arm under the opponent's left arm (2), and latches onto the triceps (3). He uses his left arm to grab the opponent's elbow, forming a "Figure 4" lock (4). Note that RIgan's right hand is now on his wrist. Rigan pishes to the side (5), breaks the grip (6), and immediately applies a wristlock (*mao-de-vaca*) using his chest (7).

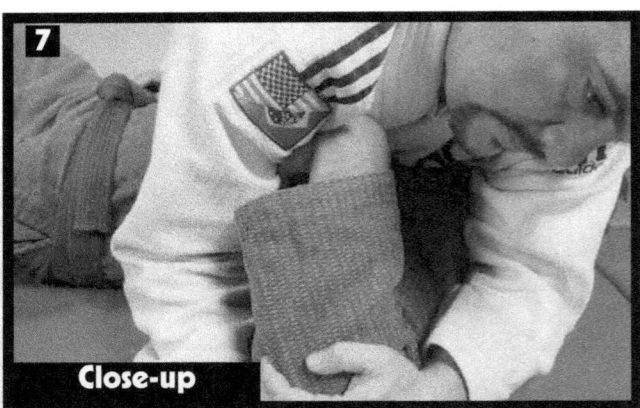

Close-up

Side Control 15

Rigan controls the altercation from the side (1). He grabs his opponent's collar with his left hand and belt with his right hand (2). Rigan pushes himself up (3), and places his right knee on the opponent's stomach (4). The opponent's tries to push Rigan's knee away with his left hand (5). Rigan reacts by hooking the opponent's left arm with his right hand (6), pulling up (7), and executing a straight armlock while standing (8).

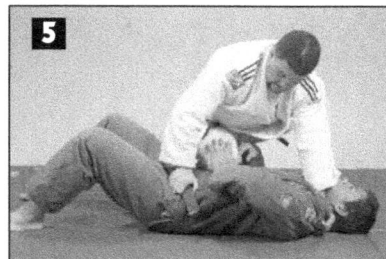
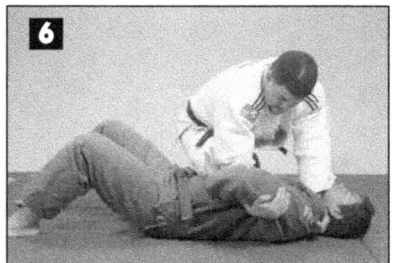

Side Control 16

Rigan controls the opponent from the side (1). Note that his left arm is under the opponent's neck. Taking advantage of this positioning, Rigan grabs his right sleeve with his left hand (2). He moves his right forearm to the front of the opponent's neck (3). Then, he applies pressure (4), and chokes him out (5).

Side Control 17

Rigan controls the opponent from the side (1). Note that his left arm is around the back of the opponent's neck. He switches arms behind the opponent's neck (2), and grabs his left sleeve with his right hand (3). In this close-up, notice how he latches onto the sleeve (4). To execute the choke, Rigan places his left forearm across the front of the opponent's neck (5).

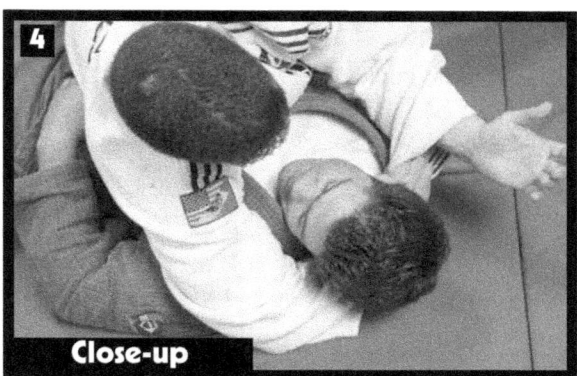

Side Control 18

Rigan controls the opponent from the side (1). He wraps his left arm around the opponent's neck (2), loosens his jacket with the right hand (3), and passes it to his left hand (4). A close-up look (5). To establish position, he moves his right hand to the other side of the opponent (6), and brings his right leg over (7). Now he can crank on the choke (8).

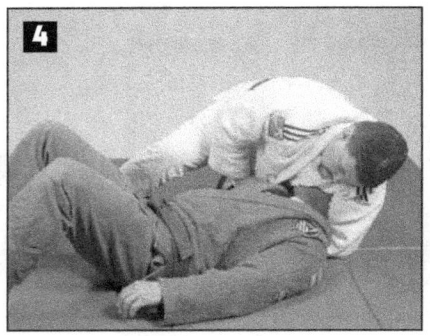
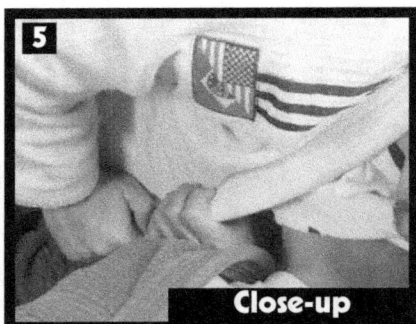
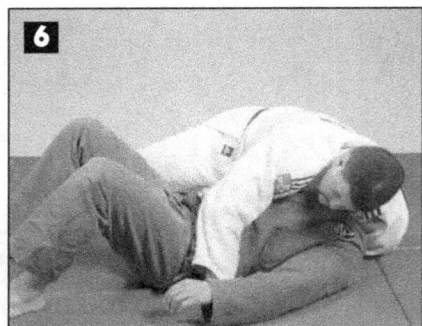

Side Control 19

The opponent has a firm grip on his own belt, which Rigan tries to break (1). Rigan circles around and moves toward the opponent's head (2). Using his left hand, Rigan lifts the opponent's left arm (3). Next, Rigan slides his left arm under the opponent's left arm and grabs his own wrist (4). He steps forward with his left leg (5), and pulls up hard on the opponent's arm, breaking the grip (6). Rigan then applies a painful bent armlock (7).

Side Control 20

Rigan controls the altercation from the side (1). He starts to wrap his left arm around the opponent's neck (2) while he positions his right arm under the opponent's armpit (3). He then grasps his hands together (4). While maintaining the hold, Rigan moves onto his left side (5), and starts bringing his right leg towards the opponent (6). He positions his leg between the opponent's legs (70. Notice how he hooks it under the left leg. This position provides leverage for a painful neck crank (8).

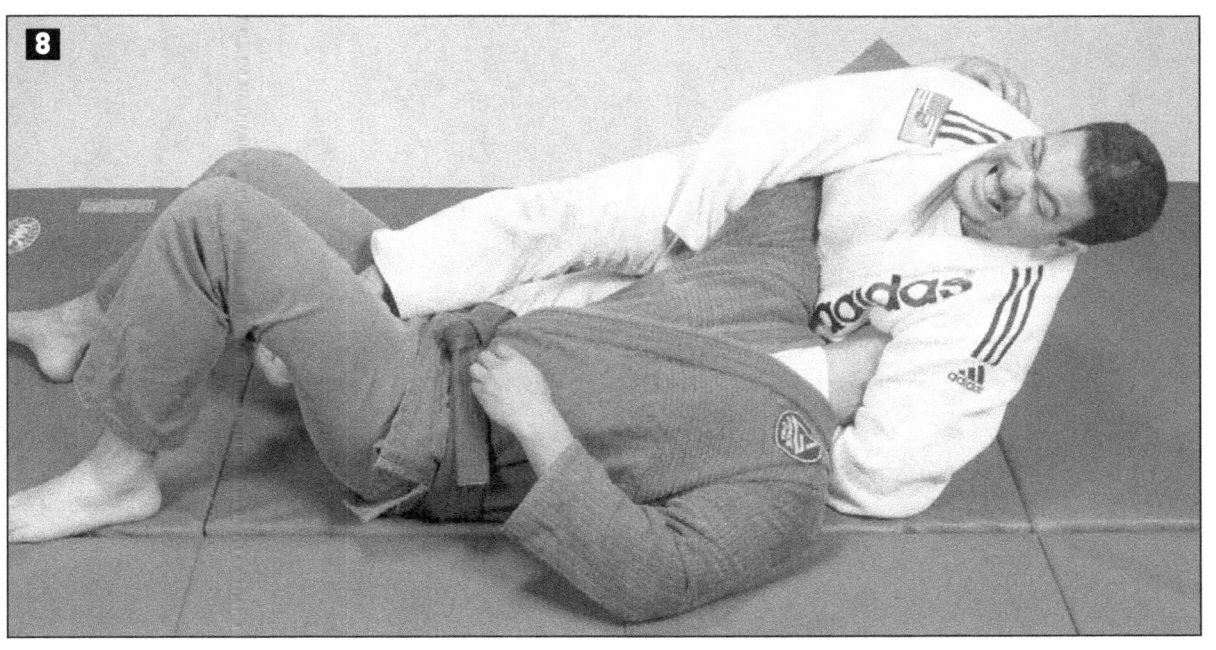

Mastering Brazilian Jiu-Jitsu 311

Side Control 21

Rigan controls his opponent from the side (1). While he starts to stand, he simultaneously grabs the opponent's right arm (2). He switches his hips to the side, brings his body over the opponent's (3), and puts his left leg over the opponent's left hip (4). He finishes with a straight armlock (5). It is important to keep the left leg close to the opponent's armpit so you can create leverage for the armlock.

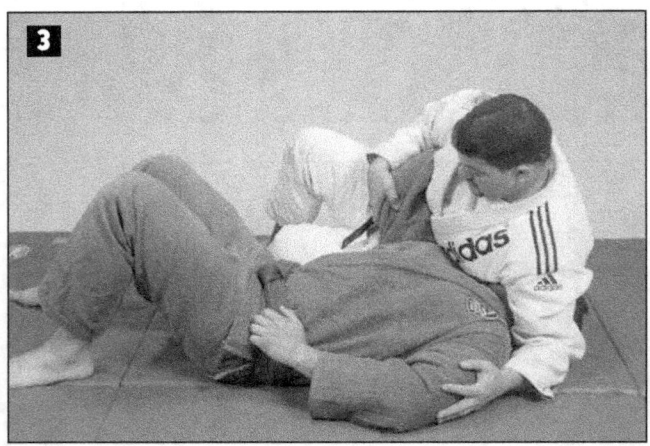

Side Control 22

Using his right hand, Rigan breaks the opponent's grip on the belt (1-2). As soon as he breaks the grip, Rigan moves his left leg over the opponent's head (3), and uses his left hand to lift the opponent's left elbow (4). He then applies a painful *kimura* (5).

Side Control 23

Rigan maintains side control and breaks the opponent's grip on the belt (1). He slides his left hand under the opponent's arm (2), and then straightens the arm (3). Notice that Rigan has grabbed his right wrist. He establishes good leverage (4), and applies a straight armlock (5).

Side Control 24a

Rigan controls the opponent from the cross-side position (1). He loosens his gi (2), and moves it to the other side (3) so he can reach it with his right hand, which is under the opponent's left arm (4).

(Continued)

Side Control 24b

He passes the uniform to his left hand (5-6), which is under the opponent's neck. Rigan immediately brings his left knee up against the opponent's neck (7), and applies a finishing choke (8).

Side Control 25a

Rigan controls the opponent from the side (1). He loosens his gi (2), and moves it across his opponent (3) so he can reach it with his right hand (4). He passes it again to his left hand (5), and switches his hips to trap his opponent (6).

(Continued)

Side Control 25b

Rigan rolls over (7o his left shoulder 9s) all the way to the front (9-10). He concludes with a finishing choke (11).

Side Control 26a

To break the opponent's grip, Rigan starts to stand (1). The opponent resists (2), and tries to bring his arm back down (3). Rigan puts his left arm under the opponent's left arm (4), and applies pressure to break the grip (5).

(Continued)

Side Control 26b

This doesn't work because the opponent's hand are still too close to his body (6). Rigan establishes his position (7), and moves his right leg forward (8). He uses his right elbow to create leverage so he can apply a bent armlock (9).

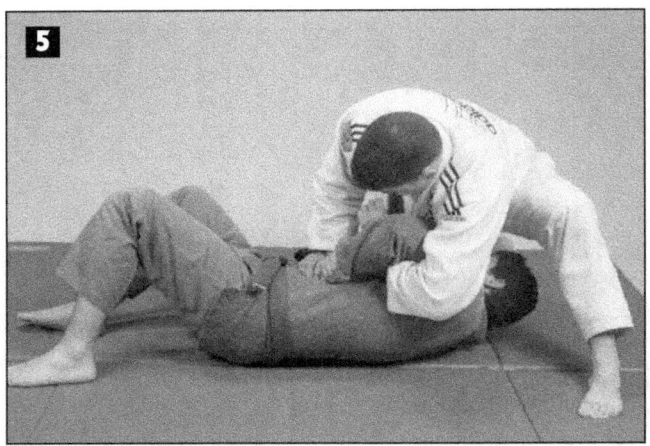

Side Control 27a

Rigan maintains control from the side, but the opponent turns to the side to avoid the attack (1). Rigan loosens the opponent's gi with his right hand (2), and grabs the uniform with his left hand (3). Notice that he traps the opponent's left arm while doing this. Using his right hand to control the opponent's right arm (4), Rigan prepares for the finishing move (5).

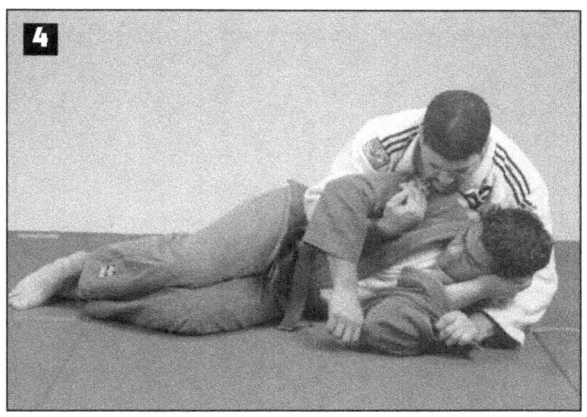

(Continued)

Side Control 27b

First, he moves his left leg next to the opponent's neck (6). Meanwhile, he controls the left arm with his left hand (7). He crosses his left leg over the opponent's chest (8), hooks his left instep under the back of the right leg (9), and applies a triangle choke from the back (10).

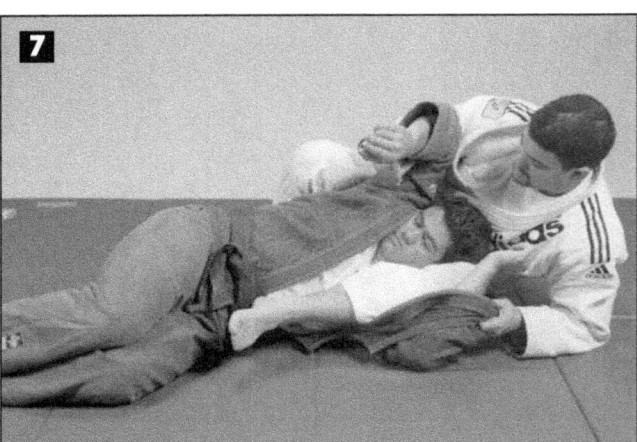

Side Control 28

Controlling the opponent from the side, Rigan loosens the opponent's gi with his right hand (1), and passes it to his left hand (2), trapping the opponent's left arm with the gi (3). He slides his right hand in to grab the collar (4), applies pressure and executes the choke (5).

Side Control 29

Rigan controls the opponent from the side (1). He sits up, slides his hips to the right and traps the opponent's right hand (2). he brings his left leg over the opponent's head, applies pressure and executes a straight armlock (3). It's important to keep your legs firmly over the opponent's arm. Also, don't put your left leg too far from the opponent's head: otherwise, he'll be able to escape.

Side Control 30

Rigan controls the opponent from the side (1). He moves slightly to the left (2) so he can switch his hips (3). Meanwhile, he tightens the grip on the opponent's collar (4). He brings his left leg over the opponent's head, pulls hard on the uniform and chokes him out (5). In this close-up, notice that Rigan creates the choke by using the gi and his left foot (6).

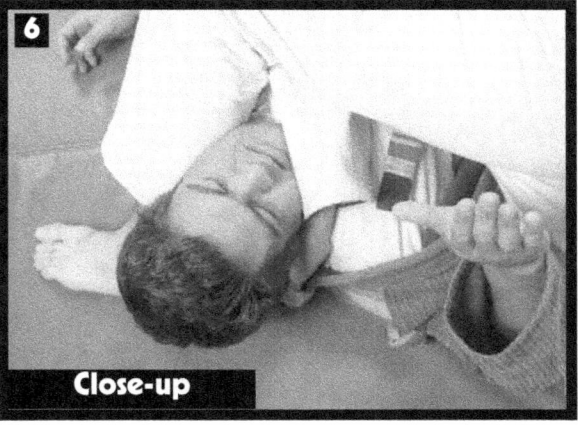

Side Control 31

Rigan controls the opponent from the side (1). He starts to stand (2), he swings his left leg over the opponent's body (3), and sits on the opponent's stomach (4). Rigan grabs the opponent's left foot with his left hand (5), and rolls to the left (6). He uses his right hand (7) to create a "figure 4" anklelock (8). A close-up (9).

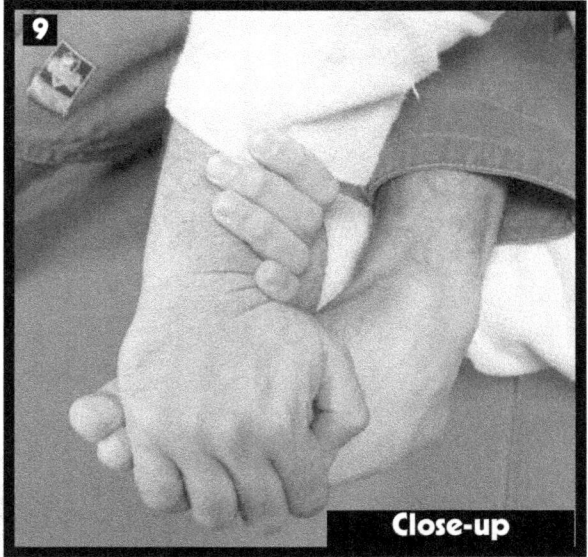

Close-up

Mastering Brazilian Jiu-Jitsu

Side Control

Side Control 32

While controlling from the side (1), Rigan brings his right knee over the opponent's stomach as he secures the left arm (2). He leans forward, allowing his body weight to drop (3). He straightens the opponent's left arm and applies a painful armlock (4).

Side Control 33

Rigan tries to control his opponent from the side, but this one rolls away from him (1). Rather than chase him, Rigan springs up, mounts the opponent (2) and sits on him (3-4). He establishes the half-mount, grabs the opponent's uniform with his right hand (5) and passes it to his left hand (6). By moving his right hand over the right side of the opponent's neck and pulling the gi with his left hand, Rigan chokes him (7).

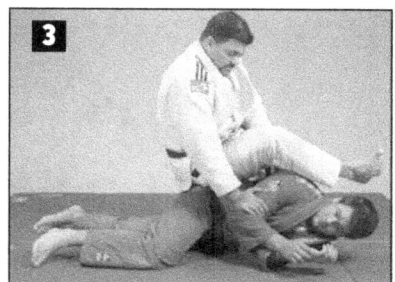

Side Control 34

Rigan controls the opponent from the side (1). Rigan uses his left arm to trap the opponent's left arm (2), and then raises up and places his left knee on the opponent's chest (3). Using his right hand to establish position, Rigan passes his right leg over the opponent's head (4), leans back and executes an armlock (5).

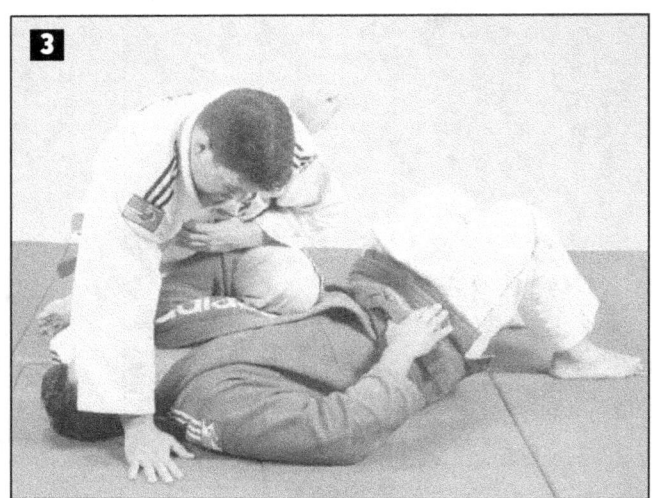

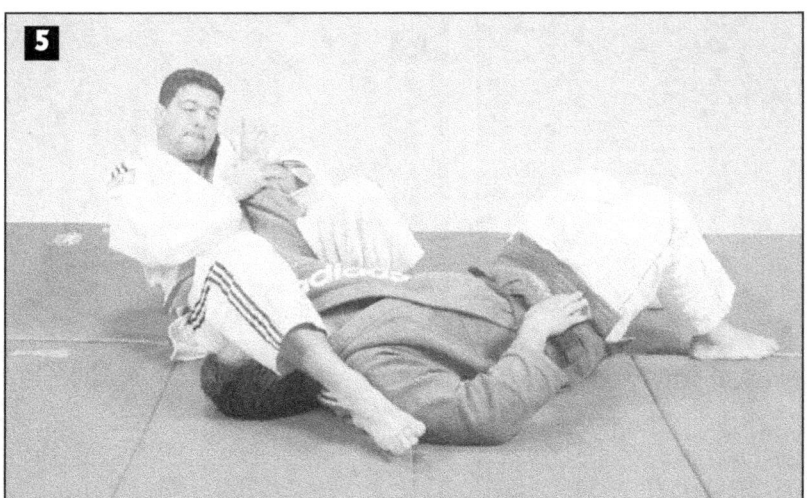

Side Control 35

From a side control (1), Rigan moves his hips back and creates room to move his left arm under the opponent's left arm so he can grab the opponent's collar (2). He slides his right hand — with the palm down — onto the other side of the collar (3). He maintains a tight grip as he prepares to finish off his adversary (4). A close look at the action (5). Rigan lowers his forearm and chokes the opponent (6).

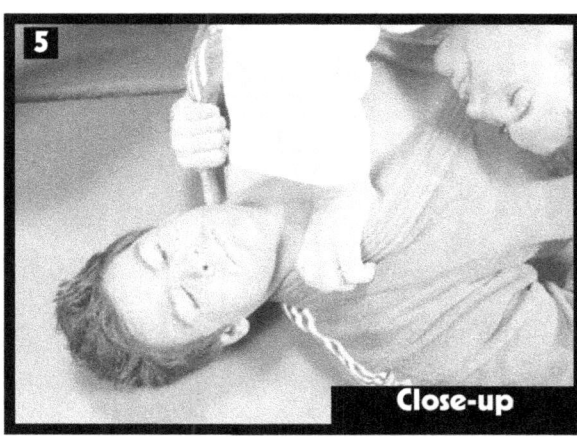
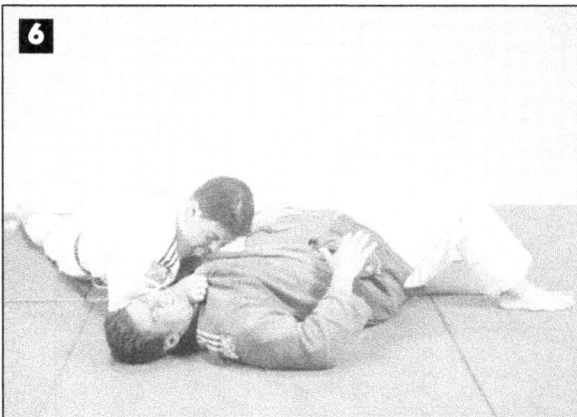

Side Control 36

Rigan tries to establish control from the side, but his opponent turns and grabs his left leg (1). Rigan circles to the right (2), and grabs the opponent's right arm (3). Rigan leans backwards (4). Then he pulls the arm all the way down (5), and finishes with a straight armlock (6).

Side Control 37

Rigan controls the altercation from the side (1) and then uses his left hand to push the opponent's left wrist down (2). The opponent uses his right hand to stop Rigan (3), who reacts by grabbing the opponent's hand (4) and pushing it down so he can trap it with his left leg (5). Rigan goes back to the left wrist (6), and applies a finishing bent armlock (7).

Side Control 38

Rigan controls his opponent from the side (1). He slides his right knee onto the opponent's chest and grabs the right sleeve (2). Rigan starts to lean backwards, applies pressure (3), moves his left leg over the opponent's neck and finishes with an armlock (4).

Side Control 39

Rigan controls the opponent from the side (1). Using a reverse grip with his left hand, Rigan grabs the right side of the opponent's collar (2), and begins to circle his left leg towards the opponent's head (3). Once he establishes his position (4), Rigan begins to apply pressure by dropping his body weight (5). Controlling the opponent's left arm with his right hand, Rigan applies even greater pressure and chokes him out (6).

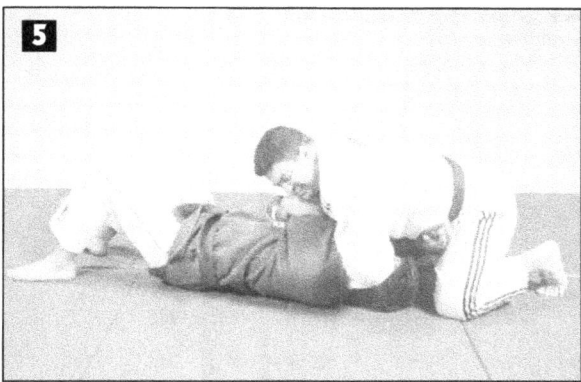
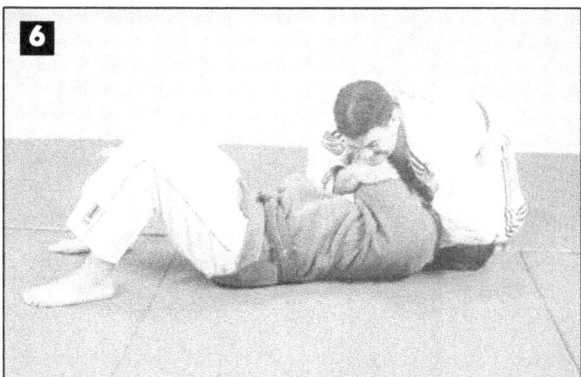

Side Control 40

While controlling the clash from the side, Rigan passes his left hand behind the opponent's neck (1), and his right hand over the chest (2). He applies pressure to execute a finishing choke (3). The close-ups show the details (4-5).

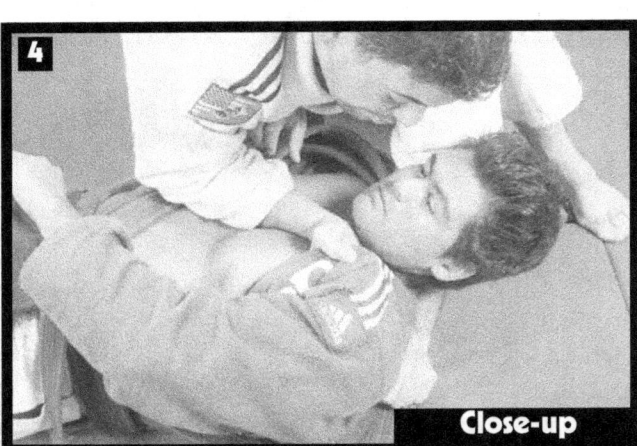

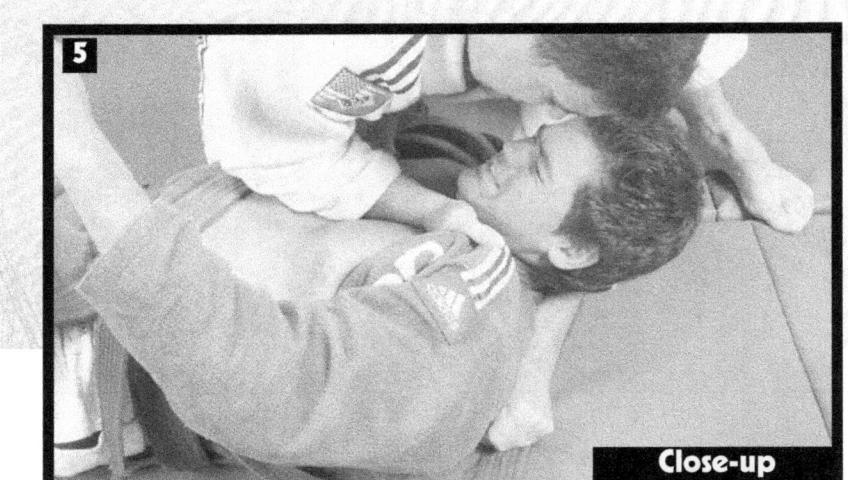

Side Control 41

Rigan controls the opponent from the side (1). Notice that his left hand is under the opponent's head. Rigan traps the right arm as he simultaneously moves his left leg to the front (2). Rigan hooks the opponent's left arm with his left foot (3), starts to lean backwards (4), and executes an armlock (5).

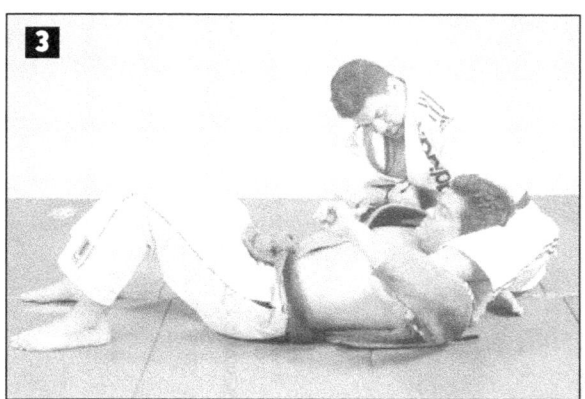

Side Control 42

Maintaining a tight grip on his opponent's jacket, Rigan establishes control from the side (1). Using his right arm, Rigan traps the opponent's left arm (2). As soon as Rigan tries to initiate the offensive to mount him, the opponent raises his right knee and stops Rigan cold (3). In response, Rigan grabs his own foot and pulls the opponent's jacket with his left hand (4). This enables him to pass the opponent's knee (5), mount him (6) and establish control (7).

Side Control 43

Rigan controls the opponent from the side with a tight grip on the jacket (1). Notice Rigan's left hand under the opponent's neck. Using his right arm, Rigan traps the opponent's right arm (2). This enables Rigan to bring him closer (3). Rigan pulls the opponent up (4) so he is between his legs (5). Rigan now has full control from the back (6). Rigan uses his left hand to grab the right side of the collar (7) and applies a finishing choke (8).

Side Control 44

Controlling the altercation from the side, Rigan reaches for the opponent's left arm (1), and pulls it closer (2). Rigan then moves his right leg over the opponent (3) as he leans forward to create space (4-5). He brings his left leg over the opponent's head (6). He can now apply a straight arm-lock (7).

Side Control 45

Rigan controls the opponent from the side (1). He raises his hips (2) so he can reach under his right leg and grab the opponent's right hand (3). Rigan sits (4), leans forward to roll (5), spins 180 degrees (6) and applies an *omoplata* from the side (7).

Side Control 46

Rigan establishes control from the side (1). He raises his hips to create space (2) so he reach under his right leg and grab the opponent's right sleeve (3). Rigan turns away from the opponent (4), and moves his left leg close to the opponent's head (5). He leans back (6), and applies an armlock (7).

Side Control 47

Rigan grabs the opponent's right arm (1), and then swings his right leg to the back (2), forcing the opponent to turn face down (3). He uses his left leg to trap the opponent's arm and then grabs the opponent's right foot (4). He finishes with a painful anklelock (5).

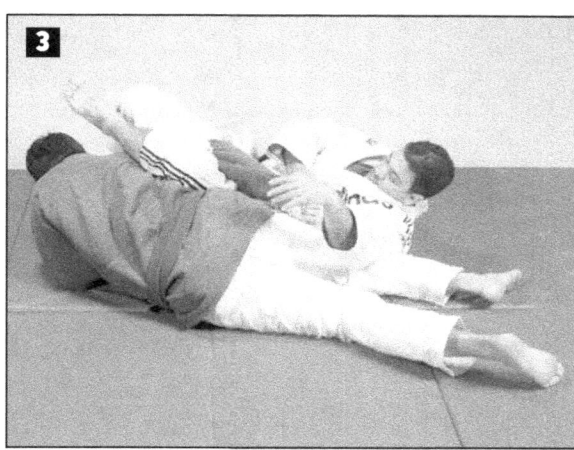

Side Control 48

Rigan grabs the opponent's right arm and leans forward (1). He rolls to the side (2), which forces the opponent upright (3). Rigan swivels his hips so he alters his direction slightly (4). He then hooks his left foot under his right knee (5), and applies a straight armlock (6).

Side Control 49

Rigan grabs the opponent's right arm (1) and rolls onto his left shoulder (2). This movement forces the opponent upright and to the front (3). Rigan then grabs the opponent's left arm (4-5). Then he pulls on the opponent's collar, submitting him from behind (6).

Side Control 50

Rigan controls the opponent from the side (1). Notice that he has grabbed the opponent's right arm. Rigan forces the arm under his left leg (2), and pulls the opponent towards him (3). Rigan quickly shifts his body, wraps his left arm around the opponent's neck and leans on him (4). Grabbing his left hand with the right, Rigan applies pressure (5), and submits his opponent (6).

Side Control 51

Rigan establishes control from the side (1). Note that he's clenching the opponent's right arm with his left hand. Rigan puts the right arm under his left leg (2), pulls the opponent's left arm (3), and maintains control by applying pressure with his body (4). With both of the opponent's arms trapped, Rigan adjusts his hips (5), brings his right knee up (6), mounts the opponent (7), and applies a finishing choke (8).

Side Control 52

Rigan controls the opponent from the side (1). He forces the opponent's right arm under his left leg (2), pulls the left arm with his left hand (3), and maintains control by applying pressure with his body (4). With both of the opponent's arms trapped, Rigan slides his hips to the right (5), and begins to push the opponent's right leg (6) with his right knee (7). To add pressure to the opponent's right hip, Rigan puts his right leg between the opponent's legs (8). Then he executes a finishing choke (9).

Side Control 53

The opponent controls Rigan (1). Using both hands, Rigan pushes the opponent to the left and slides his hips to the right (2). This opens space for him to maneuver. Rigan starts to move his left leg around the opponent's right leg as he controls the opponent's right arm (3). This helps him turn. Now facing the opponent (4), Rigan closes the guard (5).

Side Control 54

Controlled from the side (1), Rigan begins his escape by pushing his opponent away from him and swinging his left leg in front of the opponent's head (2-4). This enables him to adopt a new position and put his opponent inside his guard (5). In this movement, use your left arm to get momentum and balance yourself, as you simultaneously control the opponent's right arm, preventing him from stopping your movement.

Side Control 55

The opponent controls Rigan from the side (1). Notice that Rigan prepares to create space by pushing his opponent. Rigan rolls to the right (2), keeping the action close to the opponent's body (3). Rigan quickly turns, grabs the opponent's right hand (4), and pushes it back, nullifying the opponent's action (5). Rigan slides his left leg forward (6), and brings his opponent into the closed guard (7).

Side Control 56

Rigan's opponent controls him from the side (1). Notice that his arm is under Rigan's neck. Rigan traps the arm with his head and locks his hands to secure the opponent's right arm (2). Rigan turns to the right (3), maintaining the tight grip on the opponent's arm (4), until he is kneeling (5). Rigan moves to the left, forcing the opponent to roll (6). The opponent is now in a vulnerable position (7) so Rigan can adopt the side control to initiate the offensive (8).

Side Control 57

Rigan tries to control his opponent, who has established side position (1). As soon as the opponent moves his right arm to control Rigan's head (2), Rigan grabs the opponent's arm and belt (3). Keeping a tight grip on both (4), Rigan utilizes his hips, pulls hard to the side (5), and throws him to the other side (6). Rigan can then adopt side control to initiate an attack (7).

Side Control 58

This time the opponent assumes side control without putting his arm under Rigan's neck (1). This makes it impossible for Rigan to execute the previous escape. Instead, Rigan grabs the belt with both hands (2), and pulls hard, sending the opponent to the other side (3-4). Rigan maintains tight control until the opponent lands (5). Immediately, Rigan rolls (6) so he can assume side control and initiate the offensive (7).

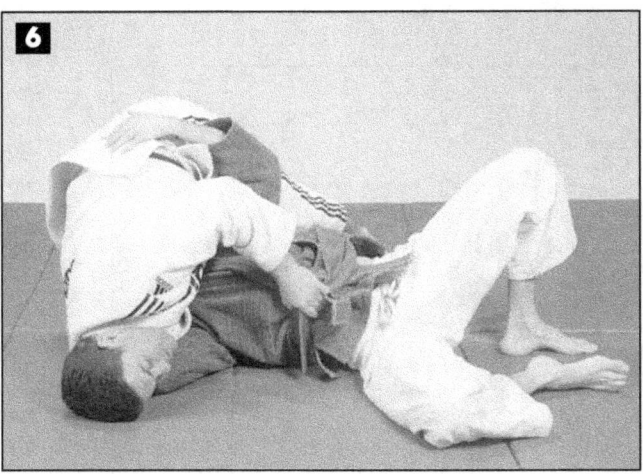

Side Control 59

The opponent controls Rigan (1). To gather momentum, Rigan lifts his legs (2), and pushes the opponent away with both hands (3). The opponent ends up flat on his back (4-5), and this enables Rigan to assume side control and begin the counterattack (6).

Side Control 60

The opponent tries to pass the guard from the side (1). Rigan reacts by grabbing the opponent's left arm and pushing it up (2). As Rigan does this, he raises his hips (3). This creates space and leverage to (4) throw the opponent over his body (5), and onto the ground (6). Rigan can now apply full side control (7).

Side Control 61

Rigan's opponent tries to initiate the offensive from the side (1). Using both hands, Rigan pulls the opponent's left arm, which unbalances him (2). Rigan slides his hips away from the opponent (3), so he can start lifting his right leg over him (4-5). Rigan starts moving to the back (6), where he can control the opponent more comfortably (7).

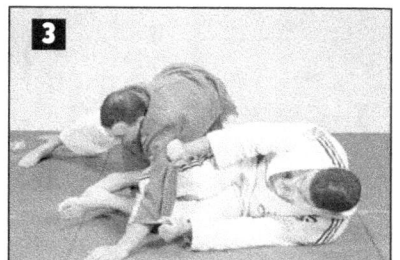

Side Control 62

The opponent controls Rigan (1). Sliding his hips away, Rigan creates some space for himself (2-3) so he can move his legs out (4). He quickly moves into a kneeling position and grabs the opponent's thighs (5). By pushing to the opposite side of the raised leg (6), Rigan forces the opponent to the ground (7), and immediately controls him from the side (8).

Side Control 63

The opponent establishes control from the side, but Rigan manages to slide back and insert his right hand between the opponent's legs and his left hand under the right armpit (1). Using these two points to establish momentum (2), Rigan begins to turn his body (3) until he's kneeling (4-5). He applies pressure with his body (6), creates space to bring his head out (7-8), and initiates the counterattack from the back (9).

Mastering Brazilian Jiu-Jitsu

Side Control 64

Rigan's opponent establishes control from the side (1). With a tight grip on the opponent's collar and belt, Rigan pushes up (2-3), and rolls him to the right (4-5). Rigan moves his left leg outside the opponent's (6), mounts him to establish better control and prepares to initiate the counterattack (7).

Side Control 65

The opponent controls Rigan from the side (1). Rigan passes has right arm between the opponent's legs and grabs the adversary's pants (2). Rigan raises the opponent's leg so he can hook it with his left leg (3). Rigan releases the opponent's right leg and immediately grabs the left ankle (4). He passes the ankle to his left hand as he grabs the opponent's left knee (5). This unbalances the opponent (6), rolling him over (7). Rigan can now initiate the final attack (8).

Side Control 66

The opponent controls Rigan from the side (1). Using his right hand, Rigan grabs the opponent's right leg (2). Notice how he reached between the adversary's legs. Rigan then pulls the leg up so he can hook it with his left leg (3). Rigan immediately switches grips and clamps onto the opponent's left leg (4).

Rigan pushes hard to the left (5), throwing the opponent to the side (6-7). Rigan scrambles up (8), and initiates the offensive from the front (9).

Side Control 68

The opponent controls Rigan from the side (1). Rigan slides his hips forward (2), and brings his left arm out (3) so both arms are on the opponent. He pushes upward with his hips (4), turns to the side (5), and escapes from the bottom (6). This enables him to go for full control from a more advantageous position (7).

Side Control 68

The opponent controls Rigan from the side (1). Rigan slides his hips forward, extricates his left arm (2), and pushes upward with his hips (3). This time he turns the opposite way (4). This move enables him to escape from the bottom (5). He goes for a counterattack from the back (6).

Mastering Brazilian Jiu Jitsu

Takedowns and Throws

Takedowns and Throws 1

Rigan adopts the orthodox right-handed sleeve and lapel grip (1). He moves closer to his opponent, releases the collar and grabs the waist (2). Next, Rigan releases the sleeve and grabs the opponent's right leg (3). He pulls up on the leg (4), creating space to begin his sweep (5-6). Ultimately, his opponent ends up on the ground (7).

Takedowns and Throws 2

Rigan uses the orthodox right-handed sleeve and lapel grip (1). Rigan steps forward with his right foot, which creates pressure on his opponent (2). He then steps forward with his left foot (3) to prepare the inside sweep (4). This unbalances his opponent (5). The adversary ends up on the floor (6-7).

Note: It is important to time the action of the leg with the pushing and control of the opponent's arms. The idea is to create a push/pull action.

Takedowns and Throws 3

Rigan employs the orthodox right-handed sleeve and lapel grip (1). To create pressure and prepare for the inside sweep, Rigan steps forward with his right foot (2) and then his left (3). Notice that he comes even closer than in the previous technique. To grab his opponent's left leg, he puts his right knee down (4-5). This facilitates the takedown (6).

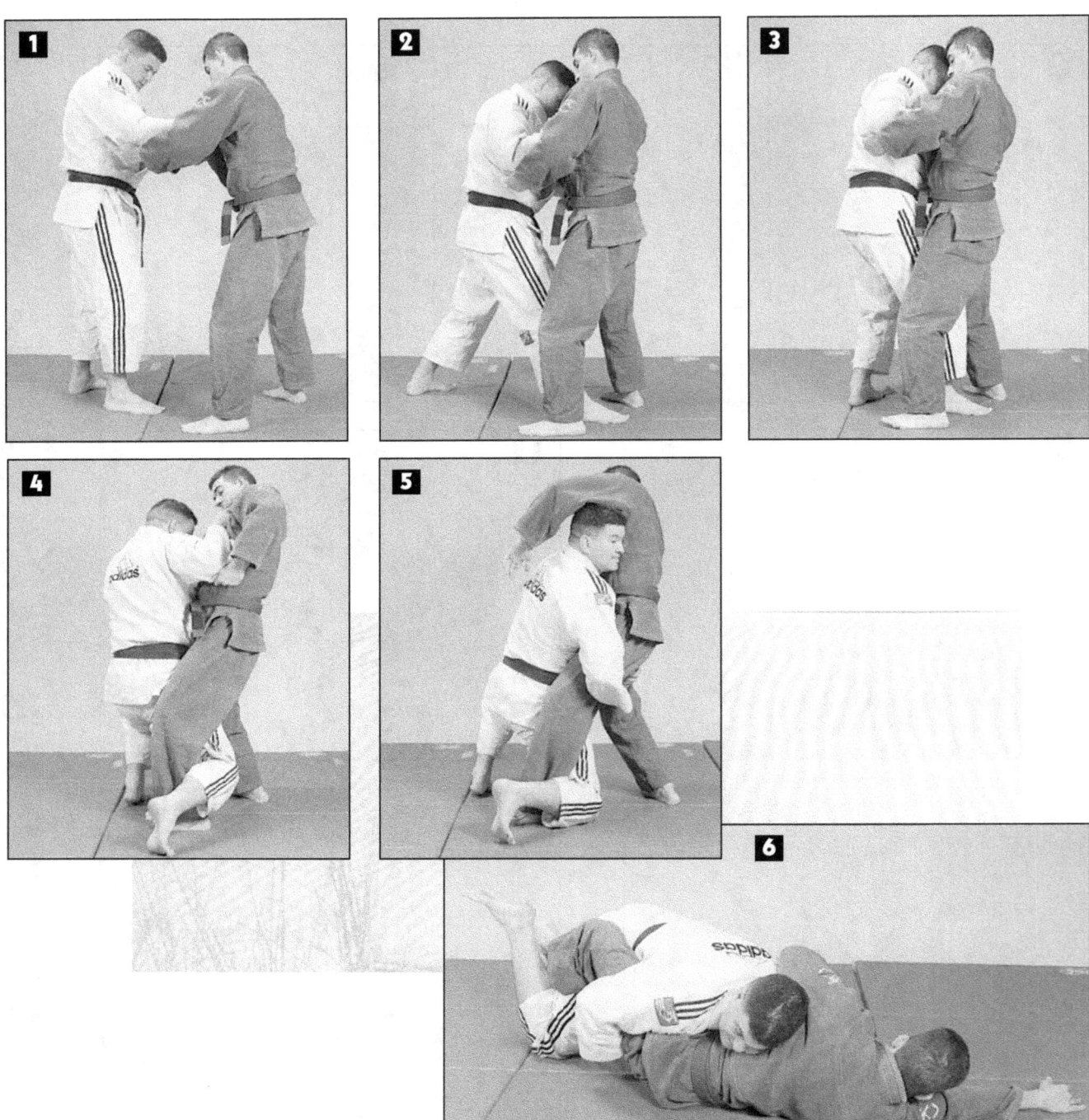

Takedowns and Throws 4a

Rigan utilizes the orthodox right-handed sleeve and lapel grip (1). To create pressure, he steps in with his right foot (2). He immediately brings his left foot forward (3) to prepare the inside sweep (4). This time the opponent feels the entry action and lifts his left leg (5), avoiding the sweep (6).

(Continued on next page)

Takedowns and Throws 4b

Rigan shifts his right foot forward (7) and begins to move his hips to the left (8) so he can control his opponent (9) and throw him. Rigan throws his opponent over his right shoulder (10-12). He controls the opponent's right arm during the action so he gets better positioning for a follow-up technique (13).

Note: Bring your center of gravity down when giving your back to the opponent. By pulling with your arm and keeping your hips low, he will be unbalanced. This will make it impossible for him to prevent the throw.

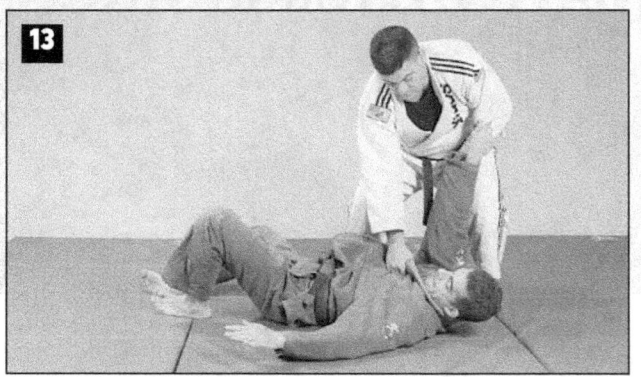

Takedowns and Throws 5a

Rigan adopts the orthodox right-handed sleeve and lapel grip (1). To again create pressure and prepare for the inside sweep, Rigan moves his right foot forward (2) and then his left (3). Again, note how close he is to his opponent. As he begins to execute the sweep (4), the opponent feels the entry action and lifts his left leg (5), escaping the sweep (6).

(Continued on next page)

Takedowns and Throws 5b

Rigan then moves his left leg to the front (7) and grabs the opponent's right leg with both arms (8). He pulls the leg up (9), unbalancing the opponent (10). Once the opponent hits the floor, Rigan can go for a finishing technique (11).

Takedowns and Throws 6

Rigan takes a firm hold on his opponent's right sleeve and left lapel (1). While raising the right arm, Rigan moves his right arm to his adversary's right hip while simultaneously moving his right leg close to the opponent's right foot (2). He grabs the opponent's right arm, moves his left leg in front of the opponent's left leg (3) and lowers his hips (4). He then throws his opponent (5-7), who lands hard on the ground (8).
Note: Your feet should be right in front of the opponent's at the time you are ready to bring your hips down for the throw. The four feet should create a "square." This will ensure that you have the correct leverage in the technique.

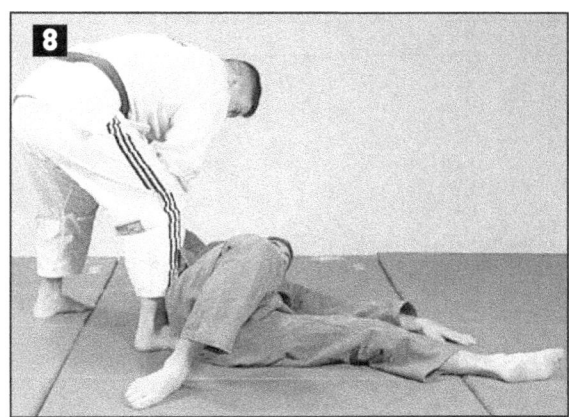

Mastering Brazilian Jiu-Jitsu

Takedowns and Throws 7

Rigan latches onto the opponent's right sleeve and left side of the lapel (1). He raises his adversary's right arm, slides his right arm in front of his opponent and moves his right foot next to the opponent's right foot (2). Once he grabs the opponent's right arm, he moves his left leg in front of the opponent's left leg (3). To get more leverage for the throw, he places his knees on the ground (4) and executes the throw (5-6). By lowering himself, he brings his opponent closer to the ground, and this facilitates the posterior throw and control (7).

Takedowns and Throws 8

Rigan adopts the orthodox left-handed sleeve and lapel grip (1). He forces his opponent's right arm down (2), releases the grip, swings his arm under and moves his left foot near the adversary's left foot (3). Once he has grabbed the opponent's left arm, he shifts his body and moves his right leg in front of the opponent's right foot (4). He lowers his hips (5) so he can start the throw (6) over his left shoulder (7). The opponent lands firmly on the ground (8-9).

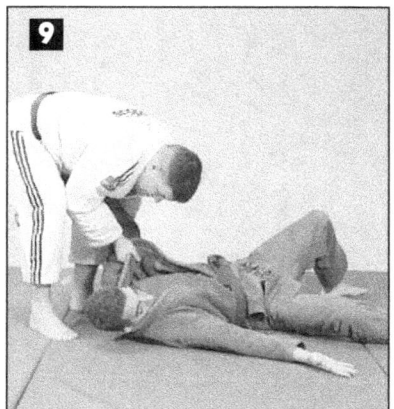

Takedowns and Throws 9

Rigan adopts the orthodox right-handed sleeve and lapel grip (1). Then he releases his grip with his left hand and quickly grabs the opponent's right wrist (2). He forces the opponent's right arm down and away (3-4) and eventually breaks the grip. Once the grip is broken, Rigan moves his left leg in front of the opponent's left foot (5) and simultaneously grabs the left arm while he places his right foot in front of the opponent's right foot (6).

He lowers his right knee to the floor (7) and then the left (8), so he can throw his opponent onto the ground (9-10).

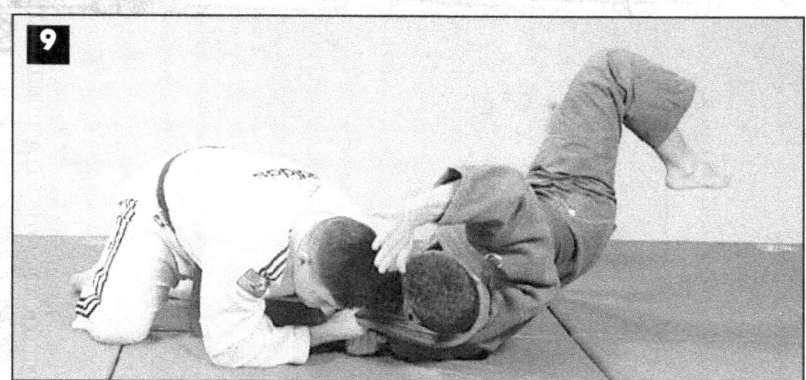
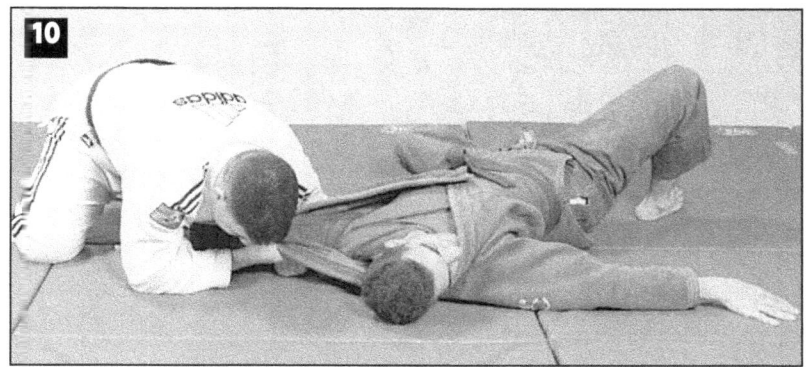

Takedowns and Throws 10

Rigan adopts the orthodox right-handed sleeve and lapel grip (1). He pulls his opponent's arms up (2) and ducks his head under the opponent's right armpit (3). He quickly grabs both of the opponent's legs (4). Using his right shoulder to apply pressure (5), Rigan pushes his opponent hard (6)

and sends him sprawling through the air (7-8). Once his opponent hits the ground (9), Rigan can start the offensive (10).

Takedowns and Throws 11

Rigan uses the orthodox right-handed sleeve and lapel grip (1). He pulls up with both hands (2) and moves his head under his opponent's right armpit (3). Then he quickly grabs both of the opponent's legs (4). Rigan puts his right foot behind his opponent's left foot (5) and pushes (6)

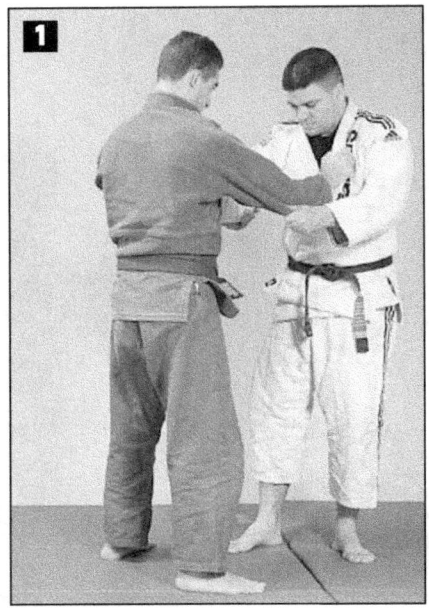

until he can hook the right leg from behind (7). Now he can use his weight (8) to unbalance the opponent, and take him to the ground (9). Here he can fully control him with his body and arms (10).

Takedowns and Throws 12

Rigan grabs his opponent's right sleeve and left side of the lapel (1). He releases the grip with his right hand (2), grabs the opponent's right leg (3) and simultaneously puts his left knee on the ground (4). He maintains control of the opponent's sleeve, so he can easily pull him over his shoulder (5), and throw him to the other side (6-7). Then, he controls him on the ground and starts his offensive (8).

Takedowns and Throws 13a

Rigan adopts the orthodox right-handed sleeve and lapel grip (1). Rigan turns his left elbow to the inside (2) and moves it under the opponent's right arm (3). This creates an opening for Rigan to pass his head under the arm (4). Simultaneously, he drops his right knee onto the floor and shoots his right arm between the opponent's legs (5). Creating a strong base, he uses his left leg (6).

(Continued on next page)

Takedowns and Throws 13b

Then, he lowers his body (7) and unbalance the opponent, who falls forward over his right shoulder (8-9). By turning to his left, Rigan brings the opponent onto the ground (10).

Takedowns and Throws 14

Rigan employs the orthodox right-handed sleeve and lapel grip (1). He releases the grip, grabs the opponent's right wrist and pushes it down (2). He releases his hold, lowers his left knee onto the floor and grabs the opponent's left leg with his left arm (3). By pulling with his right hand, Rigan unbalances the opponent (4), and starts to throw him over his shoulders (5-6). When the opponent hits the ground, Rigan initiates the offensive for the submission (7).

Takedowns and Throws 15

Rigan utilizes the orthodox right-handed sleeve and lapel grip (1). He releases the grip with his right hand and extends his arm over the opponent's left shoulder (2). He moves his left foot to the side and shifts his body closer to the opponent (3). While maintaining a tight grip on the opponent's right sleeve, Rigan raises his right leg (4) to prepare the sweep (5-6). The adversary becomes airborne (7), lands on the ground and Rigan quickly controls him (8).

Takedowns and Throws 16

Rigan adopts the orthodox right-handed sleeve and lapel grip (1). Rigan releases the collar, moves his arm over the opponent's left shoulder and grabs the gi (2). He moves his left foot to the side and brings his body close to the opponent so he can initiate a sweep with his right leg (3). The opponent blocks the attempt, so Rigan lowers his right knee to the ground (4). While dropping down, he pulls down hard with his arms, which sends the opponent onto the floor (5-6). Rigan can now start the final offensive (7).

Mastering Brazilian Jiu-Jitsu

Takedowns and Throws 17

Rigan adopts the orthodox right-handed sleeve and lapel grip (1). Rigan pulls the sleeve with his left hand (2) and moves his right elbow under the opponent's right armpit without releasing the grip (3). He uses precise footwork to place himself in the proper position in front of the opponent (4). He lowers his body (5) and begins a throw (6) that sends the opponent flying (7). The adversary lands on the ground (8).

Takedowns and Throws 18

Rigan again grabs the opponent's right sleeve and left side of the lapel (1). Rigan pulls the sleeve with his left hand (2) and moves his right elbow under the opponent's right armpit without releasing the grip (3). He uses precise footwork to place his hips in the proper position in front of the opponent (4). Rigan drops his right knee to the ground (5) and then his left (6), which unbalances the opponent. He can now throw his opponent over his right shoulder (7). Once the adversary is on the ground, Rigan goes for the final submission (8).

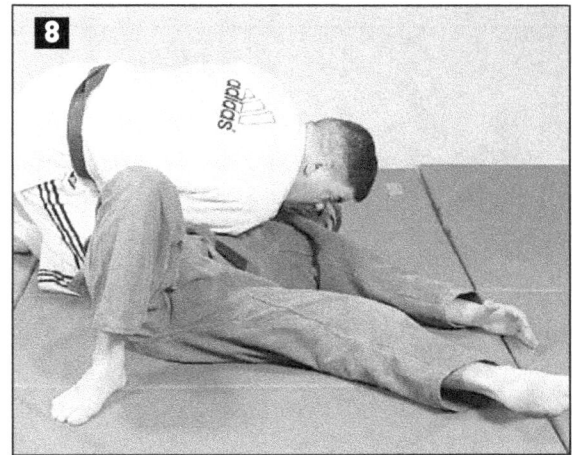

Takedowns and Throws 19

Rigan faces his opponent (1). He initiates the offensive by stepping forward with his right leg (2) and lowering his body (3) so he can shoot in uncontested (4). He grabs both legs (5) and puts his right knee on the floor to establish a base (6).

Once the base is strong, Rigan moves his left foot to the side (7) and turns to the right (8). This unbalances the opponent (9), sending him to the ground (10). Rigan then goes for the submission (11).

Takedowns and Throws 20

The opponent grabs Rigan's gi with his right hand (1). Rigan uses both hands to push the opponent's hand, which breaks the hold (2). Rigan passes his left hand behind the opponent's back and grabs the belt, as he simultaneously pulls the sleeve with his right hand (3). He inserts his left leg between the opponent's (4) and drops to the ground to throw the aggressor off balance (5). By pulling with his left hand and using the left leg, Rigan sweeps his opponent (6), taking him to the ground (7). He can now initiate the offensive (8).

Takedowns and Throws 21

The opponent unsuccessfully attempts to grab Rigan (1). Next, Rigan takes a step forward, grabs the opponent's belt (2) and pulls back to unbalance him (3). Rigan inserts his right leg between the opponent's (4), pulls back and throws him (5). Once his opponent hits the ground, Rigan turns, controls him (6) and takes the initiative to attack (7).

Takedowns and Throws 22

The opponent grabs Rigan's left collar (1). Rigan moves back (2) and uses both hands to break the grip (3). He turns to the right, takes a step forward with his left foot (4) and simultaneously twists the opponent's arm as he applies pressure on the elbow (5). If he continues to crank on the armlock (6), Rigan can take his opponent down (6).

Takedowns and Throws 23

Using the orthodox right-handed sleeve and lapel grip, Rigan grabs his opponent (1). He then takes a step forward with his right foot (2) and lowers his left knee onto the ground (3). By dropping to the ground, Rigan throws the opponent's balance off (4). Rigan inserts his right leg under the opponents left leg (5) to sweep the opponent over his body (6). By keeping his knee on the opponent's stomach, Rigan can start the offensive to gain a submission (7).

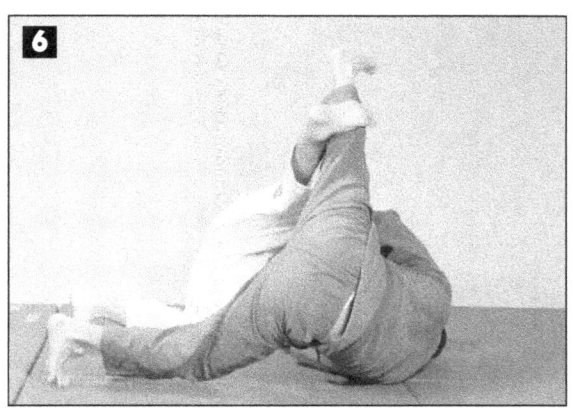

Takedowns and Throws 24

Rigan adopts the orthodox right-handed sleeve and lapel grip (1). He releases the grip with his right hand (2), reaches around the opponent's neck and grabs the opposite side of the collar (3). Using precise footwork, Rigan places his hips in front of the opponent (4), drops his weight (5) and throws the opponent over his right side (6-7). By keeping tight control of the opponent's right hand, Rigan is ready to initiate the attack on the ground (8).

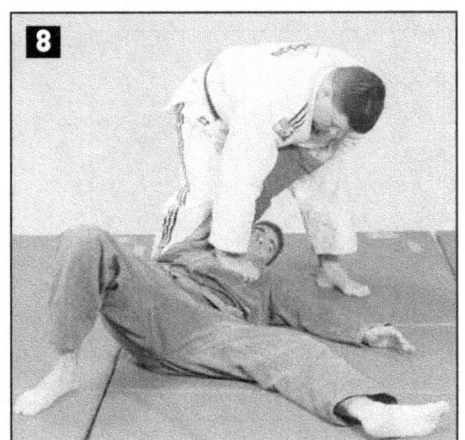

Takedowns and Throws 25

Rigan adopts the orthodox right-handed sleeve and lapel grip (1). He releases the grip with his right hand (2), reaches around the opponent's neck and grabs the opposite side of the collar. Rigan moves his right leg in front of the opponent's right side (3) and "flips" his hips to throw his adversary's balance off (4). By dropping his right knee (5), Rigan throws his opponent onto the ground (6), where he follows up with a side control (7).

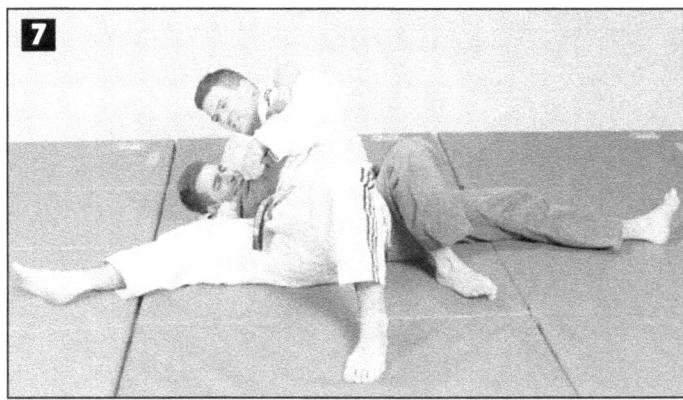

Takedowns and Throws 26

Rigan faces his opponent (1). As soon as the opponent tries to close the distance, Rigan grabs the aggressor's right wrist with his left hand (2). Next, he grabs the opponent's right elbow with his right hand (3). With full control of the opponent's right arm, Rigan side steps to the left as he releases the grip with his left hand (4) so he can grab the opponent's waist (5), and take him to the ground (6).

Takedowns and Throws 27

Using his right hand, the opponent grabs Rigan (1). In response, Rigan reaches over the opponent's right arm, grabs the collar (2) and shifts his feet so he is closer (3). Rigan raises his left leg (4) and throws his body into the air, as he simultaneously puts his right leg behind the opponent's legs (5). This unbalances the aggressor (6) and sends him to the ground. Rigan can now initiate the offensive (7).

Mastering Brazilian Jiu-Jitsu

Takedowns and Throws 28

Rigan and his opponent assume the orthodox right-handed sleeve and lapel grip (1). Rigan brings his hips forward (2) and drops onto the ground without releasing his grip (3).

Takedowns and Throws 29

Both fighters adopt the orthodox right-handed sleeve and lapel grip (1). Rigan moves forward, and using his right leg (2), pushes the opponent's left leg (3). This unbalances the opponent. Rigan drops to the ground (4), passes his left leg over the opponent's head (5-6) and applies a straight armlock (7).

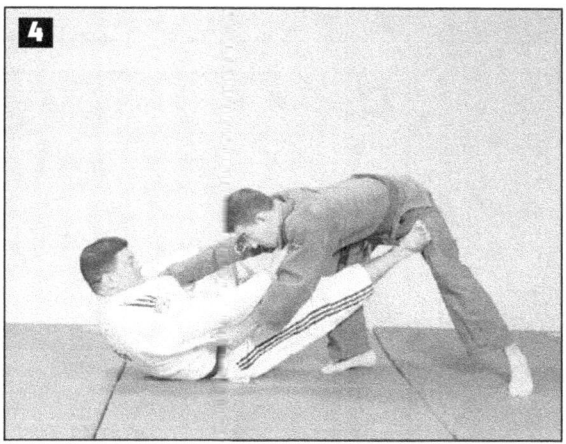

Mastering Brazilian Jiu-Jitsu

Takedowns and Throws 30

The opponent grabs Rigan with his right arm (1). Rigan moves his left foot forward and grabs the left side of the opponent's collar with his right hand (2). When the opponent tries to move away (3), Rigan pulls him back (4). Using his right leg, Rigan hits the opponent's shin (5), sweeps him (6), and throws him to the right (7). Once his adversary is down, Rigan controls him and initiates the offensive for the submission (8).

Takedowns and Throws 31

Rigan and his opponent adopt the orthodox right-handed sleeve and lapel grip (1). Rigan moves his right foot forward and circles with his left. This throws the opponent off balance (2). He moves his right leg between the opponent's (3), leans to roll forward (4), grabs the opponent's left ankle and tumbles (5). Without releasing the grip, Rigan rolls all the way over (6) and finishes with a straight kneebar (7).

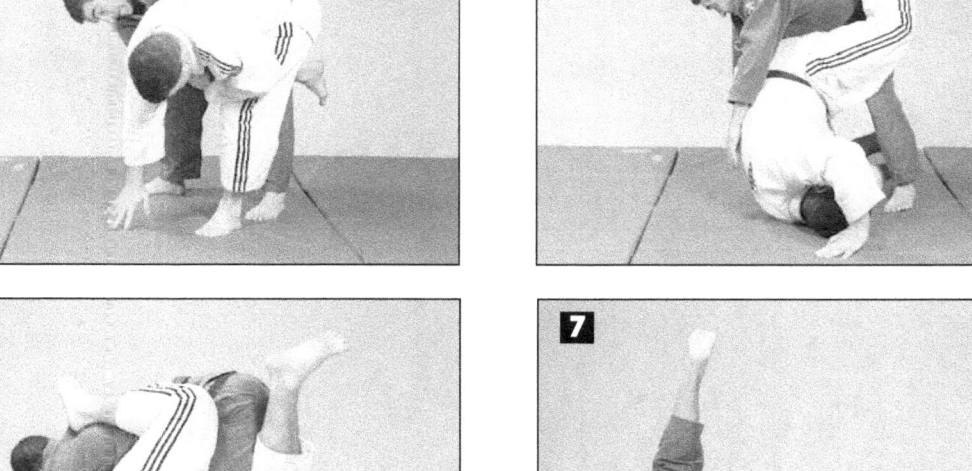

Takedowns and Throws 32

Both fighters adopt the orthodox right-handed sleeve and lapel grip (1). Rigan releases the grip from the lapel, grabs the opponent's back (2) and closes the distance with his right foot (3). He aligns the hips (4) and throws his opponent over his right side (5-6). Once the adversary is on the ground, Rigan begins the offensive with a knee-on-the-stomach side control (7).

Takedowns and Throws 33

Both fighters adopt the orthodox right-handed sleeve and lapel grip (1). Rigan releases the lapel, grabs the opponent's back (2) and latches his hands together (3). Immediately, he hooks the opponent's left leg with his right leg (4) and pulls hard as he simultaneously pushes forward with his body (5). This knocks the opponent off balance (6), and sends him to the floor (7). Rigan mounts him for a final control (8).

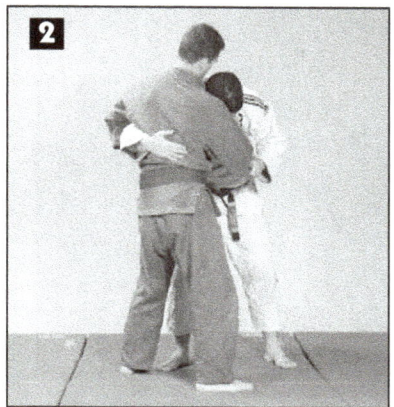
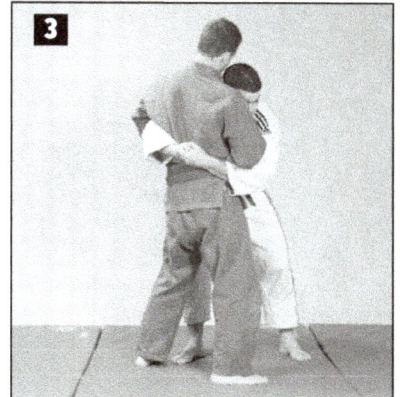

Takedowns and Throws 34

Rigan and his opponent assume the orthodox right-handed sleeve and lapel grip (1). Rigan moves backwards to create space (2) and prepares to drop to the floor (3). Once he's down, he places his right foot on the opponent's stomach (4). Rigan leans back, pulls with both hands, keeps a tight grip and sends his opponent into the air (5-6). When his opponent hits the ground, Rigan can take the offensive (7).

Takedowns and Throws 35

Rigan and his opponent adopt the orthodox right-handed sleeve and lapel grip (1). Rigan moves backwards to create space and build momentum (2). He drops to the floor and places his right foot on the opponent's stomach (3). The opponent realizes what Rigan is trying to do, so he lowers his hips to prevent the maneuver (4). Rigan reacts by sliding his hips forward, grabbing the opponent's right ankle, (5) pulling hard with his left hand and simultaneously pushing the opponent's right hip (6). This brings the opponent onto the ground (7), where Rigan initiates the offensive (8).

Takedowns and Throws 36

Rigan and his opponent adopt the orthodox right-handed sleeve and lapel grip (1). Next, Rigan swings his leg to create momentum (2). He drops down and puts his left foot on the opponent's right hip (3). Taking advantage of the momentum, he pushes the opponent into the air (4-5), and throws him to the left (6). Rigan can now start the offensive toward the submission (7).

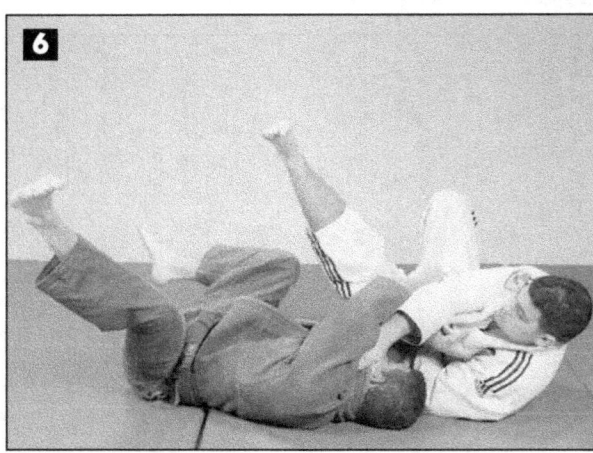

410   Mastering Brazilian Jiu-Jitsu

Takedowns and Throws 37

Rigan faces his opponent (1). Suddenly, he drops (2) and initiates the offensive by grabbing the opponent's left ankle with his right hand (3) and then his left (4). Using both hands enables him to maintain tighter control. This allows him to create a base to push with his right shoulder (5), knocking the opponent down while maintaining control of his left leg (6).

Takedowns and Throws 38

Rigan faces his opponent (1). He suddenly drops his body (2) and initiates the offensive by grabbing the opponent's left ankle (3). The opponent steps forward with his right leg (4) and tries to grab and control Rigan from the top (5). Rigan begins to sit up and this throws the opponent's balance off (6).

This maneuver allows him to grab the opponent's left leg (7). Rigan twists to the left (8) and smashes his opponent against the ground (9). Note: Always maintain control of the opponent's leg for a faster counterattack and offensive on the ground.

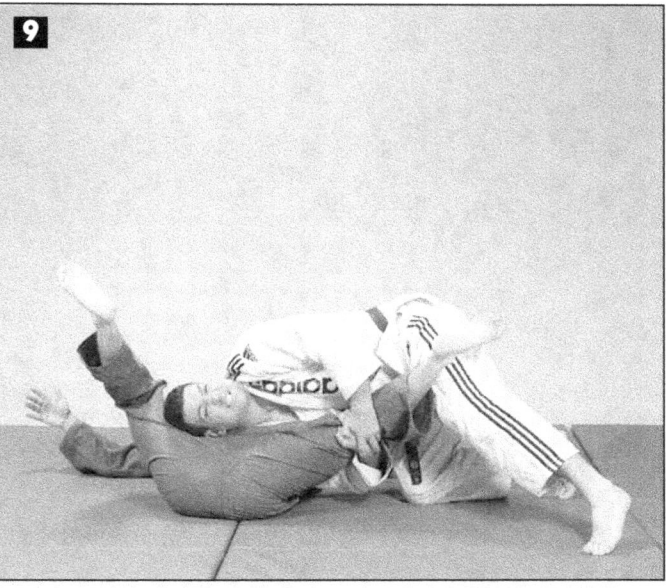

Mastering Brazilian Jiu Jitsu

414

Attacks from the Back

Attacks From the Back 1

By holding the lapel, Rigan controls his opponent from behind (1). He releases the left-handed grip and slides his hand to the right side of the collar (2). Then he releases the opponent's lapel with his right hand and grabs the left side of the collar (3). Finally, he leans forward and applies pressure with his body to choke his opponent out (4).

Attacks From the Back 2

Rigan controls the confrontation by holding his opponent's lapel (1). He releases the grip on the left side and slides his hand to the collar (2). This time he uses his right hand — not to grab the opposite side of the collar — but to control the opponent's right hand (3). Rigan leans forward and starts putting pressure on his opponent (4). To create leverage and increase the pressure, Rigan moves his right leg forward. Now he can apply a choke (5).

Attacks From the Back 3

Rigan controls his opponent from behind by holding the lapel (1). Once again, he releases the grip on the left side and latches onto the collar (2). He hooks his right arm under the opponent's right leg and exerts pressure on him by leaning forward (3). Rigan moves his right leg forward (4) and applies additional pressure for the choke (5).

Attacks From the Back 4

Rigan initiates the attack from behind (1). He grabs the opponent's left arm (2) and shoves it between his legs (3). By leaning forward, he puts pressure on the opponent's chest (4). Note how he simultaneously hooks the right arm. Rigan rolls forward over his right shoulder (5), falls on the other side of his opponent (6) and applies a choke (7). To execute the choke, he grabs the opponent's lapel with his left hand and creates leverage with his legs and right arm.

Attacks From the Back 5

Rigan initiates the attack from the back (1). He grabs the opponent's left arm (2) and forces it between his legs (3). As he hooks the right arm, Rigan leans forward and puts pressure on the adversary's chest (4). Rigan rolls over his right shoulder (5), falls on the other side (6) and reaches for the opponent's collar with his left hand (7). Note that he reaches in front — not from behind — as he did in the previous technique. He executes the choke and prevents the opponent from escaping by controlling both arms (8).

Attacks From the Back 6

Rigan controls his opponent by holding one side of the lapel (1). Using his left hand, Rigan grabs the opponent's collar (2). Next, he lifts his left leg over the opponent's head (3). To execute the choke (4), Rigan wraps his leg around the back of the opponent's head and pulls with his left hand and pushes with his left leg.

Attacks From the Back 7

To control the confrontation, Rigan latches onto the back of the adversary's collar and right arm (1). Rigan moves his left hand around the opponent's neck without releasing the grip on the collar (2). This makes the gi choke the opponent, especially when Rigan leans forward and applies more pressure to the back (3). Next, Rigan twists his body so he can slide his head under the right arm and then he grabs the opponent's left arm and cranks on it (4). Rigan keeps turning until he's flat on his back, and this enables him to choke his opponent out (5).

Attacks From the Back 8

Rigan controls the opponent from behind. Again he has both hands on the lapel (1). Rigan releases the lapel with his right hand and grabs the upper portion of the collar (2). Rigan chokes the opponent (3).

Attacks From the Back 9

Rigan controls the opponent from behind with both hands on the lapel (1). Rigan again releases the grip with his right hand and grabs the upper left portion of the collar (2). He releases the lapel with his left hand (3), slides his left arm along the side of the opponent's neck and chokes him (4).

Attacks From the Back 10

While sitting, Rigan controls the opponent from behind. He starts passing his right arm across the neck until the tip of his elbow is in the front of the opponent's chin (1). To add pressure, he closes the angle between his forearm and biceps (2). Rigan raises his left arm over the opponent's shoulder (3). To submit his opponent, Rigan tucks his arm behind the adversary's head, places his right hand on his biceps and squeezes (4).

Note: The initial movement (across the neck) of the right arm should apply enough pressure to make the opponent feel uncomfortable. The left hand secures and finalizes the technique. Bring your chest up to create leverage from behind. This technique doesn't need a lot of strength if properly applied. Leverage and proper angle are the key factors.

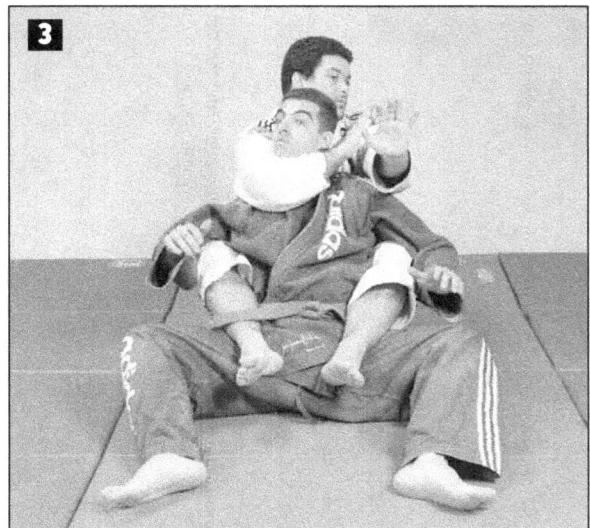

Attacks From the Back 11

Rigan's left hand controls the lapel and his right hand the opponent's right arm (1). Rigan releases the grip with his right hand and grabs the upper portion of the collar (2). He leans backwards and grabs the opponent's left leg as he applies a submission choke (3). Note: It's vital to keep a tight grip with your right hand during the entire movement.

Attacks From the Back 12

Rigan's left hand is on the collar, and his right hand is firmly on the adversary's right arm (1). The opponent's right arm prevents Rigan from directly applying a choke. Rigan releases the collar and grabs the opponent's right wrist. To create leverage as he falls backwards, Rigan grabs his own wrist (2). Once on the ground, Rigan lifts his left leg over the opponent's head (3), breaks the grip, places his left leg across the adversary's neck and applies a straight armlock (4). *Note:* To get the armlock, maintain constant pressure with both legs when breaking the grip and when pulling the opponent's arm.

Mastering Brazilian Jiu-Jitsu

Attacks From the Back 13

With both hands on the opponent's lapel, Rigan controls the confrontation (1). To create space, Rigan moves his feet to the opponent's hips and slightly pushes forward (2). He passes his right leg over the opponent's body (3), shifts to the right (4) and applies a *triangle* from the back (5).

Attacks From the Back 14

Rigan controls the opponent from behind. Both hands are again on the lapel (1). He releases the grip with his left hand, lifts his hand over the opponent's left shoulder and grabs the opposite side of the collar (2). To create space to raise his left leg over the opponent's shoulder, Rigan leans to his right (3). As he does this, he controls the adversary's right arm. Without releasing the opponent's right arm, Rigan pulls hard with his left hand, pushes with his left leg and applies a finishing choke (4).

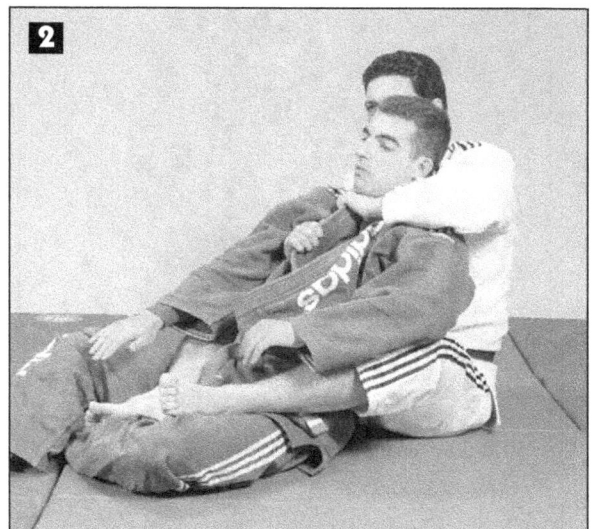
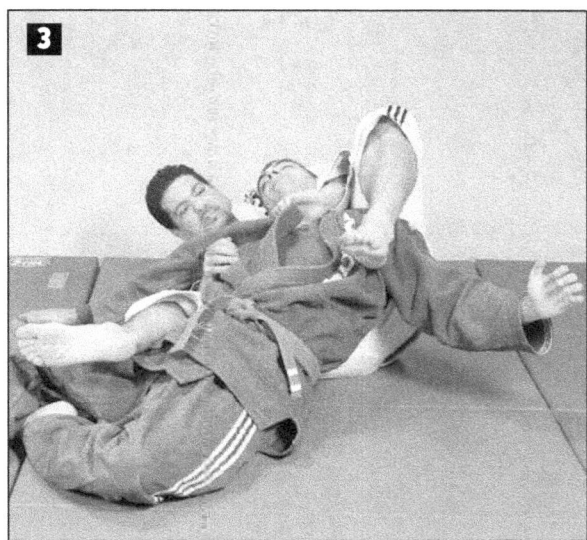

Attacks From the Back   15

While seated, Rigan controls the opponent. Both hands are on the lapel (1). He releases his left hand, pulls his arm out, slides his arm over the opponent's left shoulder and grabs the opposite side of the adversary's collar (2). As he controls the opponent's right arm, Rigan slides to his right (3). He continues to move sideways as he lifts his left shin next to the opponent's neck (4). This adds pressure and increases the leverage. Rigan pulls hard and applies the choke (5).

Attacks From the Back 16

With his right hand on the opponent's lapel, Rigan controls the confrontation from behind (1). He releases the grip with his left hand, moves his hand over the opponent's left shoulder, grabs the opposite side of the collar and leans to his right (2). Rigan raises his left leg over the opponent's head, grabs his left foot with his right hand and applies the choke (3). The choke works because the leg works in conjunction with the established grip of the left hand.

Attacks From the Back 17

Rigan controls the opponent, but his left leg is trapped inside the opponent's arms (1). Rigan slides to the right and uses his leg to break the grip (2). He leans more to create momentum and leverage so he can straighten the opponent's left arm (3). Rigan hooks the arm between his legs (4), turns over and pushes with his pelvis to apply a straight armlock (5).

Attacks From the Back 18

Rigan controls the situation, but his left leg is again trapped inside the opponent's arms (1). Rigan slides his body to the side and uses his leg to break the grip (2). He leans to the side to create momentum and leverage so he can straighten the opponent's arm (3). Because the opponent is grabbing his left leg, Rigan uses his right foot to trap the arm and break the grip (4). While using his right arm for control, Rigan moves toward the adversary's head (5). Rigan rolls forward over his right shoulder (6) until he comes up on top (7). He can now apply a finishing armlock (8). *Note:* Grab the opponent's left leg to prevent him from rolling and escaping from the submission.

Mastering Brazilian Jiu-Jitsu

Attacks From the Back 19

While the opponent crouches on the floor (1), Rigan stands and grabs the belt with both hands (2). Rigan lifts his opponent's hips into the air (3). While the opponent is up, Rigan inserts the "hooks" for better control (4). He immediately pushes forward with his hips and uses his left hand to prevent the opponent from stopping the action (5).

Once the opponent is crushed (6), Rigan removes his left hand (7) and applies a choke from behind (8).

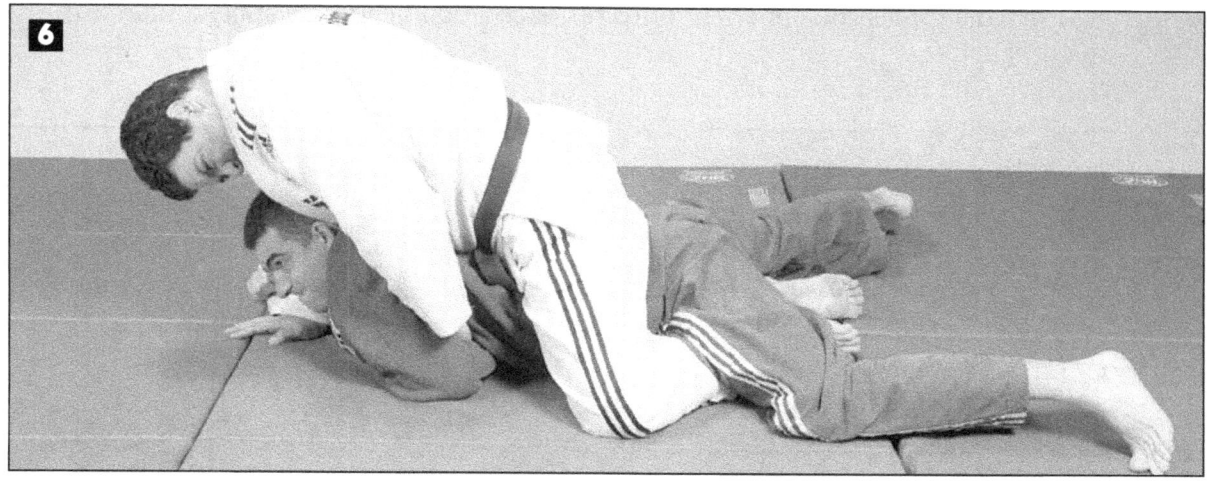

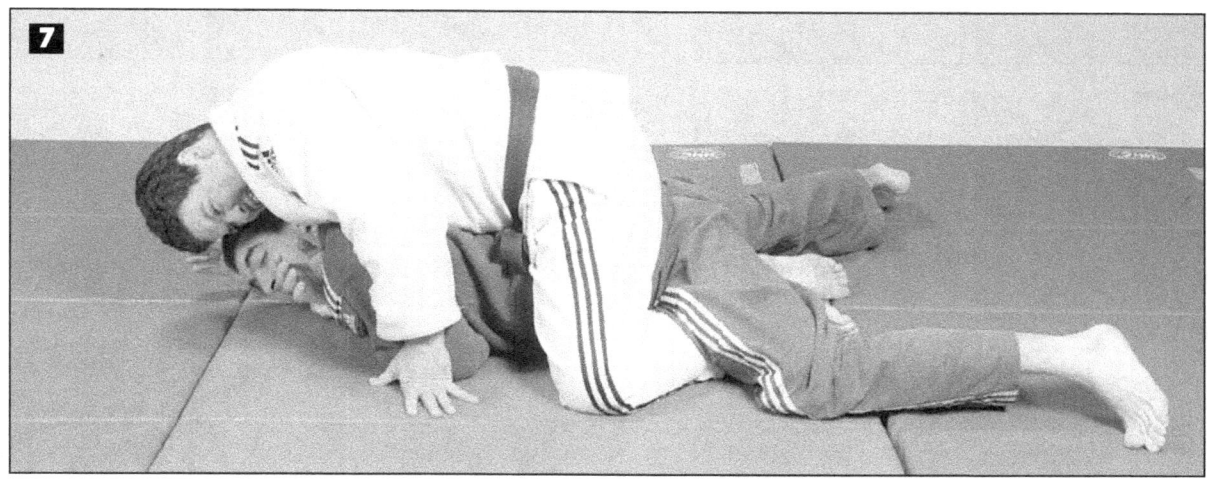

Attacks From the Back 20

Rigan controls the opponent from the back. Notice that he has the "hooks" in and his right hand is on the opponent's right lapel (1). Rigan releases the grip and starts passing his left leg over the opponent's head (2-3). Once he has a secure position (4), Rigan pushes the opponent's head with the back of his leg (5). This forces the opponent onto his back. Rigan can now apply a final armlock (6).

Attacks From the Back 21

While standing, Rigan tries to control the opponent (1). He inserts his right foot to get one "hook" in (2). The opponent prevents the second hook from going in so Rigan circles to the right and adopts a reverse position (3). Here he has easy access to the opponent's right foot (4). He grabs the opponent's foot, creates leverage with his right leg and applies a leglock (5).

Mastering Brazilian Jiu Jitsu

438

Escapes from the Back

Escapes From the Back 1

Rigan's opponent tries to initiate the attack (1). Rigan moves his left leg to the outside as he grabs the opponent's left wrist (2). Rigan rolls over his right shoulder (3), spins to the side, switches grips (4) and brings the opponent inside his closed guard (5).

Escapes From the Back 2

Rigan's opponent again tries to initiate the attack (1). Rigan moves his left leg to the outside as he grabs the opponent's right wrist (2). Using his right hand, Rigan grabs the opponent's right leg (3). Creating momentum with his body and controlling the opponent's right leg and left arm, Rigan sweeps him to the side (4-5), and controls him by leaning backwards (6) and by grabbing his right leg (7).

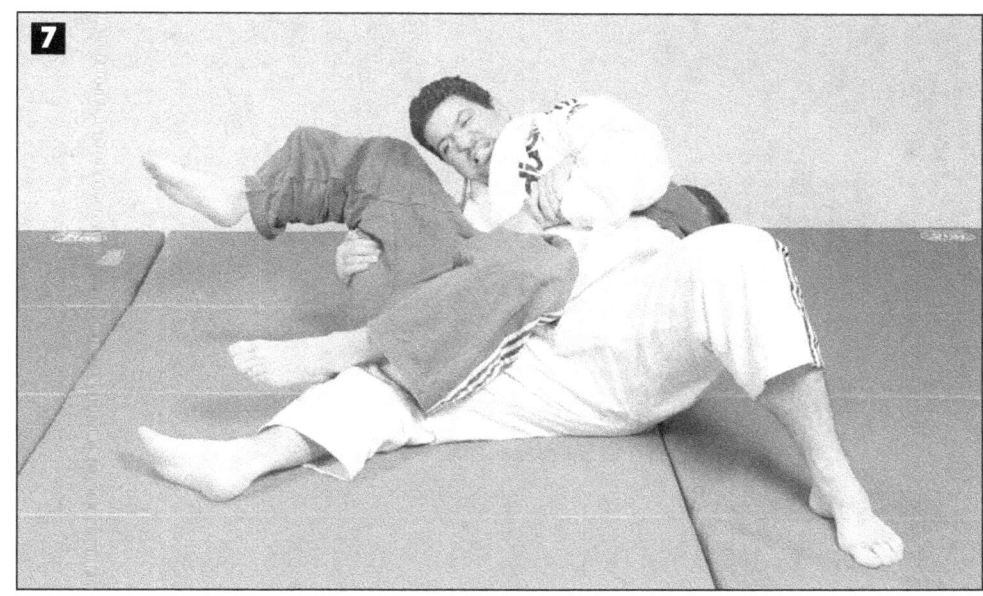

Escapes From the Back 3

Rigan gives his back to the opponent (1). With his right hand, Rigan pushes the opponent's right hand, breaking the grip and creating space (2). This enables him to bring his left leg forward (3). By turning to the right, Rigan puts his opponent inside the closed guard (4).

Escapes From the Back 4

Rigan is on his hands and feet as the opponent hooks his right leg (1). Rigan slides to the right and allows his right shoulder to roll, as he grabs the opponent's left leg with both hands (2). By turning to the left, Rigan sweeps the opponent. While executing this move, he maintains control of the leg (3), so he can apply a straight leglock (4).

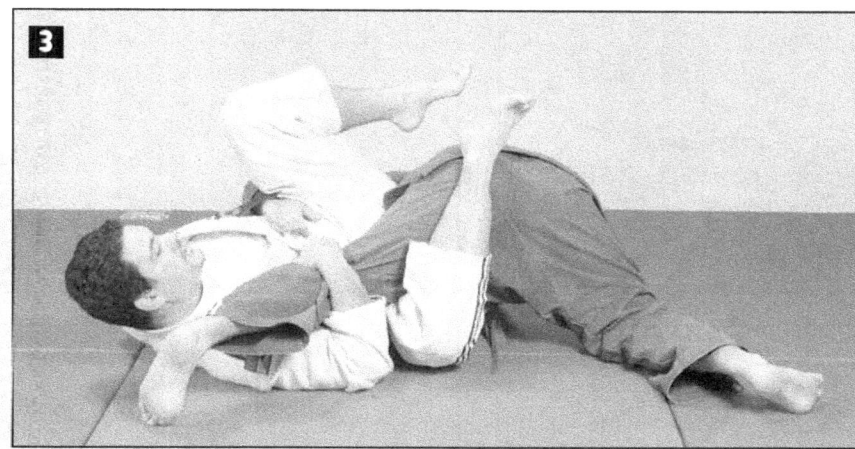

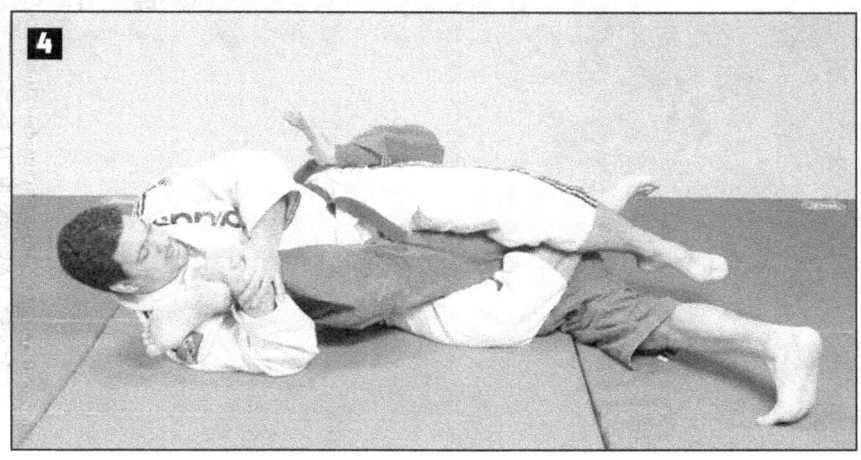

Escapes From the Back 5

Rigan's opponent initiates the attack (1). Keeping his hands and feet on the ground, Rigan pushes himself up (2), rolls forward (3-5), and escapes (6). Now he can confront his opponent from a more advantageous position (7).

Escapes From the Back 6

The opponent controls Rigan from the back (1). Rigan uses his left hand to grab the opponent's right wrist (2). He breaks the grip and grabs his own wrist with his right hand (3). This creates leverage when he turns to the right. He unbalances the opponent (4) and applies a bent armlock (5).

Escapes From the Back 7

The opponent initiates the attack from the back (1). Rigan grabs the opponent's right wrist (2). This brings the opponent closer and secures the hold. Rigan uses his left hand to grab the opponent's left leg (3). Creating momentum with his body while controlling the opponent's left leg and right arm, Rigan sweeps him to the side (4-5). Here, Rigan controls the adversary by leaning backwards (6) and by grabbing his right leg (7). Now he can initiate the counterattack.

Escapes From the Back 8

The opponent controls Rigan and tries to apply a choke from behind (1). In the process, the opponent makes the mistake of crossing both feet in front of Rigan (2). Rigan places his right foot over the opponent's feet (3). Then he puts his right foot under the back of his left knee (4), and leans backwards, creating pressure (5). By leaning to the right and stretching his body, Rigan applies a painful anklelock to his opponent (6).

Escapes From the Back 9

The opponent tries to choke Rigan from behind (1). Rigan protects his collar with the right hand and uses his left hand to grab the opponent's right wrist (2). Rigan releases the collar, grabs his left wrist (3) and applies a straight armlock (4). *Note:* When he releases his collar, Rigan slides the arm under the opponent's right arm.

Escapes From the Back 10

The opponent tries to choke Rigan from behind (1). Rigan protects his collar with his left hand, and he uses his right hand to grab the opponent's right foot (2). He moves the foot to the side (3), leans to the right (4) and throws off the opponent's balance (5). He finalizes the escape by moving his right leg outside the opponent's right leg (6). By sliding his hips (7), Rigan can begin to turn to the other side (8). This enables him to control the opponent and initiate the counterattack (9).

Escapes From the Back 11

The opponent controls Rigan from the back (1). Rigan grabs the opponent's left arm and leans sideways to unbalance him (2). He arches his back and stretches his body to create leverage (3). This enables him to move his hips to the side so he can escape from the hooks (4). By grabbing the left leg, Rigan controls his opponent's position (5). Then Rigan turns sideways and brings his opponent into the open guard (6).

Escapes From the Back 12

The opponent attacks from the back (1), but Rigan uses both hands to break the grip (2). Rigan forces the opponent's arm onto his left shoulder (3) and immediately leans back to unbalance him (4). Rigan grabs the opponent's right foot and pulls it out as he pushes upward with his hips (5). Now that he has broken the "hooks," Rigan begins to slide to the side (6) so he can initiate a counterattack (7).

Mastering Brazilian Jiu-Jitsu

Escapes From the Back 13

The opponent controls Rigan, who is on his hands and knees (1). Rigan moves his left leg to the outside and grabs the opponent's right leg with his left arm (2). This disrupts the opponent's balance and creates space for Rigan to move his right leg between the adversary's legs (3). He slides his hips forward and lifts his left leg over the opponent's right leg (4). By hooking his feet and moving his body to the side (5), Rigan forces the opponent into his half-guard (6). Now he can initiate the offensive.

Escapes From the Back 14

The opponent controls Rigan (1), who moves away (2) while keeping his hands and feet on the ground (3). As he steps forward, Rigan grabs the opponent's right leg (4). Rigan sits (5), leans back (6) and brings his opponent inside his closed guard (7).

Escapes From the Back 15

The opponent controls Rigan (1). Rigan shoots his left leg to the outside as he secures the opponent's right arm (2). Rigan slides his right leg forward (3), and immediately moves his hips to the other side; this forces the opponent's face into the floor (4). Rigan establishes control and applies a straight armlock (5).

Escapes From the Back 16

The opponent again establishes early control (1). Rigan grabs the opponent's right arm as he raises his hips to create space between himself and his adversary (2). He leans to the left and rolls, unbalancing the opponent and breaking the advantageous position (3). Rigan begins to roll to the other side (4). This gives him the proper position (5) to apply side control (6).

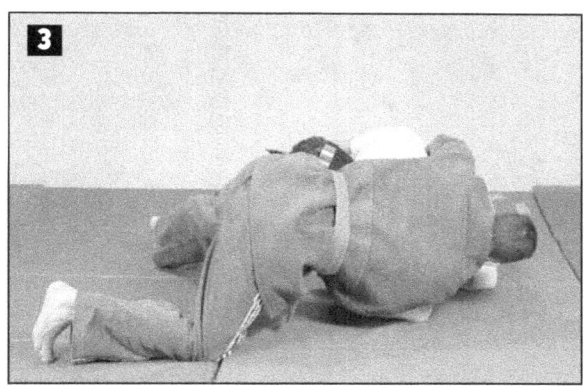

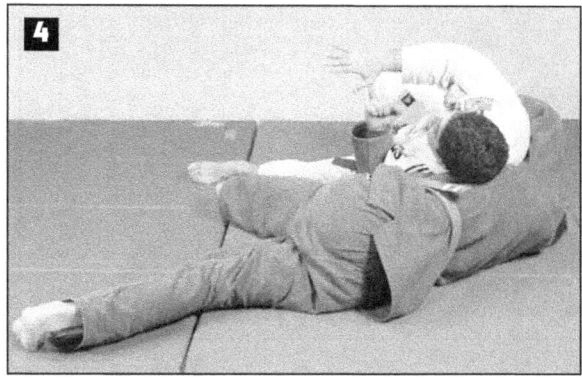

Escapes From the Back 17

The opponent is on Rigan's back (1). Using his right hand, Rigan grabs the opponent's head. Then Rigan raises his hips (2) and forces the opponent forward as he rolls (3). This brings the opponent onto his back (4) and enables Rigan to apply full side control (5).

Escapes From the Back 18

Rigan is under the opponent's control (1), so he uses both hands and feet to raise his hips (2). Using the space created by his previous movement, Rigan moves his head under the opponent's armpit and reaches for the adversary's right leg (3). Using his arm as support, Rigan moves his left leg to the side, raises his left arm (4), reaches around to the other side and moves to the opponent's back (5). He secures the position by controlling the opponent with both arms (6).

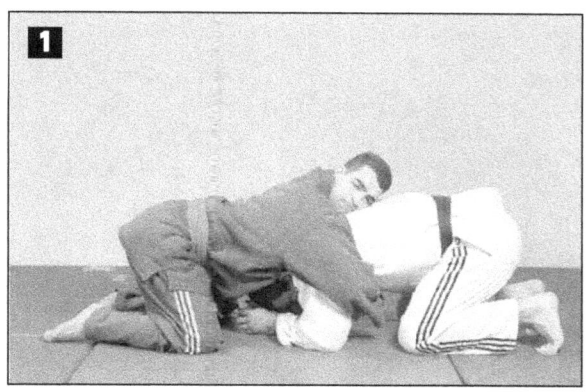

Mastering Brazilian Jiu-Jitsu

Mastering Brazilian Jiu Jitsu

Attacks from the Mount

Attacks From the Mount 1

Rigan mounts his opponent (1). With his right hand, Rigan opens the collar and then places his left hand (palm up) inside the opponent's gi (2). He slides his right hand under his left until both hands touch at the back of the opponent's neck (3). Leaning forward, Rigan applies pressure and executes the choke (4).

Attacks From the Mount 2

Rigan mounts his opponent (1). While he opens the collar with his right hand, Rigan places his left hand (palm up) inside the opponent's gi (2). Using his right hand (palm down) (3), Rigan grabs the right side of the opponent's collar (4). Leaning forward, Rigan applies pressure and chokes his opponent out (5).

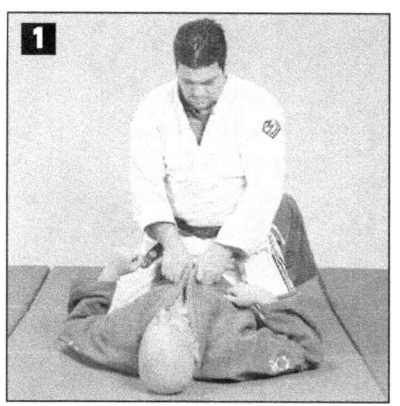

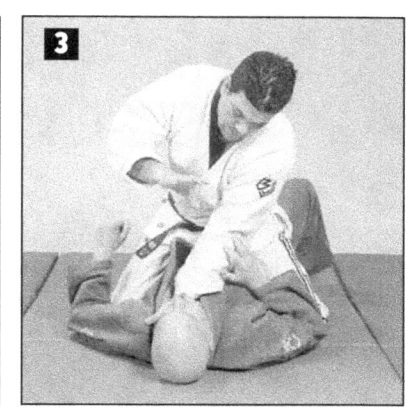
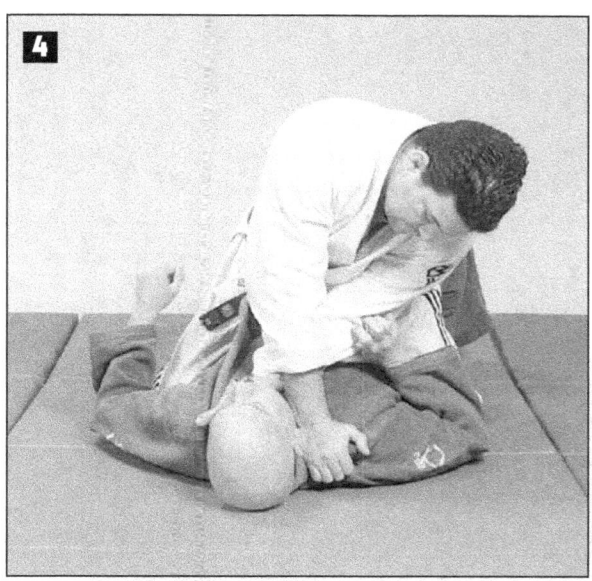
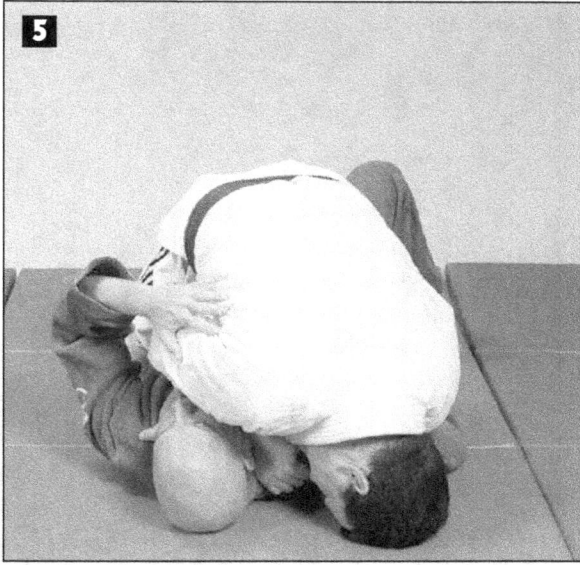

Attacks From the Mount 3

While mounting his opponent, Rigan grabs the left side of the collar (1). Again, the palm is down. Then he grabs (palm down) the other side of the collar with his left hand (2). To choke his opponent, he brings both hands together (3).

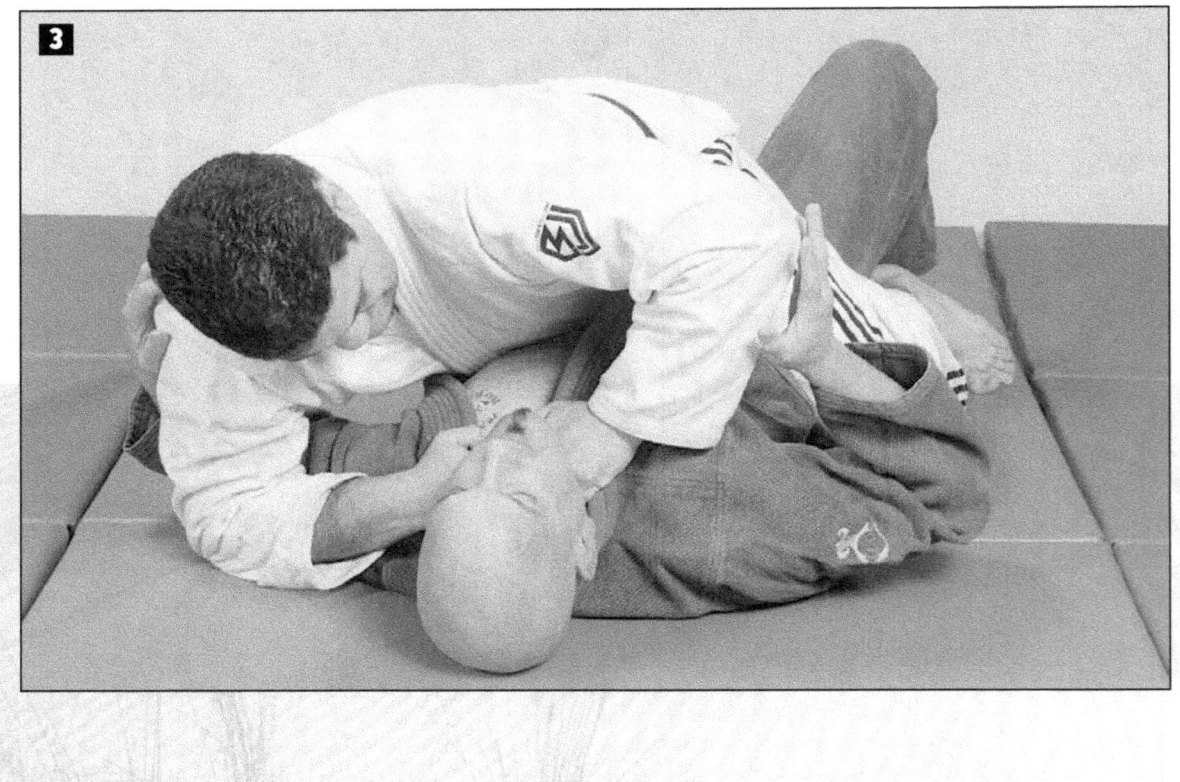

Attacks From the Mount 4

With his right arm under the neck, Rigan mounts his opponent (1). Using his right hand, Rigan grabs his left sleeve (2), and then raises his left arm adjacent to his opponent's neck (3). He places his arm across the opponent's neck, exerts pressure and chokes him with an *ezequiel* (4).

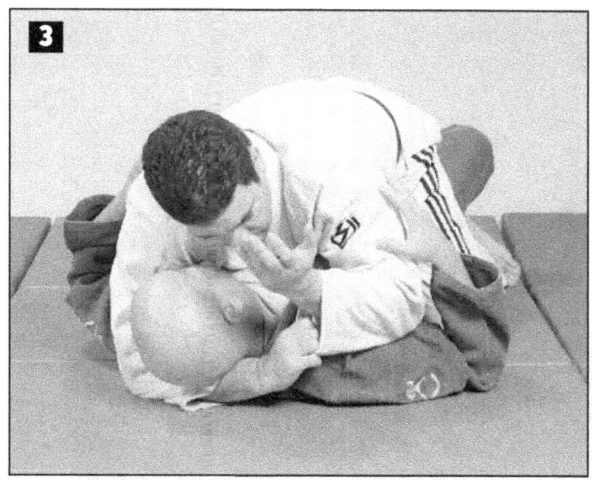
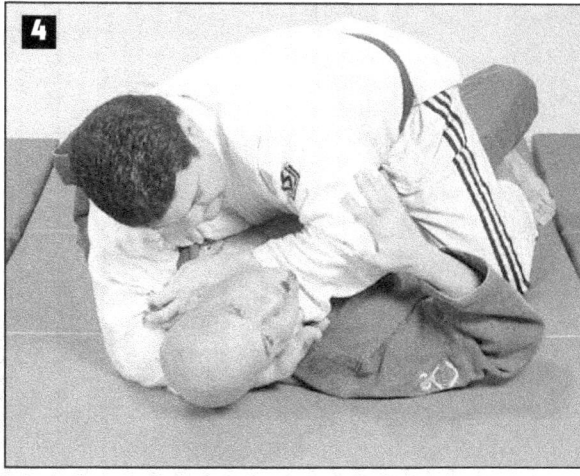

Attacks From the Mount 5

While mounting his adversary, Rigan adjusts his left leg as soon as he feels him turning to the right (1). With his left hand, Rigan opens the opponent's gi (2). He uses his right hand to grab the opponent's collar (3). To apply a finishing choke, he pulls with his right hand and crosses his left arm over the opponent's neck (4).

Attacks From the Mount 6

Rigan mounts his opponent (1). With his left hand, he grabs the opponent's left wrist (2) and forces it to the ground (3). Rigan uses his elbow to establish position (4), as he moves his right hand under the opponent's left arm so he can grab his own wrist (5). By lifting the adversary's right arm, Rigan creates pressure and applies a bent armlock (6).

Attacks From the Mount 7

As Rigan mounts his opponent, he tries to apply the previous technique (1), but the opponent turns to the right to avoid the pressure (2). In response, Rigan adjusts his position and lifts his left knee (3). Notice that he hasn't released his grip. As the opponent keeps turning, Rigan follows him (4). Rigan sits and passes his right leg over the opponent (5). He leans back and applies a finishing armlock (6).

Attacks From the Mount   8

Rigan mounts his opponent, who tries to push him away with his right hand (1). Rigan uses both hands to establish his position (2), and then he adjusts his hips as he turns to the right (3). Notice that he maintains the pressure on the opponent's chest. He moves his left leg toward the opponent's head (4), places both legs across the opponent, sits back and applies a straight armlock (5).

Attacks From the Mount 9

Rigan controls his opponent from the mounted position (1). As soon as the opponent attempts to push Rigan's left knee away so he can escape, Rigan grabs the wrist (2) and establishes position with his right arm (3). Rigan wraps his right arm under the opponent's right arm, grabs his own wrist (4) and applies a *kimura* (5).

Attacks From the Mount   10

Rigan mounts his opponent with his right hand inside the collar (1). Rigan switches his hip position, places his left elbow close to the opponent's neck, applies pressure (2), leans forward and chokes him (3).

Attacks From the Mount 11

Rigan controls the altercation from the mounted position with his right arm under the opponent's head (1). With his left hand, Rigan grabs the opponent's right wrist (2). He places his left leg between the opponent's head and his extended left arm and then grabs his ankle to secure the position (3). He switches grips and pulls the opponent's right arm as he slides his left leg behind the head (4). Moving his right leg forward so he can hook the instep of his left foot under his right leg (5), Rigan secures the position and applies a *triangle* choke from the top (6).

Attacks From the Mount 12

Rigan controls the opponent from the mounted position (1). Notice that his left arm is under the adversary's right arm. Securing his position with his left arm, Rigan slides forward and moves his right knee over the opponent's left arm (2). This creates additional pressure (3), so he can extend his body and execute the straight armbar (4). Note: It is important to maintain pressure and control on the opponent's right arm during the entire movement. Keep it tight. If necessary, grab your own gi to secure the control.

Attacks From the Mount 13

Rigan controls the opponent from a half-mounted position (1). With his left hand, he loosens the opponent's gi (2). He traps the opponent's right arm by grabbing the tip of the gi with his right hand (3). He leans back and maintains the grip with his right hand (4). Rigan releases the gi as he moves his right leg around the opponent's neck and under his left leg (5). He leans back and secures the straight armlock (6).

472 Mastering Brazilian Jiu-Jitsu

Attacks From the Mount 14

Rigan controls the opponent from the half-mount (1). Notice that he has both of the opponent's arms. He leans back (2), releases the grip of his right hand (3), and slides to the side so he can get the right angle (4) to execute a reverse *triangle* choke from the back (5).

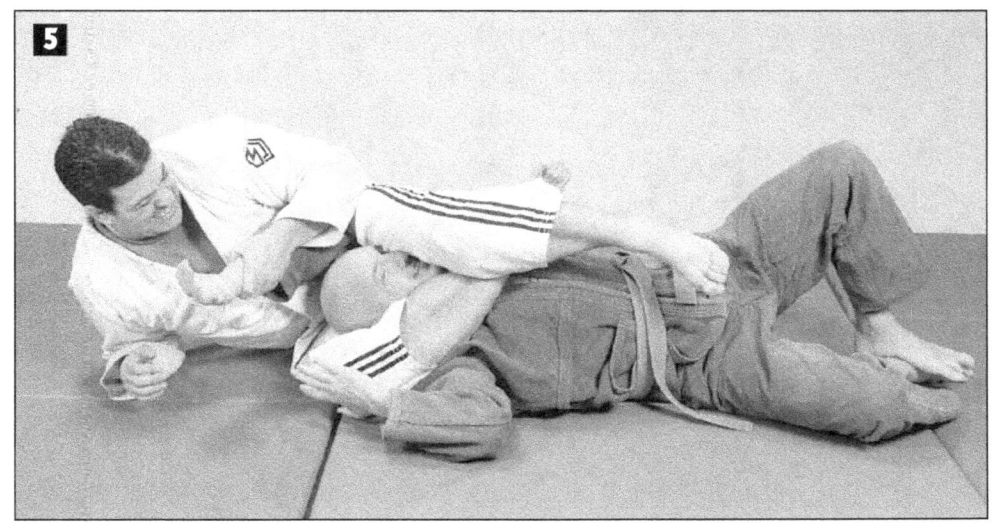

Attacks From the Mount 15

While controlling the confrontation from the half-mount, Rigan grabs the opponent's left hand (1). Rigan then pushes the opponent's arm toward the ground (2). Using his right hand, Rigan reaches around the neck and grabs the adversary's left wrist (3). To establish a better and tighter position, Rigan pushes the opponent's left elbow (4). He slides his hand to the opponent's left wrist, turns and ends up completely on his opponent's back (5-6). From here, Rigan can apply a finishing choke (7).

Attacks From the Mount 16

Rigan grabs the opponent's left hand and controls him from the half-mounted position (1). He forces the opponent's left hand to the side so he can grab it with his right hand (2). Then he pushes the opponent's left elbow to get a better and tighter position (3). Rigan sits up, adopts the back position (4), slides his arm across the opponent's neck (5), leans back, cranks on the collar and chokes him (6).

Attacks From the Mount 17

Rigan controls his opponent from the mounted position (1). To create room to move his left leg forward, Rigan pulls his opponent's sleeves (2). While maintaining the grip with his right hand, Rigan leans back and grabs his opponent's left leg (3). From there, Rigan applies a straight armlock on his opponent's left arm (4).

Attacks From the Mount 18

Rigan mounts his opponent (1). Notice that his right arm is firmly around the adversary's neck. Using his left hand, Rigan pushes the opponent's right arm across the chest (2). To establish position, Rigan leans forward and clutches his wrists (3). He starts to move his right leg to the other side. Once it reaches the opponent's right hip, he'll have better control (4). To submit his opponent, he extends his left leg and applies a choke (5).

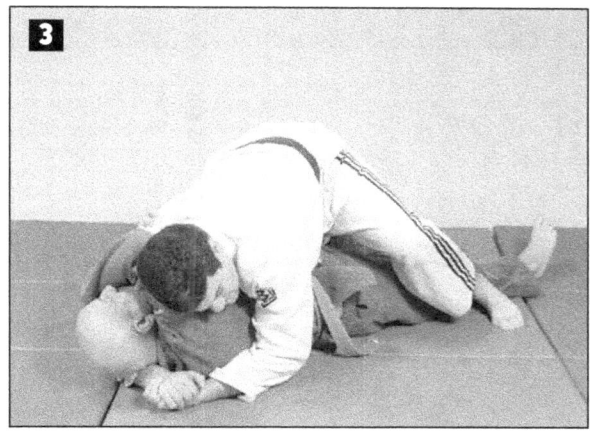

Attacks From the Mount 19

With his right hand inside the collar, Rigan controls the opponent from the mounted position (1). Using his left hand, Rigan pushes the opponent to the right (2). This enables Rigan to establish his balance (3), so he can put his left knee close to the opponent's head without losing equilibrium and control (4).

Using his left hand for support (5), Rigan places his left leg over the opponent's head (6-7), leans back and executes a straight armlock (8).

Attacks From the Mount 20

While firmly grabbing the collar, Rigan mounts his opponent (1). Rigan then sets his right leg close to the opponent's head (2-3). As soon as he feels the opponent's left hand pushing, Rigan releases the grip (4), switches hip position (5), and goes to side control (6). Here he can apply a choke (7).

Attacks From the Mount 21

Rigan mounts his opponent (1). Attempting to escape, the opponent uses both hands to push Rigan (2). Rigan takes advantage of the action and allows his body to move to the side (3). He places his left leg under the opponent's head (4), turns to the side and applies a straight armlock (5).

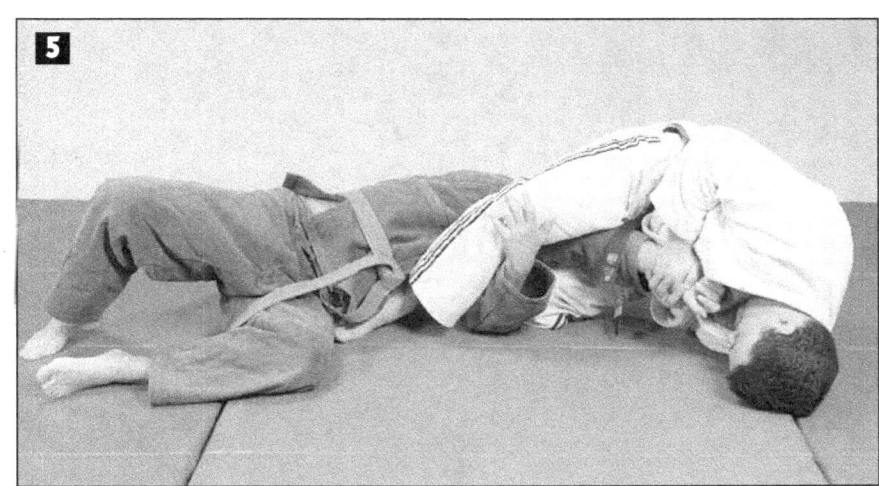

Mastering Brazilian Jiu Jitsu

482

Escapes from the Mount

Escapes From the Mount 1

The opponent controls Rigan from the mounted position (1). Using both hands, Rigan reaches around and grabs the opponent's belt (2). To create leverage, he puts his left foot between the belt and the opponent's back (3-4). As Rigan pushes, he simultaneously places his hands on the opponent's hips (5) so he can sweep him to the right (6). Rigan ends up inside the opponent's guard (7).

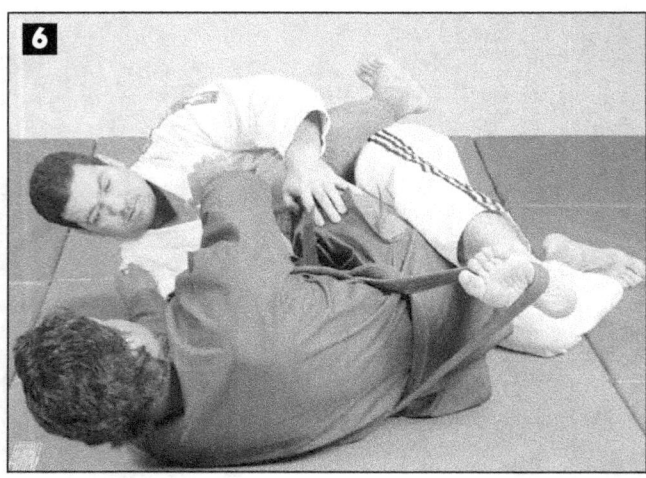

Escapes From the Mount 2

The opponent mounts Rigan (1). Taking advantage of the opponent's raised left knee, Rigan underhooks the leg with his right hand (2), pushes with his right arm and simultaneously "bridges" to get momentum (3) so he can push the opponent away from his chest (4). While holding the opponent's left leg, Rigan starts to turn (5) so he can initiate the counterattack (6).

Escapes From the Mount 3

The adversary controls Rigan from the mounted position (1). Rigan grabs the opponent's pants with his right hand (2) and "bridges" as he pulls the leg up (3). This creates space for Rigan to move his left leg under the opponent's leg (4). He uses his right foot to push the opponent's left leg away (5-6). When the adversary hits the ground (7), Rigan can escape (8).

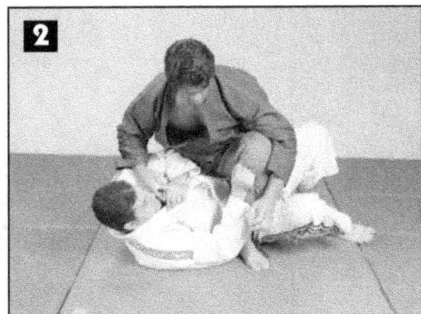

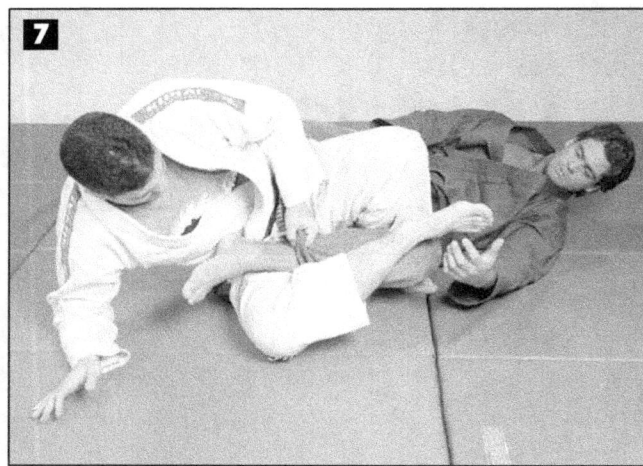

Escapes From the Mount 4

Using the mount, the opponent controls Rigan (1). As Rigan passes his left arm under the opponent's left leg and latches on, he simultaneously grabs the pants with his right hand (2). Using these grips as support, Rigan "bridges" (3) and turns to the side to escape (4). He is now behind the opponent (5), and he can initiate the offense (6).

Escapes From the Mount 5

Employing the mount, the opponent controls Rigan (1). Utilizing his elbows to keep the opponent's knees away from his armpits, Rigan moves his hips to the right as he pushes the opponent's left knee away (2). This enables him to plant his right foot behind the opponent's left leg (3). To create space, Rigan moves his hips to the right (4) as he pushes the opponent's right knee away (5). He wraps his left leg around the opponent and closes the guard (6).

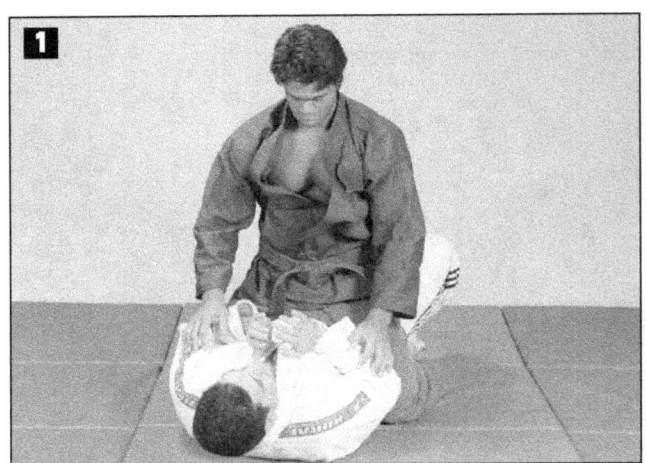

Escapes From the Mount 6

The opponent mounts Rigan and places his right hand inside the collar (1). Using his right hand, Rigan controls the opponent's right hand. With his left, he secures the opponent's right elbow (2). Then he "bridges" to the left (3), which throws the opponent onto the ground (4-5). Rigan continues to roll until he is in the opponent's closed guard (6).

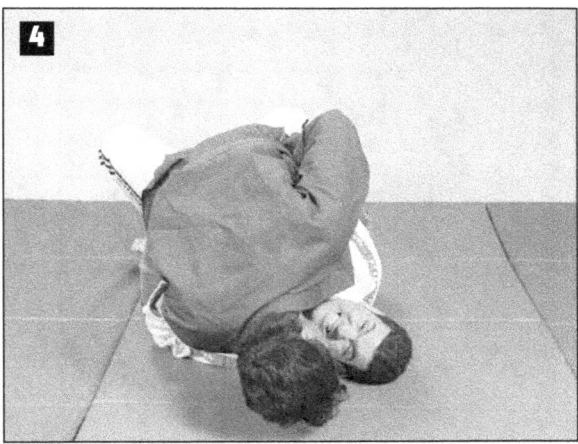

Mastering Brazilian Jiu-Jitsu

Escapes From the Mount 7

The opponent controls Rigan from the mounted position (1). Rigan grabs the opponent's belt with both hands (2) and pushes up as he "bridges" to create some space (3). This enables him to bring his right knee toward his chest (4), place his foot on the opponent and push him away (5). When the adversary hits the ground, Rigan applies an anklelock (6).

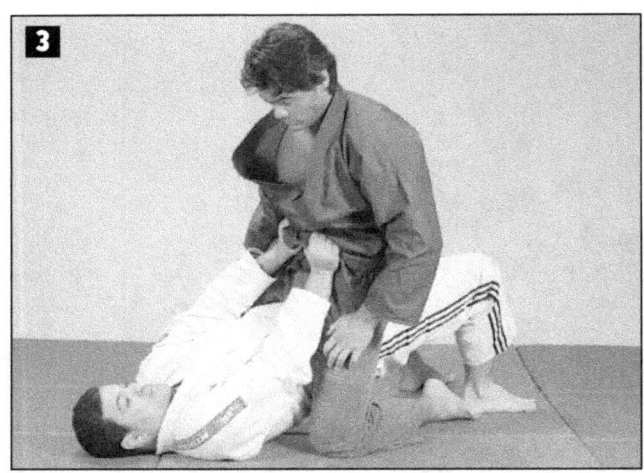

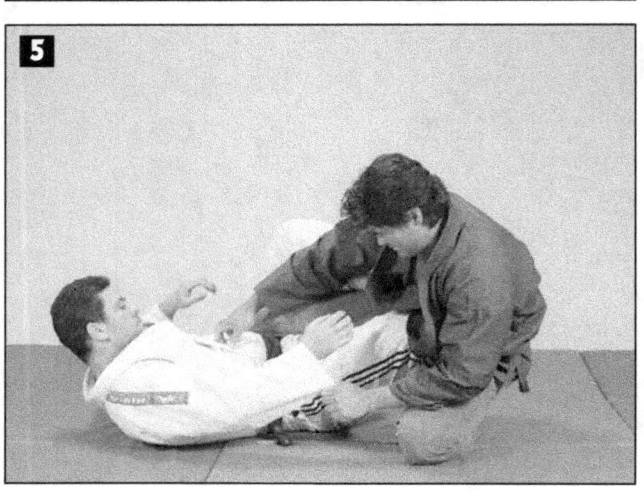

Escapes From the Mount 8

The opponent mounts Rigan (1). To create space, Rigan "bridges" and pushes the opponent away (2). He raises both legs (3), places them in the opponent's armpits and pushes (4). Rigan quickly moves to his hands and knees and grabs the opponent's right foot (5). He circles his right arm around the opponent's foot (6) and applies a footlock (7).

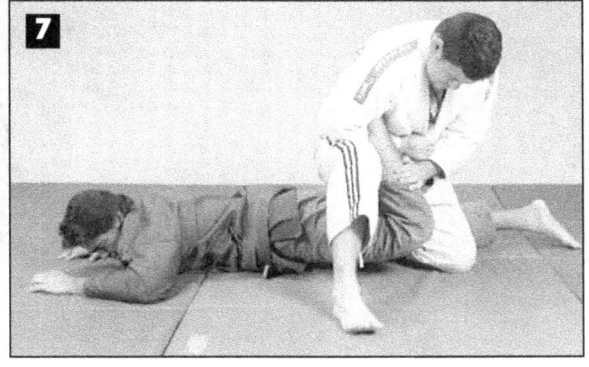

Escapes From the Mount 9

Mounted by the opponent (1), Rigan tries to escape using the "bridge" (2). However, the opponent shoots his right leg to the outside and blocks Rigan's attempt (3). In response, Rigan moves his left knee towards his chest (4). Now he can either sweep the opponent (5) or bring him into his half-guard (6).

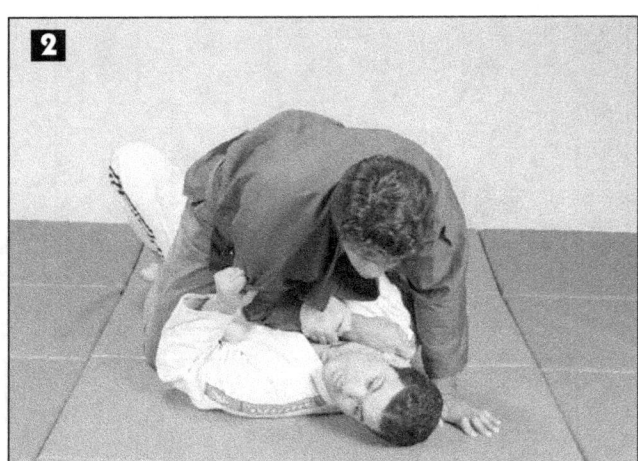

Escapes From the Mount   10

The opponent establishes control by mounting Rigan (1). To escape, Rigan brings his left knee up (2), turns his hips to the side (3), hooks the opponent's left foot with his heel (4) and secures the leg with his right leg (5). Rigan slides his hips to the other side and extricates his right knee (6). He hooks the opponent's left leg with his right foot as he starts to move his left knee outside (7). Finally, he adopts the closed guard (8).

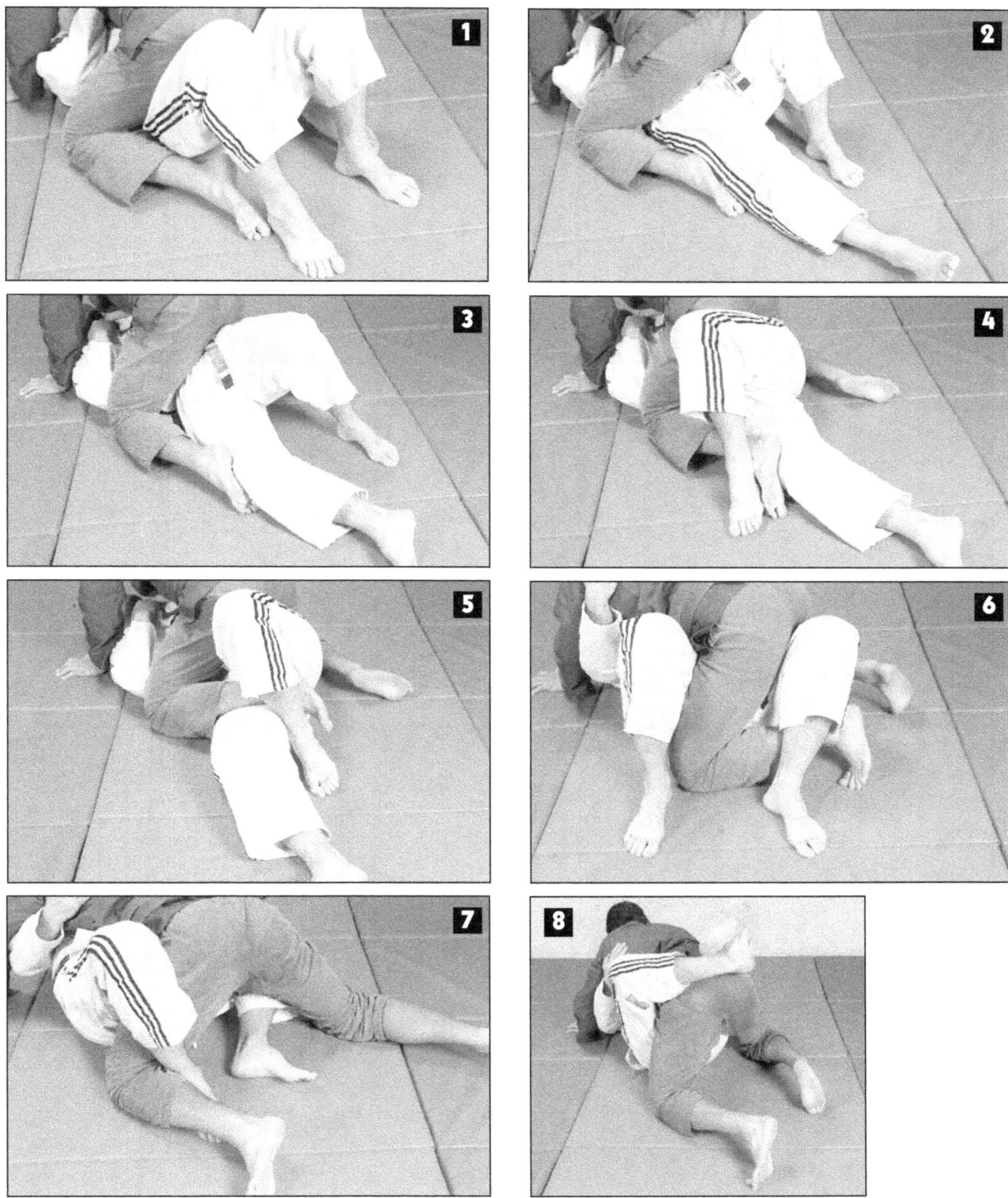

Escapes From the Mount 11

The opponent mounts Rigan (1). To create space, Rigan brings his left knee up (2) and turns his hips to the side (3) so he can hook the opponent's left foot (4). Rigan brings the foot over his right leg and secures it with his left heel (5-6). As he controls the opponent's left leg with his left foot (7), Rigan slides his hips to the outside (8) so he can extricate his left leg. Wrapping both legs around the opponent, Rigan puts him in his closed guard (9).

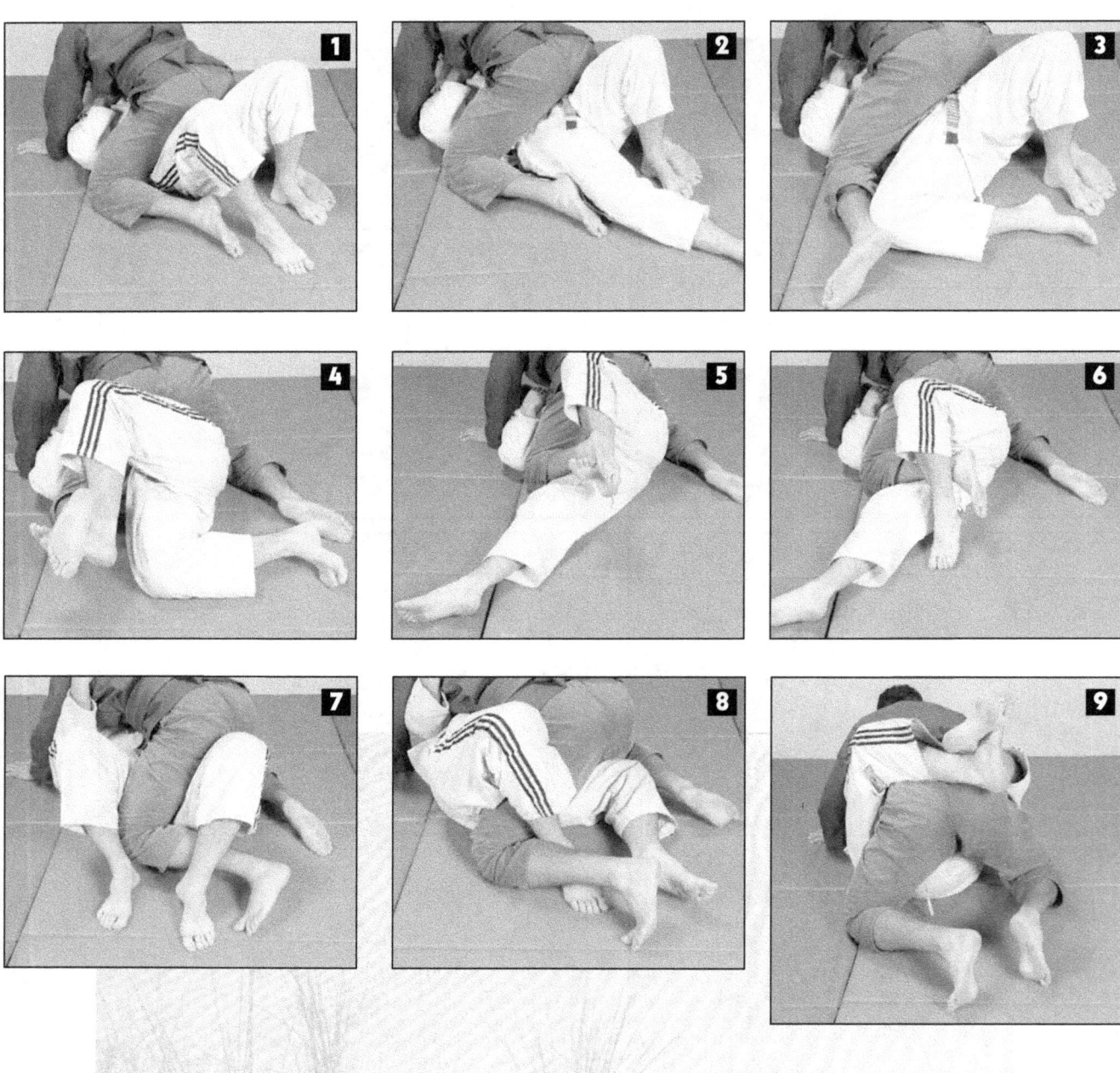

Escapes From the Mount 12

Using his "hooks," the opponent prevents Rigan from reversing the position (1). In response, Rigan kicks out with his right leg (2). This frees his right leg and enables him to break the hook by kicking the opponent's right foot (3-4). Rigan turns his hips on an angle (5) as he shifts his left leg to the outside (6). Notice that he is controlling the opponent's right leg with his right leg. While Rigan now uses his left foot to control the opponent's right leg, he pushes the opponent's left thigh (7). This gives him space to extricate his right knee, and he pulls his opponent into the closed guard (8).

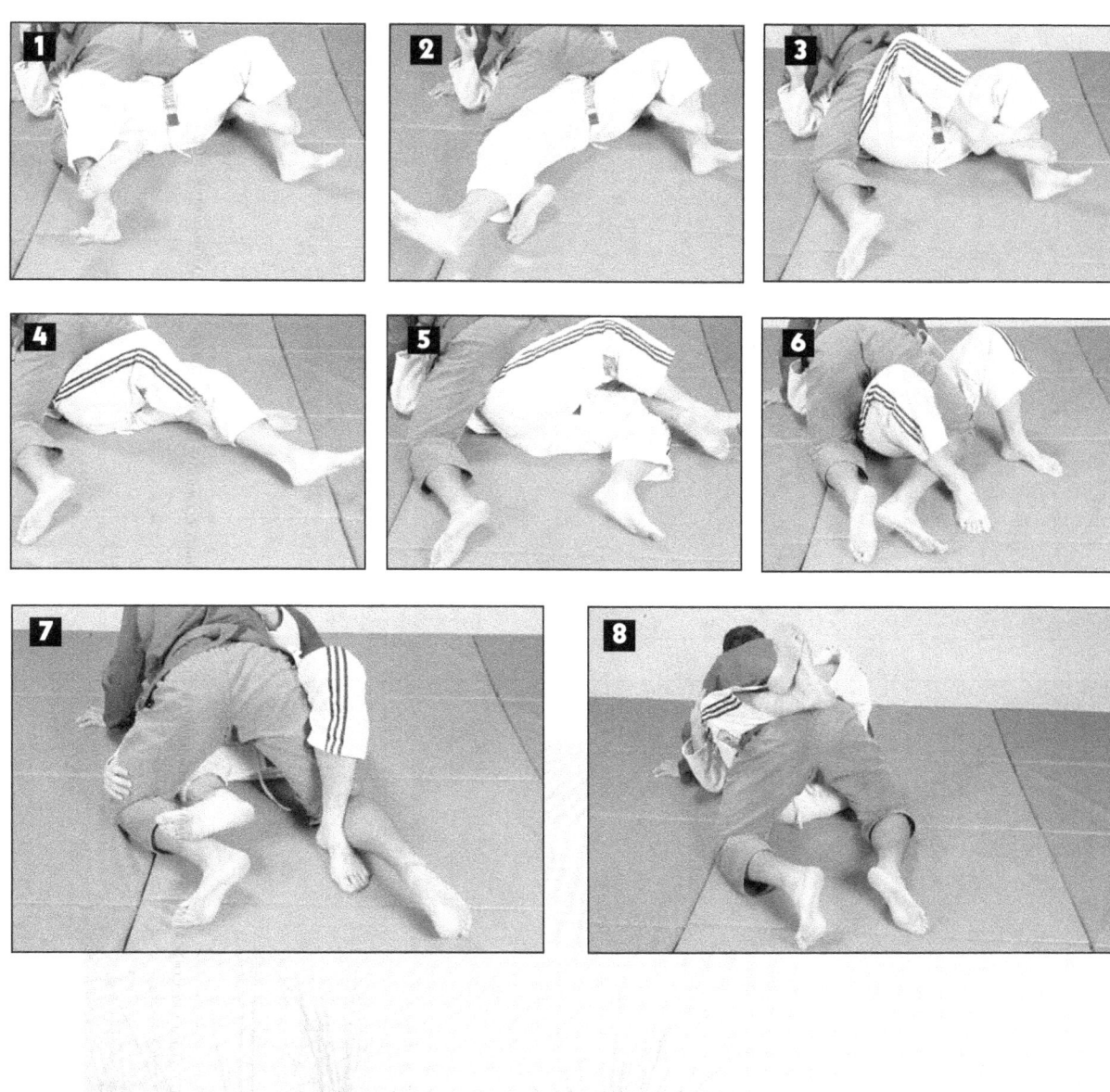

Mastering Brazilian Jiu-Jitsu

Escapes From the Mount 13

The opponent hooks both feet close to Rigan's buttocks. This prevents Rigan from using "footwork" to reverse the position (1). To create momentum and space, Rigan raises both legs (2), breaks the "hooks" and pushes the opponent's right leg away (3). Rigan twists his hips (4) and traps the opponent's right foot (5) between his legs (6). During this maneuver, Rigan maintains control of the foot with his right foot. Once he has established this position (7), Rigan slides his hips to the other side (8), moves his right leg outside and pulls the opponent into his closed guard (9).

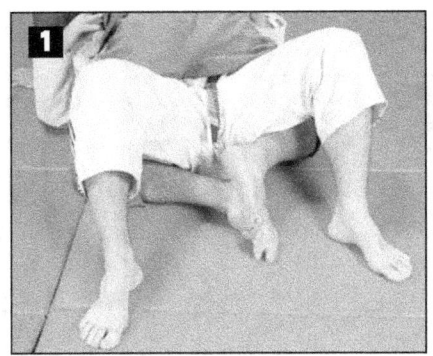 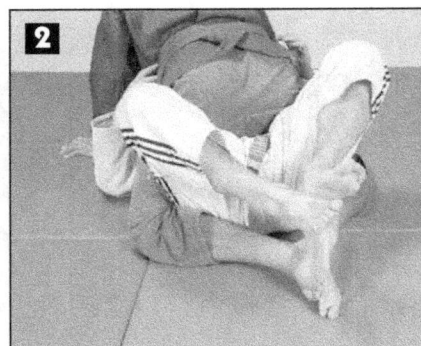 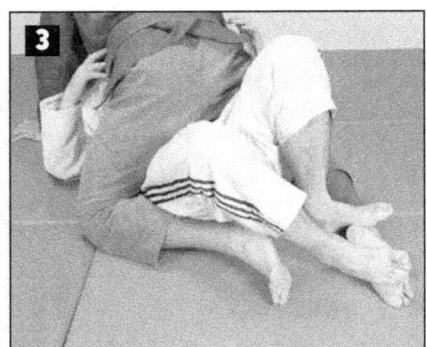

 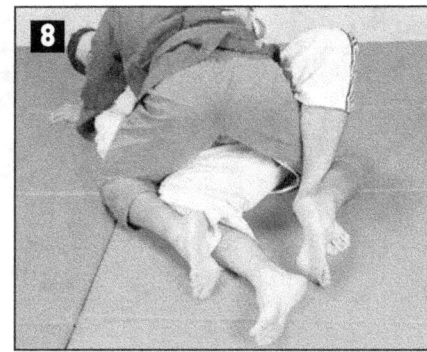 

Escapes From the Mount 14

The opponent mounts Rigan (1). In response, Rigan secures the opponent's left arm. This is a close-up (2). Using his left hand, Rigan grabs the opponent's belt (3). To support himself when he "bridges" and to prevent the opponent from breaking the grip, Rigan moves his head to the ground (4) and then sweeps him to the right (5). Rigan rolls with him (6) and ends up inside his closed guard (7).

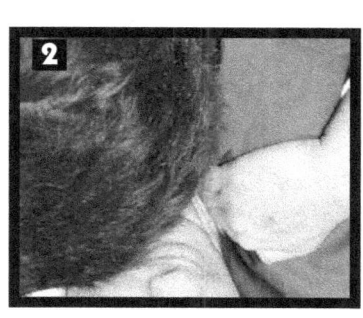
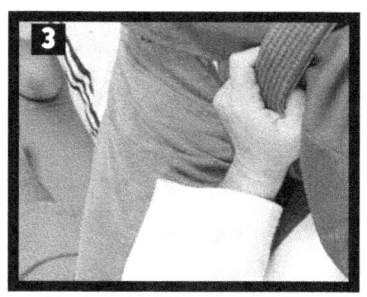

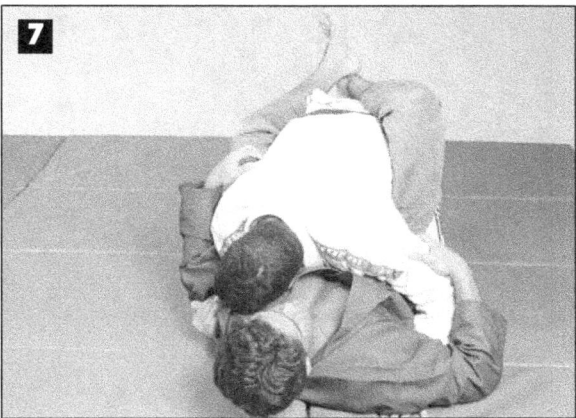

Mastering Brazilian Jiu-Jitsu

Escapes From the Mount 15

While supporting himself with his hands, the opponent controls Rigan (1). Using his right arm, Rigan hooks the opponent's left arm (2), and he secures the grip with his left hand (3). He pulls the opponent's arm down (4) to keep it close to his body (5). Despite the opponent's attempt to stop him, Rigan executes a "bridge" (6). The opponent falls to his side (7). Rigan ultimately ends up in his opponent's closed guard (8), where he can initiate the offensive response.

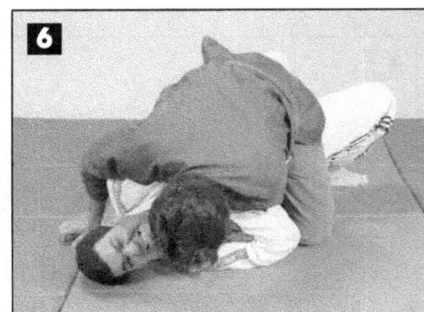

Escapes From the Mount 16

Rigan tries to control his opponent, who has established side position (1). As soon as the opponent moves his right arm to control Rigan's head (2), Rigan grabs the opponent's arm and belt (3). Keeping a tight grip on both (4), Rigan utilizes his hips, pulls hard to the side (5), and throws him to the other side (6). Rigan can then adopt side control to initiate an attack (7).

Mastering Brazilian Jiu Jitsu

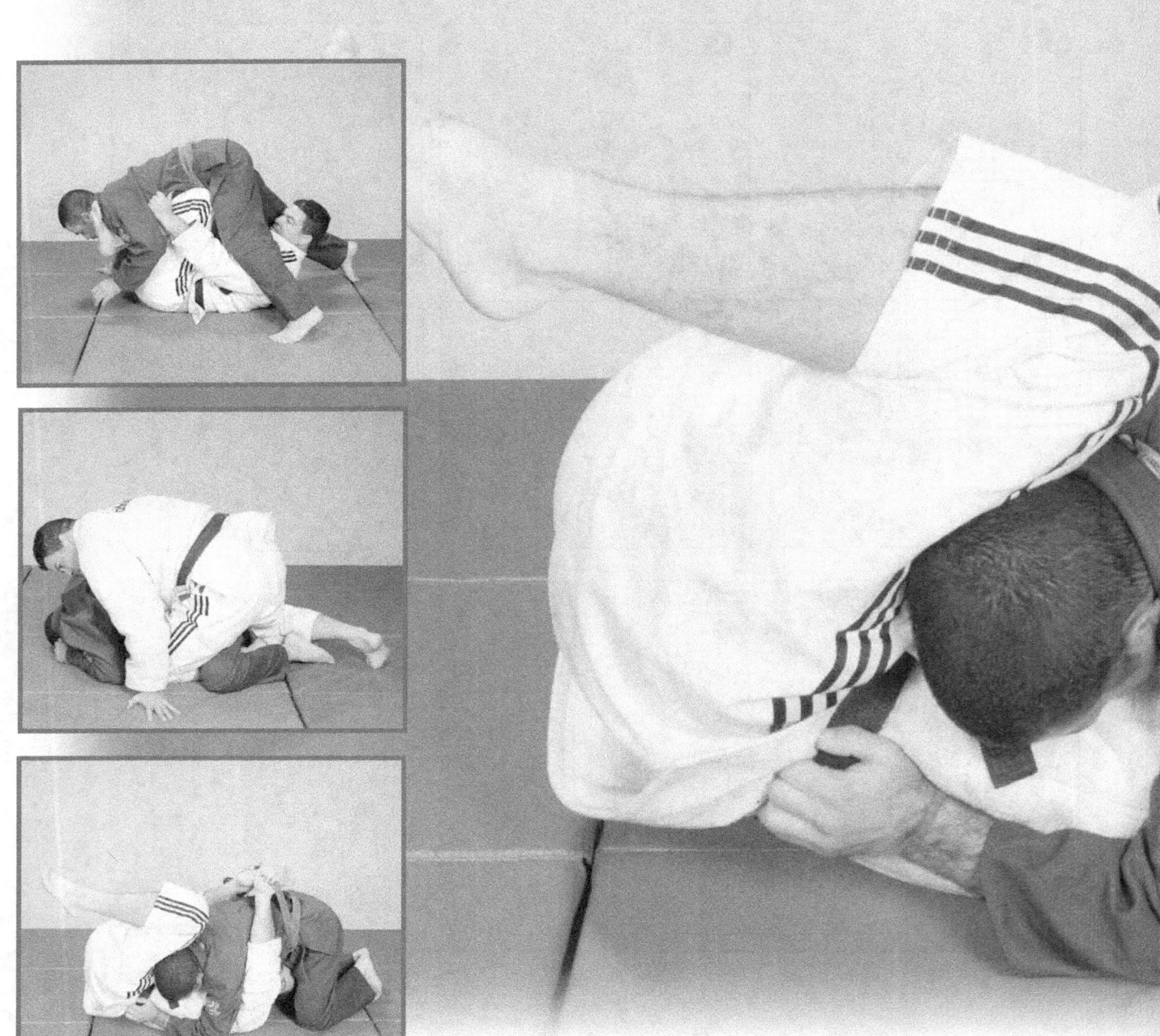

North & South

North & South 1

The fighters are in the north-south position, and Rigan is on the bottom (1). Employing his left hand, Rigan grabs the opponent's belt (2). Then he slides slightly away, reaches up and grabs his right foot (3-4). He traps the opponent's belt with his right foot (5), and uses it as support (6) to move away (7).

Rigan slides his head out (8), turns around (9) and puts the opponent inside his open guard (10).

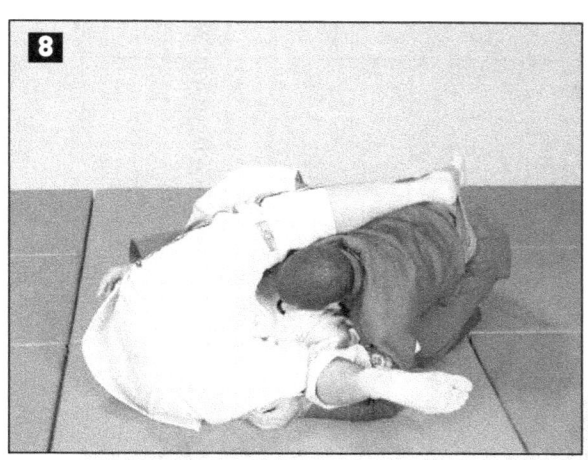

North & South 2

Rigan is again under the opponent's body (1). Rigan "bridges" and pushes the opponent away with both hands (2). Keeping his knees close to his body, Rigan raises his legs (3), pivots to the right (4), and escapes (5). He can now put the opponent in the open guard (6).

North & South 3

The combatants are in the north-south position, and Rigan is on the bottom (1). Utilizing both hands, Rigan "bridges" and pushes the opponent away (2). He raises his legs, keeps his knees close to his body (3) and pulls the opponent forward (4). During this maneuver, Rigan controls the adversary with his legs (5-6). While maintaining control, Rigan grabs the opponent's right leg (7) and applies a straight kneebar (8).

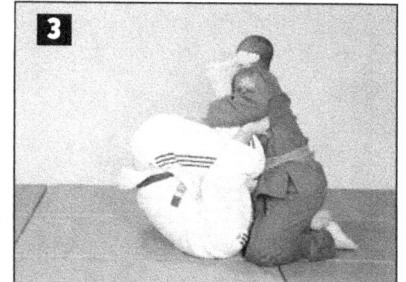

North & South 4

While in the north-south position, Rigan starts underneath (1). Rigan immediately "bridges" and pushes the opponent away (2). He lifts both legs, keeping his knees close to his body (3). Then he puts his right foot under the opponent's right armpit (4), and his left in the left armpit (5).

By simultaneously pulling with his hands while pushing with his feet (6), Rigan disrupts the opponent's balance (7). The adversary ends up on the ground (8), where Rigan can initiate the offensive (9) from the side (10).

North & South 5

The fighters are in the north-south position, and Rigan is on the bottom (1). Using both hands while he "bridges," Rigan pushes the opponent away (2). Keeping his knees tight to his chest, Rigan raises his legs (3-4), and passes his right leg under the opponent's left armpit (5).

This gives him leverage to spin to the left (6), as he simultaneously pulls himself into the opponent's guard (7-8). Rigan grabs his left foot with his right hand (9), and applies a *triangle* choke (10).

North & South 6

The fighters begin in the north-south position (1). Rigan again is underneath. Rigan "bridges" and pushes the opponent's hips away (2). By swinging his legs, Rigan generates momentum (3) to place his right leg under the opponent's left leg (4). Rigan immediately traps the leg by closing his legs (5). While grabbing the opponent's belt, Rigan slides forward (6), moves to the opponent's left (7), and initiates the offense from the back (8).

North & South 7a

Rigan is on the bottom as the fighters begin in the north-south position (1). He grabs the opponent's left leg (2) and secures the hold with his right hand (3). This provides leverage to prevent the opponent from standing (4). Once he controls the opponent's body, Rigan moves his knees closer (5), slides his body and head under the opponent.

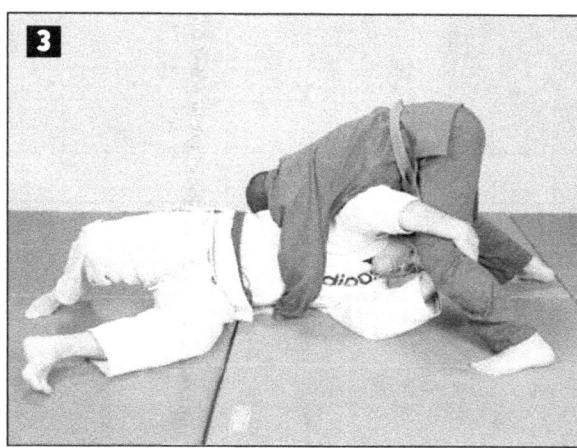

(continued on next page)

North & South 7b

Then he throws him (6-8) to the right (9). Rigan controls the opponent's legs (10), and initiates the attack from the side (11).

North & South 8

The fighters are in the north-south position, and Rigan is under the opponent (1). As he grabs the opponent's left leg, Rigan slides away (2). Using his left hand to support himself, Rigan starts turning to the side (3) until he is on his hands and knees (4). He grabs the adversary's left leg, shifts to the right (5), raises his head (6) and escapes (7). He immediately seizes the opportunity to turn (8) and mount the opponent from behind (9).

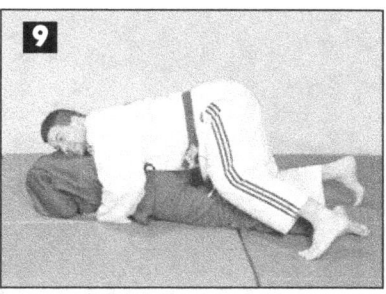

North & South 9

The combatants begin in the north-south position, and Rigan is on the bottom (1). Rigan grabs the opponent's left leg and slides away (2). Using his left hand for support, Rigan flips over until he is on his hands and knees (3). Utilizing his right arm, Rigan grabs the opponent's left arm (4). Rigan raises his body (5), turns to the right (6-7) and throws his opponent (8). After assuming side control, Rigan initiates the offense (9).

North & South 10

Rigan is on the bottom as the pair begins in the north-south position (1). Rigan grabs the opponent's left leg, pushes himself away (2), twists and gets on his hands and knees (3). Rigan sits in front of the opponent (4), places his left foot inside the opponent's legs (5) and sweeps him to the side (6). Rigan rolls with him (7) and assumes side control so he can initiate the attack (8).

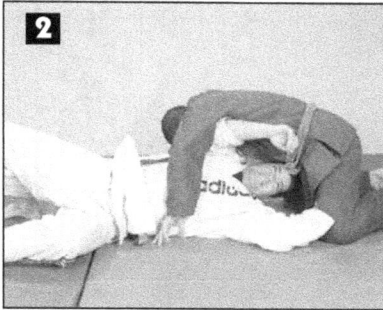

North & South 11

While in the north-south position, Rigan controls the opponent (1). Rigan moves backwards, gets on his feet and grabs both of the opponent's armpits (2). He stands (3), pulls the opponent upright (4) and quickly starts to sit (5). Once Rigan is on the ground (6), he quickly "hooks" the opponent (7). Note the position of his feet. Employing his right hand, Rigan opens the opponent's collar (8). He uses his left hand to grab the lapel, and he cranks on the choke (9).

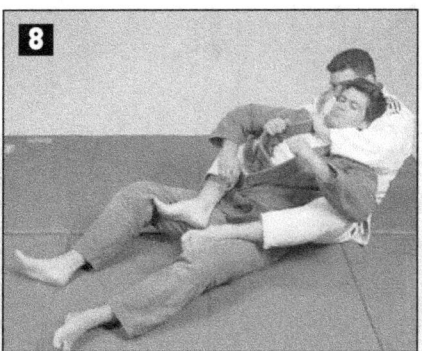

North & South 12

Rigan is under his opponent in the north-south position (1). To avoid the pressure, Rigan pushes the opponent's hips with both hands and slides his hips forward (2). He raises his legs (3) and escapes from the bottom (4). He scrambles to the opponent's back (5) and gets ready to initiate the attack (6).

Mastering Brazilian Jiu Jitsu

Breaking the Grip

Breaking the Grip 1

The opponent prevents Rigan from getting an armlock by grabbing his own wrist (1). With his left arm under the opponent's arms (2), Rigan slides his right arm under and grabs the opponent's left hand (3), twists to the side and simultaneously pulls back. This creates a wristlock that allows him to break the opponent's grip (4). He leans back, pulls the arm and executes the final armlock (5).

Breaking the Grip 2

Utilizing the "fingers-with-fingers" grip, the opponent prevents Rigan from getting an armlock (1). As Rigan grabs his own gi to secure the grip, he moves his left foot onto the opponent's right arm (2). As he pushes the arm with his foot, he releases his gi, grabs the opponent's hands and pulls (3). He breaks the grip (4), leans back and applies the straight armlock (5).

Breaking the Grip 3

By grabbing his own forearms, the opponent prevents Rigan from getting an armlock (1). Rigan places his left leg inside the opponent's arms as he secures both arms with his right hand (2). Then he pulls the opponent closer (3), leans back, guides the opponent's head closer (4) and executes a *triangle* choke (5).

Breaking the Grip 4

To prevent Rigan from getting an armlock, the opponent grabs his own arms (1). Rigan places his left leg on top of the opponent's arms (2) and hooks his left foot under his right leg to apply pressure (3). As he pulls back with his hands, he pushes down with his legs, breaking the grip (4). He now executes an armlock (5).

Breaking the Grip 5

The opponent prevents the armlock by grabbing Rigan's legs (1). Using his right hand, Rigan grabs the opponent's right arm (2). He then leans forward (3) and mounts his opponent as he maintains control of both arms (4). Rigan quickly switches positions (5), swings his left leg over, leans back and applies a straight armlock to the opposite arm (6). Note: Keep total control of both arms while you are moving from side to side. If you lose the grip, you will lose control.

Breaking the Grip 6

To prevent the armlock, the opponent grabs his lapel (1). To create some maneuvering room, Rigan slightly moves his hips (2). Employing his right hand, Rigan grabs the opponent's collar (3), pushes forward (4) and breaks the grip (5). Now he can execute the final armlock (6).

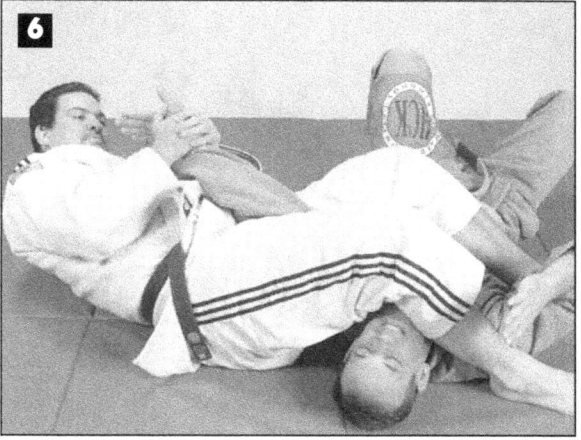

Breaking the Grip 7

To prevent Rigan from getting an armlock, the opponent grabs his own forearms (1). Rigan clutches his hands together (2). Note that his left arm is between the opponent's arms. He pulls back (3), and keeps leaning until he breaks the grip (4). He can now apply an armlock (5).

Breaking the Grip 8

The opponent prevents Rigan from getting an armlock by grabbing his own triceps (1). Rigan places both hands on the opponent's right triceps (2) and pulls hard. This creates pressure in the wrists, which eventually will break the grip (3). To assist in this maneuver, notice how he uses his left leg to generate additional pressure (4). He hooks his left foot under his right leg (5) and easily applies a reverse straight armlock (6).

Epilogue

Now that you have finished this book, what have you learned? Hopefully nothing less than a series of practical and efficient techniques for becoming a successful Brazilian Jiu-Jitsu practitioner. These methods and training practices will help you succeed in competition and also to learn and grow after each defeat. These techniques have been developed by world-class competitors who have successfully applied them in elite competition. By using these same methods, you can also enjoy success in your own matches, even if you're not a world-class competitor. But simply reading through these pages is not enough. You must consistently practice each technique with a training partner, exploring all the possibilities of each position, until you obtain the desired results based on your body style, athletic ability, and physical attributes. Not all positions and techniques will work for every practitioner. Once you have a basic framework in place, you must fine- tune each position until it fits your game. The enjoyable part of Brazilian Jiu-Jitsu is that everyone can adapt and personalize it. While the basics are the same, the application of the basics is as different and varied as each practitioner. When practiced under the guidance of a qualified instructor, or with the assistance of a willing training partner, the principles and methods explained in this volume will be effective. This is because they have been tested and proven for decades in the laboratory of practical experience and the crucible of real competition. Your task now is simply to go out and have fun with them!

— The authors

MASTERING BRAZILIAN JIU JITSU

• Vol.1: LEGLOCKS • Vol. 2: CHOKES • Vol. 3: HALF-GUARD

A world Brazilian Jiu Jitsu champion and trainer of many top Mixed Martial Arts and Brazilian Jiu Jitsu fighters, Rigan Machado reveals the techniques, training, and strategy for dominating your opponent from the half-guard and submitting him with leg locks and chokes. Time-tested in real competition, Rigan's DVD series is considered by many experts as the ultimate guide, and a "must" for all BJJ practitioners and Submission fighters. It includes many detailed techniques and comprehensive information that will vastly improve the practitioner's ability to finish the opponent.

#206 - $24.95 – ISBN-13: 978-1-934347-10-2
#207 - $24.95 – ISBN-13: 978-1-934347-11-9
#208 - $24.95 – ISBN-13: 978-1-934347-12-6

NO-GI SUBMISSION GRAPPLING

Vols. 1-2-3

This is a complete presentation of the principles and applications of the best elements and techniques of all grappling methods, demonstrated by one of the most sought-after Submission Grappling masters of all time, Rigan Machado. The DVD series explores the techniques and science of Submission Grappling. There is a detailed breakdown of the offensive and defensive skills used in no-gi grappling competitions, and the tactical elements of timing, control, positioning, etc.... The unique principles and techniques of no-gi Submission Grappling as taught by Rigan Machado are fully described in these authoritative DVDs. This series has a great deal to offer to all grappling students, from beginner to black belt level, as well as being a unique and enjoyable way to learn about the sport of Submission Grappling. It is a true gem by one of the best grappling masters of our time.

#215 – US $24.95 – ISBN-13: 978-1-934347-23-2
#216 – US $24.95 – ISBN-13: 978-1-934347-24-9
#217 – US $24.95 – ISBN-13: 978-1-934347-25-6

TO ORDER VISIT
www.em3video.com

ENCYCLOPEDIA OF LEGLOCKS

A world Brazilian Jiu Jitsu champion and trainer of many top Mixed Martial Arts and Brazilian Jiu Jitsu fighters, Rigan Machado reveals the techniques, training, and strategy for dominating and submitting your opponent with leglocks. Time-tested in real competition, Rigan's book is considered by many experts as the ultimate guide to leglock submissions, and a "must read" for all Submission fighters. It includes hundreds of photos and comprehensive information that will vastly improve the practitioner's ability to finish the opponent with devastating leglocks. This unbeatable volume is the only book you'll ever need to learn the leglocks submissions for Mixed Martial Arts and Brazilian Jiu Jitsu.

#214 – US $29.95
7 x 10 – 280 pages
ISBN: 978-1-933901-14-5

TO ORDER VISIT
www.empirebooks.net